A NARRATIVE OF GOD'S POWER

JUDGES

CYRIL J. BARBER

A NARRATIVE OF GOD'S POWER

JUDGES

CYRIL J. BARBER

An Expositional
Commentary

Foreword by Dr. Ray Stedman

LOIZEAUX BROTHERS
Neptune, New Jersey

Library of Congress Cataloging in Publication Data

Barber, Cyril J.
    Judges: a narrative of God's power: an expositional commentary/ Cyril J. Barber
        p. cm.
    Includes bibliographical references.
    ISBN 0-87213-025-8
    1. Bible. O.T. Judges—Commentaries. I. Title. II. Title:
    Narrative of God's power, Judges.
    BS1305.3.B37 1990
    222 '.3207—dc20
                                                                      89-2763
                                                                         CIP

Printed in the United States of America

10 9 8 7 6 5 4 3 2 1

With appreciation and affection,
to my dear friends
Jack and Jean Gamble
of Belfast, Northern Ireland

CONTENTS

FOREWORD

Mirrors are useful objects: they show us truth about ourselves that we could not otherwise know. Sometimes the truth we learn encourages us; more often it humbles us. But one thing is always true of a good mirror—the truth it reveals is there. If we want to deal with life realistically, we must accept what the mirror reveals.

Scripture is like that, says the apostle James (1:23–25). To peruse its stories, poems, sermons, or prophecies is to see basic human nature revealed as it truly is. We miss much of this revelation, however, particularly in the Old Testament, because of the cultural and technological differences between the world of the Bible and our modern age. Here is where the gift of teaching comes in. A skillful teacher can bridge the gap and allow modern readers to see themselves reflected accurately in the ancient stories about God's people. This is what Cyril Barber does outstandingly with the book of Judges—one of the least understood (and least read) books of the Old Testament.

The parallels between the times of the judges and our modern difficulties and challenges are often uncanny. We learn that today's problems are not new, but neither are they insolvable. Barber skillfully analyzes the Israelites' terrible problems of depression, homosexuality, apathy, occultism, child abuse, and widespread hostility. He also clearly traces paths to recovery and renewal, which are as valid today for individuals and societies as they were then.

The great heroes and heroines among the judges (Gideon, Samson, Deborah, and the rest) appear in these pages as full-fleshed humans, beset by weaknesses but manifesting the elements of faith and courage that make for greatness. With vivid imagination Barber clothes the biblical facts with color and insight, making us feel as though we know the judges personally. They become as real as the characters of popular television programs, but with much more positive influence, for we suddenly see that they are us. The biblical mirror has then fulfilled its purpose.

These cameos would prove particularly useful for group study or for pastors and teachers who wish to make their preaching and teaching live. Anyone who reads this book will never forget the lessons of the judges and their pertinence to life in today's world.

Ray C. Stedman

PREFACE

In 1615, Richard Rogers published his *Commentary Upon the Whole Book of Judges,* a collection of expository messages that filled 970 pages. Although authors since Rogers have written on Judges, people today tend to neglect this portion of scripture. Because each generation needs to apply the truth of God's inerrant word to its own needs, I believe a fresh approach to the book is justified.

I began these studies in 1981 while serving as a consultant to the International Christian Graduate University. Each Wednesday morning the library staff met for Bible study and prayer. After a few sessions, they asked me to lead the discussion. The group knew that a publisher had invited me to write a commentary on the book of Judges. That manuscript, however, was not published. Later, at a Christian Booksellers' Association convention, I mentioned my work to Marie Loizeaux, then editor for Loizeaux Brothers. She suggested that I submit my manuscript to them for consideration. After reviewing my material, Loizeaux Brothers encouraged me to expand it to meet the needs of a wider circle of readers, which I have done.

Many see Judges as a dismal record of Israel's failure, but to me it illustrates God's power, a message both timely and relevant.

I have explained the theme of Judges in a nontechnical way to encourage laypeople to study this period of history for themselves. Working through each section of this book and discussing the important truths in this book with a friend or two will enrich each reader (cf. Mal. 3:16–18). Using your own experiences, you will be able to expand areas of application to which I have only been able to allude.

Pastors who find the contents of this book meaningful will appreciate the notes at the end. These resources will enable them to flesh out topics of interest that I have only touched on.

Over the last five years I have spent an average of fifty hours per week helping people with their problems. My work as a counselor has given me a deeper understanding of our shared humanity and the relevancy of God's word to our needs. And so I have written this book for average Christians, *not* for scholars or seminarians.

Judges, more than any other book of the Bible, illustrates the way God works through ordinary people to accomplish his purposes. This should inspire us with confidence, particularly as we

study each passage in light of the apostle Paul's words in 2
Corinthians 3:5 and 4:7:

> Not that we are competent in ourselves to reckon anything [i.e.,
> any success or adequacy for the task] as [coming] from oursel-
> ves, but our competency [is] of God . . . in order that the
> excellency of the power may be of God and not of us.

Judges may be seen as an illustration of the power of God at
work in us. The Holy Spirit still sovereignly empowers believers to
accomplish his purpose.

Several years have passed since I first arranged my material
on this book, and some who helped at that time may no longer
recognize their contributions. Nevertheless, I am indebted to Mrs.
Steven (Janet) McCracken and Mrs. Michael (Marilyn) Moore. In
addition, I would like to thank Miss Marie Loizeaux (who mean-
while, and in spite of my protests, retired from an office she had
held for many years) for her encouragement and confidence.
Special thanks likewise is due my good friend Dr. Ray Stedman,
senior pastor of Peninsula Bible Church, Palo Alto, California, and
chairman of the Council on Bible Exposition, for graciously taking
time out of his busy schedule to read the manuscript and write the
foreword. I especially wish to acknowledge the loyalty and support
of my wife, Aldyth. The words "Thank you" do not adequately
express my appreciation!

INTRODUCTION

Freedom! The word stirs our emotions. Our nation was founded to secure freedom from tyranny and oppression. In 1986 Americans observed the centennial of the Statue of Liberty, a symbol of freedom. An estimated six million people in New York and millions around the world participated in the extravaganza of "Miss Liberty's birthday." She symbolizes hope for people everywhere.

The spectacular celebrations provided an opportunity for us to reflect on our heritage. Words of praise and appreciation from people in all walks of life reminded us of the benefits of freedom. Only those who have endured the abuse of authority can fully appreciate what many of us take for granted. However, the liberty we enjoy is like a bag filled with sand. If there is a hole in it, all the sand will eventually run out. If any group of people is denied their rights, sooner or later all groups stand to lose their rights.

William Harvard (1710–78), the English poet and dramatist, pointed out, "the greatest glory of freeborn people is to transmit that freedom to their children." This may be harder to do than we imagine.

Ben Stein, a writer for the *Los Angeles Herald Examiner,* spent more than a week interviewing students on the campus of one of Southern California's most prestigious private universities. When asked what they valued most in life, some replied success and others said power or influence. All of them believed that money was basic to happiness. When questioned about freedom, however, many became flippant and cynical. Their answers revealed the shallowness of their thinking. One student even commented, "If the Russians come here and take over America, I suppose we will all have to learn Russian."

These interviews point out that the abandonment of traditional beliefs corresponds with a decline in values. Some people take lightly the privileges we enjoy and wish to pass on to our children—including freedom of worship, speech, and press. John Philpot Curran's words "eternal vigilance is the price of freedom" have lost their meaning in our culture.

Judges deals with a people who lost their freedom—not all at once, but gradually. By Samson's time the Israelites were content to let the Philistines rule over them. Judges clearly describes the reasons for this spiritual and moral, personal and national decline. It began with compromise.

When the godly leaders of Israel died, the people's commitment to God's revealed will steadily decreased until it was no longer sufficient for the crises that arose. A cycle of apostasy, oppression, repentance, and, by God's grace, deliverance resulted.

We can better understand the significance of God's deliverers if we consider how the Jews viewed their leaders. About 190 B.C. Jesus Ben–Sirach wrote:

> Let us now praise famous men. . . . The Lord hath wrought great glory by them through his great power from the beginning (Ecclus. 44:1–8).

He then lists the names of several leaders. All of these won fame in their own generation and were the pride of their times.

During the period of the judges (c. 1381–1058 B.C.), the people had an agrarian economy. Farm lands surrounded each small village. Boundary stones, not fences, divided one owner's property from the neighbor's.

Economically the Israelites had not prospered. Some of the nations in the land had retained control of the major highways (i.e., the trade routes).[1] And with certain valleys in the hands of those with horse–drawn chariots, the Israelites had no place to live but in the rocky highlands. Unable to trade with other countries, they sold their farm produce in nearby cities.

Most people were poor. Their hope of inheriting a land flowing with milk and honey had faded (cf. Exod. 3:8, 14; Deut. 6:3, 10–11). Instead of driving out the inhabitants of Canaan, the Israelites had been intimidated by them. They had lapsed into a "peaceful" coexistence. As a result of their disobedience, they experienced hard times instead of God's blessing.

Culturally the Israelites lagged as well, whether in art, pottery, buildings, writing, or in the manufacture of tools, weapons, and farm implements. Not until the time of David did the Israelites master the art of smelting iron, and by then the Philistines had profited from the process for more than two and one–half centuries.

Politically, instead of maintaining unity as a nation, the tribes of Israel had been cut off from one another. Each went its own way. Only when a common enemy opposed them did some tribes cooperate with one another. No wonder they only partially conquered the land.

The Israelites' inability to maintain unity may be traced back to their failure to expel the Amorites and the Canaanites from the land. With the valleys and portions of the highlands in the hands of the enemy, the Israelites controlled only the area allocated to the tribe of Judah (and Simeon), sections of the hill country, and the portion of land north of the Valley of the Esdraelon.

Religiously, they had drifted into apostasy. Israel's inability to stamp out idolatry combined with her hard-pressed economy resulted in inadequate support for the priests and Levites. Consequently, the sons of Aaron, instead of teaching the law, became apathetic toward spiritual realities. They either "gave up the ministry" and took to farming or sought out wealthy patrons.

In this setting, idolatry gradually became socially acceptable. It promised people the hope of material prosperity, and it appealed to their senses. The sanctuaries of the heathen and their forms of worship were more spectacular than the staid and somewhat somber worship of Yahweh. Cultic prostitution of both sexes was a prominent feature of heathen worship. The sensual attraction, therefore, made righteous living very unattractive.

We tend to think that the events of the book of Judges happened in prehistoric times. But the needs during that era,[2] though we are more than three millennia removed from it, were not too different from our own. The people needed to master the forces that confronted them, use their economical resources wisely, stay abreast of technological advances, maintain a social milieu in which to rear their children, and try to regulate political issues that affected their well-being. And their society, like ours, had the potential for the abuse of power.

God's people also feared the sudden attack of Bedouin tribesmen who might raid their small villages, drive off their cattle, or take captive their wives and children. In a similar way, we fear aggressor nations that threaten national security or jeopardize the well-being of our citizens.

The Hebrews could have served as a light to other nations in their ethical and legal systems (Deut. 4:7–8). Their relationship with the true God lifted them to a higher ethical plane than any people of that time. Their failures were obvious, but they occurred in the same general areas as ours. We have much to learn, therefore, from this period of biblical history as we see God display his power (cf. Rom. 15:4; 1 Cor. 10:6–11).

DIVINELY APPOINTED LEADERS

Who were these judges? What was their function? How did their duties differ from the duties of judges who sit on the benches of our courts today?

The Hebrew term *šōpᵉṭîm* ("judges"; LXX *kritaí,* "ruler"; cf. Acts 13:20) comes from the verb *šāpat* ("to judge"). Judges 2:16 and 18 explain it in part. In times of adversity, when God's people succumbed to the oppressive policies of nations more powerful than themselves, God sent deliverers (cf. 2 Sam. 7:11; 2 Chron. 17:10). They were to make God's will known among the people (2 Chron. 17:6) and to serve as military commanders. Although they differed from magistrates selected by the individual tribes (cf. Deut. 1:16–17; 16:18; 19:18–19), there was some overlap in function (Judg. 3:10*a*; 4:4). After a judge delivered his people, he ruled over them for the rest of his life.[3]

The tendency has been to emphasize the martial role of the judge, but those whom God raised up to deliver his people did not also occupy unique judicial roles (cf. 12:7, 9, 11, 13–14; 1 Sam. 7:6, 16–17).

THEME

Although the content of the book of Judges may at first seem to emphasize only the repeated failures of the Israelites, the biblical writer's theme lay much deeper. He wanted people to see how the *power of God* operated through ordinary men and women whom He chose to speak and act on His behalf. The key, of course, was the ministry of the Holy Spirit. In Old Testament times He came to selected individuals (now, however, He indwells all believers). The way the Holy Spirit equipped people to accomplish his purpose in the period of the judges should encourage us when we are compelled to face opposition or unbelief.

The judges were theocratic leaders, and the word theocracy comes from two Greek words, *theos* ("God") and *kratein* ("to rule," which is familiar to us in words like "auto*cratic*" or "demo*cratic*"). Theocracy may be defined as God's "rule over the earth through his divinely chosen representatives who speak and act on his behalf."[4]

The first words of the trinity, recorded in Genesis, lay a foundation for our understanding of the theocracy:

> And God said, "Let us make man in our image, according to our likeness; and let them *rule* over the fish of the sea, over the birds of the heavens, over the cattle, over all the earth, and over all the creeping things that creep (lit., 'is creeping') on the earth." And God created man in his image, in the image of God he created him; male and female he created them. And God blessed them, and God said to them, "Be fruitful and multiply, fill the earth, and *subdue* it, *and rule over* the fish of the sea, over the birds of the heavens, and over all creeping beasts on the earth" (Gen. 1:26–27; cf. 2:19–20).

Adam and Eve were "rulers" over the earth.[5] God gave to both of them authority (Gen. 1:26) commensurate with their responsibility (Gen. 1:28), along with accountability (Gen. 3:13). This is the basis of the theocracy.[6] It has never been rescinded (cf. Rom. 11:29). We, like our first parents, are to rule the earth on God's behalf. It is a sacred trust. We are his representatives.

After sin entered the world, God promised a redeemer[7] who would remove sin and suffering from the earth (Gen. 3:15; Rom. 5:12–21; 1 Cor. 15:22–24, 45). From what follows we realize that his redemptive (priestly) program and the administration of the earth (later identified as his kingly rule) now run concurrently.

After being thrust out of the garden of Eden, Adam and Eve cherished the hope of a redeemer. At the birth of Cain, Eve exclaimed, "I have gotten a man, even the Lord" (Gen. 4:1).

Cain, however, was not the longed-for savior. Later his brother Abel was born. The offerings of Cain and Abel may have indicated who God's new representative on the earth would be (cf. Gen. 4:3–8; Heb. 11:4). With the murder of Abel, Cain fled from the presence of the Lord, journeyed as far from his birthplace as possible, and founded his own civilization.

The descendants of Cain opposed the truth. Evil became embedded in the fabric of their lives. In time God added a new line of the theocracy by raising up prophets. Enoch, we read, boldly denounced the trend of his times (Jude 14–15). Three separate offices were now in effect: prophet, priest, and ruler.

Scripture reveals that Noah also served in the line of the theocracy (1 Peter 3:20; 2 Peter 2:5). After the flood God reaffirmed and redefined his rule over the earth through human government (Gen. 9:1–17).[8] His words to Noah echo his original intent (Gen. 1:26–27).

In time the people rejected the authority of God and his right to be worshiped (Gen. 10:8–10; 11:1–9; cf. Rom. 1:18–32). God then chose one man from among the nations, Abraham, to bring his program to completion.

The covenant God made with Abraham (Gen. 12:1–3), and later amplified, is still in effect today (Rom. 11:29).[9] It promised personal, national, and universal blessings to Abraham and his descendants. In time this basic covenant became the foundation on which the Palestinian (Gen. 12:7; 17:7–8; Deut. 30:1–10), Davidic (Gen. 12:2; 13:16; 17:2–6; 2 Sam. 7:11, 13, 16; Jer. 31:35–37; 33:20–21), and New Covenants (Gen. 12:3; 22:18; Jer. 31:31–40; Gal. 3:16; Heb. 8:6–13) were built.

The authority of God's representative comes into clearer focus when we trace biblical history through Genesis and into Exodus. Speaking to Moses, God said he would be "for" or "in the place of" God to Aaron (Exod. 4:16). In Exodus 7:1 we read:

And Yahweh said to Moses, "See, I have made you [as] Elohim [God] to Pharaoh; and Aaron your brother shall be your prophet."

In other words, whatever Moses said or did was looked on as if God himself had said or done it. And whatever the people said or did to Moses was looked on as if they had said or done it to God.

After God delivered his people from the slavery of Egypt, they journeyed through the wilderness. God gave Moses, as his representative (cf. Exod. 12:43; 13:1; 14:1 et al.), remarkable power. He had authority over nature (Exod. 14:16) and the power to work miracles on behalf of God's people (cf. Exod. 17:1–7; such evidences of the presence of God did not recur until the time of Elijah/Elisha. The ability to work miracles ceased until the ministry of Christ and his apostles).

Furthermore, what happened to those who opposed Moses illustrated the respect due Moses as God's representative (cf. Num. 16:1–35). This extended even to his own family (Num. 12:1–12; Deut. 24:9).

Moses had the power to delegate divine responsibility to others (Exod. 18:13–27; Deut. 25:1–3). He gave the Holy Spirit to those who served as judges of the people (Num. 11:17–25). He also appointed Joshua as his successor (Num. 27:18–23) and predicted that the messiah would be like him (Deut. 18:18–19).

All divine revelation points to Christ who, as prophet, priest, and king, will bring revelatory history to completion. In establishing his kingdom, "He will appoint judges as at the first" (Isa. 1:26)—men and women empowered by the Holy Spirit who will speak and act on his behalf.

We also stand in the line of the theocracy in that the Holy Spirit indwells each believer. It is our responsibility to reverently, and with godly fear, serve the Lord in our homes, neighborhoods, and places of employment. In this respect the book of Judges gives us great encouragement and hope when we note how God sovereignly worked through ordinary men and women. The diligent study of this book, therefore, is not a dry, academic exercise; it is an exciting adventure in learning more of what God in Christ has revealed for us.

GOD'S PLAN FOR HIS PEOPLE

We are accustomed to complex and elaborate administrative hierarchies involving executive, legislative, and judicial forms of government. But God's plan for his people was simple and efficient. He delegated authority to the tribes; and, as Dr. Leon Wood observed, "All the Israelites had to do was obey the heavenly Ruler and the most attractive future ever enjoyed by a nation awaited them"[10] (cf. 1 Sam. 8:9–18; 10:17–19, 25). Further validation comes from the writings of British scholar Dr. Andrew R. Fausset:

> The extraordinary judges, in delivering the chosen people from their oppressors, were not arbitrarily sent forth to their work, but were chosen to vindicate Jehovah's righteousness, that is, His faithfulness to His covenant, in behalf of Israel. His eternal principle is, when His people return to Him in penitence, He

returns to them in mercy. His salvation and His righteousness go hand in hand (Isaiah 45:8). Thus they were Judges of righteousness not only in, but for, Israel . . . . The Judges were the vice-regents of God in carrying out part of that particular providence, which characterized His moral government of Israel, in contra distinction to the Gentile nations, whose idols were utterly unable to help them.[11]

EXTENT OF THE PERIOD OF THE JUDGES

Bible scholars have sharply debated the extent of the period of the judges' rule (Ruth 1:1). Gleason L. Archer's *Survey of Old Testament Introduction*[12] summarizes the evidence well.

It is probable that the conquest of Canaan began around 1405 B.C. and was completed seven years later (Josh. 14:7, 10). From that time on each tribe was responsible for occupying its allotted territory. If we allow about ten years for Joshua's rule (deceased c. 1390 B.C.), another decade for the lives of the elders who outlived him, and eight years for the oppression under Cushan-rishathaim, then the period of the judges would have begun about 1373 B.C. with Othniel's deliverance of his people.

The end of the period of the judges is more difficult to determine. Eli (born c. 1165 B.C.) discharged the functions of priest and judge from 1105–1067 B.C., and Samuel (born c. 1105 B.C.) was a contemporary of Samson and succeeded Eli, continuing into Saul's reign (deceased c. 1022 B.C.). Samuel continued to serve as a judge to the end of his days (1 Sam. 7:15), but the period of the judges may have officially ended with the accession of Saul to the throne (1043 B.C.; cf. Acts 13:20).

THE PARTS THAT MAKE UP THE WHOLE

The book of Judges has three main parts. The first (1:1–3:6) is introductory in nature and provides a "flashback" to the time of Joshua (1:1–2:5). Then it gives a foretaste of the repetitive cycle of events in the remainder of the book (2:6–3:6).

The second part (3:7–16:31) chronicles seven oppressions by surrounding nations and seven deliverances.

OPPRESSOR	DELIVERER	YEARS OF OPPRESSION
1. Cushan-rishathaim	Othniel (3:9–11)	8
2. Eglon of Moab	Ehud (3:12–30)	18
3. Philistines	Shamgar (3:31)	—
4. Jabin, king of Canaan	Deborah/Barak(4:4–5:31)	20
5. Midianites	Gideon (6:2–8:28)	8
6. Ammonites	Jephthah (11:1–12:7)	18
7. Philistines	Samson (13–16)	40

The judges during this period were both military and civil. Those of whom much has been written (Ehud, Deborah/Barak, Gideon, Jephthah, and Samson) are called "major" judges. The others (Shamgar, Tola, Jair, Ibzan, Elon, Abdon) are called "minor" judges because little has been recorded of them.

The third part of the book (17:1–21:25) is a supplement or appendix. It details two incidents that typify the attitudes of the people throughout the entire period. These incidents occur early in the settlement of the people in the land (c. 1370 B.C.; cf. 3:11 and 18:30 with Ps. 78:60–61 and 1 Sam. 4:11) and illustrate their spiritual and moral decadence. The "captivity" referred to may well have been the capture of the ark of the covenant by the Philistines (c. 1047 B.C., approx. 320 years later). The near destruction of the tribe of Benjamin probably occurred around 1360 B.C.

THE PERSON BEHIND THE BOOK

Commentators and scholars have greatly debated the authorship of Judges.[13] According to the Talmud (*Baba Bathra* 14b), Samuel wrote it. Judges 1:21 indicates that the Jebusites were still living in Jerusalem. The book must have been written, therefore, before David captured the city (1004 B.C.; 2 Sam. 5:6–10). Judges 3:3 has Sidon rather than Tyre as the chief city of Phoenicia. This points to a time before the twelfth century B.C. All this indicates an era "when there was no king in Israel" (cf. 17:6; 18:1; 19:1; 21:25). Samuel's ministry preceded his anointing of Israel's first two kings. His knowledge of his people's history would certainly qualify him to write this book. If he did not do so, perhaps it was written by one of the young men in the School of the Prophets that he established.

PRINCIPLE LESSONS

Failure of the Tribal Confederation

People accustomed to a monarchy or who view it as ideal are quick to point out the deficiencies of a democracy.[14] They use the book of Judges to bolster their point of view, especially the verses that intimate there was no king in Israel in those days. Such a theory, however, ignores the *theocratic* principle that underlies God's dealings with his people. It sets up an artificial dichotomy between monarchial and democratic forms of government, misuses the book of Judges, and implies failure on the part of Israel for not fulfilling God's grand design (of which the people, at this period in their history, were totally ignorant).

Advocates of this view also ignore the fact that it was God who made his people a nation. He gave them laws to govern their lives. He allotted to each tribe its inheritance and told the people to take possession of the land. If their failure was due to their tribal confederation, why did the angel of the Lord at Bochim (Judg. 2:1–5) not make this clear to them?

In the administration of the theocracy, God made adequate provision for the delegation of authority. The elders were responsible for the internal administration of the cities and tribes. The priests were responsible for the spiritual instruction of the people. And God raised up prophets as occasion required to reprove both the priests and the people.

The Lord Jesus Christ did use negative illustrations to warn his followers of certain dangers (e.g., Matt. 7:15; 16:6, 11–12; Mark 8:15; 12:38; Luke 12:1, 15; 20:46), but they were not the primary thrust of his teaching. It is unlikely, therefore, that God would devote an entire book of the Bible—covering one of the longest periods of Israel's history—to illustrate the failure of the theocracy and the importance of a monarchy.

Advocates of a monarchy would do well to see this period of history in light of God's progressive revelation. They should also realize that if we are to set aside the tribal confederation because of its supposed failure, we must do the same with the monarchy, for the kings of Israel and Judah (with few exceptions) were corrupt, self-seeking, vacillating failures.

Retribution and Reward

Other writers believe the purpose of Judges is to illustrate and enforce the doctrine of retribution. One of the first stories concerns Adoni–bezek (1:4–7), and the events surrounding his inclusion in the sacred narrative clearly illustrate the principle of retribution. Realizing that this view also carries with it a negative emphasis, commentators who favor it have added the corresponding truth of reward. They point to Caleb (Judg. 1:12–13) and emphasize the blessings of the Lord that accompany faithful service. They then attempt to show how each recurring cycle presents the ideas of retribution and reward.

The validity of the principle should be recognized, but Judges does not maintain the theme with any degree of consistency. Retribution–reward should be viewed as one of the subordinate lessons of the book rather than as the central unifying theme.

Closely associated with the retribution–reward view is the theory popularized by the late Dr. V. Raymond Edman:

> The long period of the Judges showed how faithless mankind can be, and, by the same token, how faithful and merciful God can be. He kept the light of His truth burning even in the days of utter spiritual declension. It is most heartening to know that among the heroes of faith referred to in Hebrews 11, the Judges like Gideon, Barak, Samson, and Jephthah, are included. From a study of their lives, we learn how human, frail, and inconsistent they could be on occasion, and yet God records them as men of faith.

Dr. Edman then advanced his opinion that the theme of Judges illustrated Proverbs 14:34: "Righteousness exalts a nation, but sin is a reproach to any people" (RSV).[15]

The period of judges certainly illustrates this truth, but so does the period of the kings.

Antidote to Materialism

Still others believe that the teaching of Judges powerfully counteracts the self-centered fallacies of our hedonistic and materialistic culture. Slogans such as "Do your own thing" or "If it feels good, do it" or "Reach for all the gusto you can get," express what has evidently become our national lifestyle. Such attitudes, coupled with the infection of relativism, affect the way we think, the type of activities we engage in, our recreation and personal ambitions, and the way we rear our children. The book of Judges provides a powerful corrective to this kind of thinking, and this, too, is one of its subordinate themes.

Human Depravity

Others have observed the recurring cycle of apostasy and use this portion of the book to illustrate the depravity of the human heart because the Lord had to reprove Israel for their unfaithfulness on three occasions (2:1–4; 6:7–10; 10:10–14). Dr. Fausset showed that God raised up judges to coincide with Israel's ever-deepening oppression by the enemy from without and the mutual severance of the tribes from within. Under Othniel and Ehud, all Israel joined forces against the oppressor. Under Deborah and Barak, Reuben, Gilead, Dan, and Asher took no part (5:15–17). Furthermore, only with difficulty was Gideon able to raise an army. Jephthah experienced a similar dilemma, and Samson stood alone. We see further evidence of disunity in that only with difficulty was Gideon able to appease the sensitivity of the tribe of Ephraim (8:1–3) and Jephthah was forced to defend himself against their unprovoked attack (12:1–6).

On separate occasions the Spirit of God came on one chosen of God to save Israel (2:1–5 and 3:10; 6:11, 34; 10:10–16 and 11:29; 13:3–25). Some writers have referred to these events as times of "revival." If this is so, a plunge into apostasy followed them. As a result, the length of the people's servitude increased. Each period of oppression also increased the degree of national humiliation, and the opposing forces came closer and closer to actually occupying the land itself. In the fifth, sixth, and seventh oppressions (by the Midianites, Ammonites, and Philistines), the Israelites' suppression became progressively harder to bear and lasted for seven, eighteen, and forty years, respectively.

The primary cause of such spiritual languor may have been the Israelite's ignorance of the things God had chosen to reveal to them. They had neglected the law and were guilty of disobedience. When they refused to repent, God had to discipline them. Because sin robs us of God's blessing—whether nationally, as with Israel, or personally—the message of this Old Testament book is particularly appropriate today. Relativism in ethics, expediency in politics, pragmatism in business, and secularism in education characterize our age. This portion of God's inspired revelation provides a necessary antidote to these tendencies.

Two Biblical Principles

Of paramount importance is how God viewed this period of history. In this regard, scripture presents two important truths.

First, following the failure of the sons of Israel to drive out the inhabitants of the land, the angel of the Lord came up from Gilgal to Bochim and rebuked the Israelites for their faithlessness and disobedience.

> And also I have said, "I shall not drive them [the nations] out before you, but they shall become [adversaries] to your sides, and their gods shall become to you a snare" (2:3; cf. vv. 21–23)

The reason God left these nations in the land was to test Israel (to give experience to those who had not fought in the wars of Canaan, 3:1–2). One of the purposes of Judges may be to emphasize that liberty, freedom, and justice are not without cost, and that we must continuously prove ourselves blameless and innocent, the children of God, living above reproach in a crooked and perverse world (cf. Eph. 6:10–18); Phil. 2:15.

This is a hard lesson to learn. Many of us have developed a *passive dependence* on the Lord. We have been told that to be victorious in the Christian life, the Lord must do everything and that we do nothing. We must "let go, and let God." Instead, the book of Judges emphasizes an *active dependence* on the Lord. Although such teaching may at first be hard for us to accept, these principles run throughout scripture and in no way negate God's sovereignty or place undue stress on man's responsibility.

The second truth the text gives is that the era of the judges anticipates the future. Dr. Fausset drew attention to the ideal state of the theocracy. He pointed out that the Lord himself was Israel's king, and his "princes" (i.e., the elders of the different tribes) ruled in judgment.[16] These princes exercised administrative authority. The priests and Levites served the spiritual needs of the people; prophets, when necessary, rebuked princes, priests, and people. In other words, Israel had all they needed. They could live their lives in tranquility, contentment, and service.

God's ancient people forfeited their blessings because of their disobedience. Such blessings will be restored when Christ returns to the earth and establishes his kingdom (Isa. 1:26).

When we compare all the different theories of government with one another, the theocracy represents the ideal.[17] In such an administration God rules through those whom He has appointed (cf. 1:1–2, 4, 9, 22; 2:1–4, 7, 11, 16–23; 3:1, 4, 7–11, 12, 15; 4:1–3, 6–8, 14–15, 23; 6:1, 7–10, 12, 14, 16, 21, 25–27, 34 et al.).

Summary

Ultimately, the book of Judges illustrates *the power of God* working through his representatives who speak and act on his behalf. With each person empowered (i.e., controlled) by the Holy Spirit, and each ministering according to his or her special gifts, God's people will enjoy righteousness, peace, and a measure of prosperity.

1 TAKING THE OFFENSIVE

Judges
1:1–2:5

Speaking at the International Congress on Biblical Inerrancy in San Diego, Dr. Walter C. Kaiser, vice-president and dean of the Trinity Evangelical Divinity School, shared with those present his observations on the state of Christianity in America today. He pointed out that while we as evangelicals do deference to the whole canon of scripture in our creeds and confessions of faith, we nevertheless favor certain books of the Bible and neglect others.

For example, we favor the New Testament over the Old. When it comes to the gospels, we elevate John's gospel over those written by Matthew, Mark, and Luke. Among the Pauline epistles we prefer the letter to the Romans. And when studying the general epistles, we give Hebrews a position of prominence. By ignoring large portions of God's word, we fail to avail ourselves of the "whole counsel of God" (Acts 20:27).[1]

As a result, God's people are again perishing for lack of knowledge (Hos. 4:6) and simply because they have slighted large portions of scripture that the Holy Spirit inspired people of old to write (2 Tim. 3:16; 1 Peter 1:25a; 2 Peter 1:21).

God, in his infinite wisdom, moved someone (possibly Samuel) to inscribe the book of Judges; therefore we should treat it with respect (Rom. 15:4). We should recognize in this portion of the

Bible a revelation of God's will for us. Then, as we read what has been written, we will find that it contains a message which applies to us today.

TAKING TIME

But what relevance can this record from remote antiquity possibly have for us?

We are all familiar with the stories of Gideon and Samson; our Sunday school teachers told us about them. However, most of us know little about principles that God intended to teach us through their lives. And because of this we have not discerned the lessons that lie latent in this portion of the Bible. We have also failed to benefit from that which God intended to communicate to us.

Some erroneous theories prevail about the theme of Judges. Most scholars see in it a record of failure—a lack of success on the part of the Israelites to possess the land. We can even rally scripture to support such a view. Judges 2:6–3:6 appears to be concerned with this theme. But if the Bible is a disclosure of the nature and will of God, what are we to derive from a rehearsal of Israel's repeated failures? At this point we become subjective. Because a theme of failure does not fit our success-oriented society, we conclude that the book of Judges is irrelevant to our needs.

To make this study worthwhile, we need to ask the Holy Spirit to illumine the sacred pages for us. We need to picture the human element in each scene. We need to conjure up before our minds the flesh-and-blood reality of the events the writer describes. When we do this, we will appreciate the original writer's genius. We will also find in these pages from Israel's past a graphic record of the power of God. This will give us confidence as we face the trials and difficulties of life. We will see the biblical writer's descriptions as both apt and relevant, his portrayal of events as real to everyday life, and his appreciation of God's acts as a source of continuing encouragement (cf. 1 Cor. 10:11).[2]

The writer, in developing his theme, divided the introductory section (1:1–3:6) into two parts: (1) 1:1–2:5, which deals with the experiences of the Israelites while Joshua was still alive; and (2)

2:6–3:6, which provides a pattern of the recurring cycle of apostasy and deliverance.

In this chapter we will consider Israel's early experiences under Joshua.

EARLY VICTORIES (1:1–15)

The Arrogance of Power (1:1–7)

The opposition Israel faced initially came from one who epitomized the arrogance of power.

Inspired by the thought of conquest and a possession in the land, the sons of Israel inquire of the Lord[3] as to who should be the first to engage the enemy. The term "go up" is a Hebraism for a military expedition (cf. Isa. 7:1; Jer. 50:3). God directs the tribe of Judah to go first (Gen. 49:8). They are the most numerous and powerful of all the tribes, and their success will encourage the other tribes.

In Judah's selection lies an important principle of good leadership. Those who have developed a reputation for certain prowess and have been given positions of prominence should be ready to set an example to others. They should not neglect the Lord's counsel; otherwise they might repeat the mistake when the Israelites attacked the city of Ai (Josh. 7).

By seeking the Lord's leading, Judah is assured of victory. God's words—"I have delivered the land [i.e., their inheritance] into their hand"—will give them courage when the contest is at its height and the outcome (from man's point of view) uncertain.

Because the tribe of Simeon received an inheritance within the borders of Judah (Josh. 19:1), they naturally worked together with Judah. These two tribes also were descended from the same mother (Gen. 29:33, 35) and so could be expected to help each other. Although some commentators have seen in this early association evidence of Judah's weak faith, Matthew Henry had an interesting comment on their relationship:

> Observe here that the strongest should not despise but desire the assistance even of those that are weaker. It becomes Israelites to help one another against Canaanites; and all Christians . . . to

JUDGES 1:1 – 2:5

strengthen one another's hands against the common interests of
Satan's kingdom.[4]

The first encounter of the men of Judah and Simeon is with the
Canaanites and Perizzites at Bezek.[5] This Canaanite coalition is
under the leadership of despotic king Adoni-bezek (*Adoni*, "lord,"
of Bezek).[6] Clarence Edward Macartney described his arrogance:

> This monster amused himself with the savage mutilation of the
> princes whom he conquered in battle, cutting off their thumbs and
> great toes, thus rendering them unfit for military service. To
> cruelty and mutilation, he added insult and degradation by com-
> pelling them to grovel about his table in the palace, where he threw
> crusts of bread to them as if they were dogs.[7]

Adoni-bezek rules one of the strongholds of the Canaanites
that Israel had not taken at the time of Joshua's rapid conquest.
Having conquered seventy other city-states, Adoni-bezek is able
to field a large army.

The Israelites rout the forces of Adoni-bezek and pursue the
monarch until they capture[8] him. Then, in a very elementary form
of *lex talionis* (Lev. 24:19–20; 1 Sam. 15:33; Isa. 33:1), they subject
him to the same humiliation.[9]

Recognizing the justice of such retribution, the disabled monarch pathetically reflects on his past: "As I have done, so God
[Heb., '(the) gods'] has [have] repaid me." It is a striking acknowledgement, drawn from a guilty conscience.

The people of Judah then go up against the city of Jerusalem.
Whether or not Adoni-bezek is taken there to illustrate to the
Jebusites the fate that had befallen one who opposed the people
of God, we have no means of knowing. We do know that he dies
there.

In these opening verses of Judges we notice three important
principles: First, in any endeavor we should seek the Lord's counsel at the outset (cf. Prov. 3:5–6). God longs to lead and direct us.
All too often we only entreat him to help us when a task seems too
difficult for us. The example of the Israelites (1:1) and the success
they achieved should motivate us to constantly seek God's will in
the specific situations we face.

Second, God can give us the victory whether by many (as
illustrated here) or by few (as with Gideon). The tribe of Judah

may have lacked courage to be the first on the field of battle. Up until now Israel had fought together with all twelve tribes united in a single endeavor. Perhaps this is why the people of Judah asked Simeon to accompany them. The Lord blessed their cooperative efforts and delivered the Canaanites and Perizzites into "their" hand. He considers the frailty of our human natures, particularly when this causes us to ally with those who have similar beliefs and values.

Third, the judgment that came on Adoni-bezek illustrates the principle of retribution in kind. As he had done to others, so it was done to him. The whole incident is a striking example of the New Testament teaching that "whatever a man sows, that shall he also reap" (Gal. 6:7; cf. Judg. 1:5, 16–20, 9:52–54; Prov. 1:17–19, 25–27).

Sometimes, from our human perspective, justice is slow of foot. Evil prevails and we wonder whether righteousness and equity exist in the world anymore. The ancient Greeks observed the same process. They also perceived the inevitability of divine retribution. According to one of their writers, "The mills of the gods grind slowly, but they grind exceeding fine." Justice inevitably overtakes the proud and the arrogant. In a pathetic display of cowardice, Adoni-bezek tried to hide from his pursuers, but his efforts were futile. His time had come. His sins had caught up with him. His confession was a striking acknowledgement of justice served.

The Advantage of Position (1:8)

The victory at Bezek is only the beginning. The task facing the tribe of Judah is far from over. They succeed in conquering one monarch. Next they must turn their attention to Jerusalem, a strategically situated city—one having the advantage of position.

Jerusalem sits on a hill with steep valleys surrounding it. Throughout its long history it has been a very difficult city to capture,[10] but no natural advantages can secure it against those who have the Lord of hosts on their side. Judah defeats the Jebusites and burns their city.

Following this destruction of Jerusalem (c. 1395 B.C.),[11] the Israelites do not occupy the site, and the Jebusites repossess and reinforce it. It remains in their possession until David takes it in 1004 B.C. (2 Sam. 5:6–9).

The Israelites failed to capitalize on their God-given victory. Whatever reason(s) Israel may have offered for not occupying Jerusalem, subsequent history showed the fallacy of their decision.

It is easy for us, when God gives us some notable success, to forget the process by which we gained the victory. When this happens, we soon forget the lessons we should have learned. The result is that we have to fight the same spiritual battles over again. For some of us this may go on for years and prevent us from reaching true spiritual maturity.

The Acceptance of a Possession (1:9–15)

With these victories behind them, the tribes of Judah and Simeon assess the strength of the other towns and villages in their territory, which divide geographically into three areas:

(1) the hill country—a rugged and mountainous region between Jerusalem and Hebron
(2) the Negev[12] or south(land)—a semiarid region between Hebron and Kadesh-Barnea
(3) the lowland—probably the Shephelah[13] or region of foothills running north and south between the coastal plain and the central mountain range

Different people inhabited these areas, so Israel had to use different strategies to defeat the inhabitants.

Attack on the Hill Country. The capture of the city of Hebron[14] (formerly known as Kiriath-Arba, or "city of four," Josh. 14:15; 15:13) contrasts with the capture of Jerusalem. Hebron was the home of Anak and his three sons (cf. Josh. 14:6–15).

Caleb, the man who had been sent with Joshua forty-seven years earlier to spy out the land of Canaan (Num. 13), attacks it. Because Caleb wholly followed the Lord his God, Moses promised that Hebron would be his inheritance. Now the promise is fulfilled. Caleb dispossesses the Anakim from their stronghold and kills those who had caused the Israelites to feel like grasshoppers (Num. 13:32–33).

Hebron is a populous city to this day.[15] Hallowed by Abraham, Isaac, and Jacob, it sits nineteen miles southwest of Jerusalem. Following the defeat of the giants, it becomes Caleb's home.

Earlier, when the tribes of Judah and Simeon had attacked and captured the city of Jerusalem, they did not possess the city. Caleb, however, when he wrested Hebron from the control of the Anakim, did possess it. His action illustrates how we, too, should make the most of the victories God graciously gives us.

A spiritual diary can be very helpful in reminding us of the way that the Lord has led us. Ronald Klug, in *How to Keep a Spiritual Journal*, explains how this may be done. The journal is valuable because it reminds us of the lessons we have learned. It also provides us with a solid basis for mature reflection, which aids our spiritual growth.

Attack on the Southland. Having described the way that the tribes of Judah took Hebron (a city representing the "hill country," v. 9*a*), the author now turned to one of the campaigns launched against a city in the Negev (or southland, v. 9*b*).

He introduced Othniel, whom we will read about later. Beginning with verse 11, the author described the capture of the city of Debir (ancient Kiriath-sepher)—a city which, if we may judge from the names it bore (*Debir*, meaning "oracle"; and *Kiriath-sepher*, meaning "city of books"), was evidently an ancient center of Canaanite learning, or what we would call today a "university town."[16]

The biblical text "then from there he went against the inhabitants of Debir" presupposed that Caleb led the forces of Judah against Hebron (cf. Josh. 14:6–15).

With Hebron secured for Israel, Caleb reconnoiters the city of Debir. He then issues a challenge: "The one who attacks Kiriath-sepher and captures it, I will give my daughter Achsah for a wife." As the great Irish commentator Andrew Robert Fausset pointed out, "The greatness of the reward was in direct correlation to the difficulty of the undertaking."[17]

Othniel is successful. He is a brave, resourceful warrior, who later will prove to be an able judge. He captures this center of pagan culture, and Caleb gives Achsah to him as his wife.

Judges passes quickly over the attack on Debir, but it records in more detail an incident concerning Othniel and Achsah. At the time Achsah comes to live with Othniel, she seeks to persuade him to ask her father for a special field, which she wants as an addition to her dowry. Apparently Othniel hesitates.[18] Having already been given the daughter of the leader of his tribe, he is reluctant to ask for more. Achsah feels no such reluctance. She quickly "alights from her donkey." The word *sānah* is and literally means "to leap forth." It implies an eager impulse.

Noticing this, Caleb asks his daughter what she desires. Achsah responds politely and precisely. She first states her request generally ("give me a blessing") and then specifically ("since you have given me the land of the Negev, give me also springs of water"). "And Caleb gave her the upper springs as well as the lower springs" (1:15b). Both Achsah and Othniel would be well provided for. In the dry season the upper springs would probably dry up first, but then Achsah's husband's herdsmen would still have the lower springs to water their flocks and herds.

Othniel's wife illustrates the power of intercession. Knowing her father's generosity, she readily asked that he give her that which would sustain life during the hot, dry summer months. She did not complain about her lot or imply that there was any inadequacy in the dowry he had given her.

Based on anticipated need, her request was simple and to the point. In making her petition, Achsah chose the right time (after Caleb had fulfilled his promise of v. 12) and approached her father in the right way. Her statement revealed her awareness of a possible solution. She based her petition on their relationship, and the petition was well within her father's ability to grant. This account also illustrates the response of a kindly father and shows on a human level the higher principles that apply to our intercession before our heavenly Father.[19]

LATER FAILURES (1:16–36)

Quest for Security (1:16)

With Debir possessed by God's people, the biblical writer introduced a seemingly unrelated, though vitally important, fact.

The Kenites,[20] a nomadic group who accompanied the Israelites on the wilderness march, have earlier settled in the vicinity of Jericho.[21] Because they are accustomed to living in tents, they do not need to rebuild the city. They remain there for some time. In seeking a permanent place to settle, they keep themselves informed of the military successes of each tribe. With Judah's success in conquering Adoni-bezek, taking Hebron, and occupying the cities in the Negev, the Kenites, descendants of Moses' father-in-law, decide to throw in their lot with Judah. It is a wise political move. The Kenites will be on the side of the tribe noted for its power and military prowess.

Unfortunately these descendants of Jethro do not share the same convictions as the people of Israel and do not obey the command of the Lord (Num. 33:50–56; Deut. 7:1–5, 16, 24–26; 9:3; 12:2–3, et al.). Instead of expelling the Amorites from the Negev, the Kenites move into the southland and live among them. Their compromise goes unnoticed by those who are busy engaging the Canaanites in battle and seeking by steady progress to bring the land under control. It does introduce a somber note, however, and before long the victories previously experienced become harder and harder to achieve—and eventually disappear altogether.

On leaving Kiriath-sepher, the tribes of Judah and Simeon attack Zephath, a city located about twenty miles southwest of Hebron. They are successful and completely destroy it. They change its name to Hormah (meaning "devoted to destruction," 1:17). Possibly Caleb had returned to Hebron before the assault on the city, for the author did not mention Caleb as leading the attack (cf. 1:11, 17). Furthermore, according to Deuteronomy 7:22, the process of subjecting the land was to proceed gradually; and it was not uncommon for men to return to their cities or farmlands on a rotation basis. Others would then take their places. Although Caleb had served as "prince" of his tribe for many decades, he was now approaching ninety years of age; so he might naturally leave greater responsibility in the hands of younger men.

Settling for Second Best (1:17–36)

Having taken the cities and villages in the hill country (cf. 1:9*a*) and the Negev (1:9*b*), the tribe of Judah, unaided by Simeon,

JUDGES 1:1 – 2:5

attacks the lowland cities (1:9c; cf. vv. 18–20).[22] The Judahites take
the chief centers of the Philistines but then encounter difficulties.
They find themselves unable to drive out the inhabitants of the
valley because of their iron chariots (cf. Deut. 7:17–23). (Leon
Wood believed the valley inhabitants intimidated the Israelites by
the maneuverability and speed of their chariots.)[23] Rather than
risk an engagement with this kind of weaponry, the Israelites
rested in their accomplishments. The ancient Jewish historian,
Josephus, supported this view in part. He wrote:

> After this the Israelites grew effeminate as to fighting any more
> against their enemies, but applied themselves to the cultivation of
> the land, which producing them great plenty and riches, they
> neglected the regular disposition of their settlement, and indulged
> themselves in luxury and pleasures.[24]

Another possible explanation may be that in much the same
way that presumption resulted in defeat at Ai (Josh. 7), so here
compromise brings about a weakening of resolve. The Israelites
lose the divine perspective. And without the aid of the tribe of
Simeon, it is easy for the men of Judah to look at the obstacles
rather than to the Lord. As a result they lack the faith to believe
that God will give them victory over those who have superior
weapons.

Judah's vacillation sets a pattern for the other tribes. Benjamin
is next to experience failure. The Canaanites have retaken and
rebuilt Jerusalem, and Benjamin is unable to expel them.[25] Important trade routes, therefore, remain in the hands of the enemy.

The descendants of Joseph go up and attack Bethel[26] and, by
using strategy, take the city. Manasseh and Ephraim both encounter difficulties and meet with partial success. Manasseh fails
to control the important trade route through the valleys of Jezreel
and the Esdraelon;[27] and because the Canaanites hold this stra-
tegic plain, a wedge is driven between the tribes. This wedge
separates those to the north of the valley from their brethren to
the south.

The tribe of Ephraim does not take the strategically situated
city of Gezer,[28] eighteen miles west of Jerusalem, on a low spur of
the Shephelah (or coastal foothills). [29] They gain entrance to the
city but have to allow the Canaanites to live among them.

The tribes whose allotment lay to the north of the valley of Jezreel were Zebulun, Asher, and Naphtali. The Canaanites have cut them off from the other tribes, and their failure to dispossess the Canaanites spirals in its effect.

The people of Zebulun do not drive out the inhabitants of the cities. This places them at a disadvantage. The Zebulunites follow an agrarian economy, which forces them to trade with those who control the commerce and industry. Furthermore, those Hebrews who live in the cities have all the disadvantages of newcomers. They move into an already established power structure and have to find their place at the lower end of the pecking order.

The Asherites fare even worse since the Canaanites retain control of the land, compelling them to live in isolated groups. Neither are the people of Naphtali able to drive out the inhabitants of the principal cities. As a result the centers of the worship of the sun god, Baal, and the fertility goddess, Anath, continue.[30] Later these false forms of worship will cause Israel's downfall.

Finally, the author of Judges turned southward to the tribe of Dan, who the Canaanites force to migrate northward outside of the portion God has assigned to them. The Danites, whose inheritance borders that of Judah, have difficulty even gaining a foothold. Eventually they take up residence in a single city far to the north (cf. chap. 18).[31]

It is easy to discern the biblical writer's design; he noted the increasing powerlessness of the Israelites and the progressive deterioration of their situation. Each of the successive tribes fared worse than its predecessor. Eventually, the Canaanites dominated the Israelites. And in the case of the Danites, the Canaanites completely dispossessed them. This was the result of political— and religious—compromise.

TIMELY WARNING (2:1–5)

God, however, is loathe to leave his people in their sin. Dr. Alfred Edersheim described what happened: "Israel was settling down in this state, when their false rest was suddenly broken by the appearance among them of 'the Angel of Jehovah'."[32] God summons them to Bochim. There, in a theophany,[33] He confronts his people with evidence of their infidelity and reproves them for their failure.

The nature of the reproof (2:1–3) strongly supports the idea that Israel had broken the covenant or treaty they had with the Lord (cf. Deut. 7:12–14).[34]

In suzerainty treaties of this period, a definite pattern or formula is discernible. The king or suzerain declared to his vassals his character and mighty works on their behalf. Then, in the main body of the treaty, he outlined the stipulations. The most important of these was that those under him must give him loyal obedience. Certain blessings and curses were then invoked. (Many contemporary Bible scholars see parallels to this form of treaty in Exod. 20–23, Deut. 1–28, and Josh. 24.)[35]

The emphasis in the opening verses of chapter 2 is clear. The Lord was faithful in fulfilling his promise. He demonstrated his power by bringing the Israelites out of Egypt. He fulfilled his word to the patriarchs by giving them the land. He helped them conquer their enemies. No blame could attach to his name, but his covenant with them had been broken. Israel had failed to obey his commands.

God took notice of this. Because the Israelites lacked watchfulness, they were unaware of his growing displeasure. Little by little his power had been withdrawn from them. As a consequence, defeat followed on defeat. Frustration and uncertainty began to mount.

The people no longer possessed the confidence that the Lord was indeed with them. This caused them to turn to the gods of the Canaanites for the blessing and prosperity that the Lord had promised to give them. Intermarriage with the pagans also occurred on a wide scale.[36]

God's displeasure was evident in the punishment He placed on them. Their disobedience rendered them impotent before their enemies. No one thought of calling on the Lord to find out why He withheld his blessings (cf. Josh. 7:6–12).

On hearing the indictment of the angel of the Lord, the Israelites give way to loud weeping. They turn from their sins and offer sacrifices. Then each person returns to his inheritance to do as the Lord has commanded.

JUDGES 1:1 – 2:5

ABIDING VALUES

The Israelites were locked in the same kind of conflict we face as we try to grapple with political, social, and economic forces. They had to distinguish between the temporal power of the pagans and the eternal enabling of God.

The epitome of the abuse of power was Adoni-bezek. He was proud, haughty, arrogant, and cruel, and he wielded his power with despotic fervor. He had no allies, only conquered kings over whom he gloated with depraved zeal (cf. Prov. 10:9, 24, 27; 16:5, 18). He was like many today who seek to climb the corporate ladder by trampling others under their feet.

The Jebusites in Jerusalem possessed a different kind of power. They had the advantage of position. They felt secure in their situation. And because they controlled the trade routes in the hill country, they enjoyed all the advantages of the wealthy (Prov. 10:15; 11:28; 15:25a; cf. 21:22). People with social position and political influence find it easy to flaunt their power over others.

Then there are those who, as with the Canaanites in the hill country, the southland, and the lowlands, are comfortable in their depravity. Theirs is the power of association. As the apostle Paul pointed out in Romans 1:32, they know that their deeds are evil and yet encourage one another in wickedness. Years later Solomon would write: "There will be no future for the evil man; the lamp of the wicked will be put out" (Prov. 24:20; cf. 14:11, 26–27; 21:12; 29:16, 25).

True power, influence, or ability is intrinsic rather than extrinsic. God gave to his people everything they needed (cf. Deut. 7:6–8, 13–14). First, they enjoyed a unique feeling of security, for they were his special possession (Deut. 14:2). They belonged to him. He was their God, and they were his people. He pledged himself to help them. All they had to do was avail themselves of his omnipotence.

Second, not only did Israel sense their security but also their significance (cf. Deut. 16:11; see also Judg. 2:1–3). God had chosen them above all the other nations on the earth. They were to bear his name among the nations. He had established his covenant with them. All this gave them a sense of confidence.

Third, God had promised the Israelites success (cf. Deut. 1:8, 21; 30:5). All they had to do was obey him. By obeying him they enjoyed a feeling of competence. He was on their side to help and to protect them.

The source of true power is the same regardless of the period of history. The really influential people have not always been numbered among the noble or the mighty (cf. 1 Cor. 1:20–21, 26–27 and 2 Cor. 2:14; 3:5). They have often stood in the minority.

As we draw parallels from God's unique relationship with Israel, we see a distinct correlation between their experience and our own (cf. 1 Cor. 10:11).

First, as a result of Christ's death on the cross, we can have a new relationship with God the Father (Eph. 2:1–7). We have access to his presence (Eph. 2:13–18). He has made us members of his family (John 1:12); we have the privilege of calling him "Father" (Rom. 8:15; Gal. 4:6); and we can approach him with confidence (Heb. 4:16). In a very real sense, we belong to him. He is the source of our assurance.

Second, our true worth is not based on anything we have done or can do (Eph. 2:4–7). We cannot merit Christ's approval. Our value can only be gauged by the price He paid for our redemption (1 Peter 1:17–19) and by reflecting on the fact that He has made all believers fellow-heirs of his eternal glory (Rom. 8:17; Titus 3:7). This is the measure of our worth. He is the source of our confidence.

Finally, the Holy Spirit indwells and equips us for every task (cf. Acts 1:8; Phil. 4:13). Through our yieldedness to him, we are made competent. He is the source of our ability.

All He requires of us is our obedience to his word. The excellency of the power, therefore, is of God and not of us (cf. 2 Cor. 4:7). Ours is the responsibility to live under the authority of his word so that we may bring praise to his glorious grace (Eph. 1:4–6).

Israel's experiences admonish and encourage us (cf. Rom. 15:4). Disobedience in any form causes the Lord to withdraw his power from us. Only through repentance and a renewal of our commitment to him can we turn defeat into victory.

2 THE PATTERN OF HISTORY

Judges
2:6–3:6

Chuck Swindoll, in his book *Growing Strong in the Seasons of Life,*[1] related an incident that happened in his high school chemistry class. The instructor placed a frog in a beaker of cool, clear water. Then he placed a Bunsen burner beneath the beaker and very slowly heated the water. For over two hours the frog stayed happily in the beaker as the temperature increased. Before it sensed what was happening, it died from the rising water temperature. The change took place so gradually that the frog felt no discomfort and did not jump out of the beaker.

Since World War II, dangerous, almost imperceptible, changes have occurred in our society. Although we have profited greatly from the advances made in science and industry, moral erosion is now evident. Like the frog, we were unaware of what was taking place. But looking back, the deterioration alarms us.

Since the fundamentalist-modernist controversy of the 1920s, there has been a continuing decline in knowledge of the word of God and our understanding of it as "God-breathed and profitable."

Humanism has affected almost every area of life. Some of its influence has been helpful, but certain of its basic assumptions have had a negative effect on education, politics, ethics, medicine, and business. The change has been so gradual, however, that only with the benefit of hindsight can we begin to discern the process that has brought us to our present moral and spiritual chaos.

Increased "freedom" has resulted in the discarding of traditional values. The frequency of couples living together in an alternative life-style (without the benefit of the commitment to each other that marriage requires) has grown to the point where it no longer arouses more than an idle comment. Riding tandem with this is the increased incidence of single women deliberately choosing to have children without regard for the balance and direction that two parents can give.

Homosexuality is gaining acceptance in our society. In some cities the homosexual life-style is protected by law.

The church is no longer a significant force in the community, and moral values have declined as integrity has fallen into disrepute. The number of fetuses aborted in a single year exceeds all the Americans ever killed in wars. Increased child neglect, drug use, and problems of the elderly are the results of the subtle decline in values. If we ignore these changes and fail to take action we will suffer the same fate as the frog in the beaker of water.

From Judges 2–3 we realize that one of the gravest dangers facing us as Christians today concerns how parents impart biblically based beliefs, values, and goals to their children. When parents neglect divinely ordered principles, their children grow to adulthood having a form of godliness but lacking a knowledge of its power. Parents have not prepared their children to withstand the problems and pressures that they will surely face. Lacking a spiritual dynamic to give direction to their lives, they will fall prey to materialism and hedonism and be particularly vulnerable to a variety of cultic teachings.

THE BENEFIT OF A SECOND CHANCE (2:6–10)

New Opportunity (2:6)

The people of Israel are now repentant. The angel of Yahweh has rebuked them at Bochim. Following this event Joshua probably summons them to Shechem where the events of Joshua 24:1–28 take place. Judges 2:6 is, therefore, a summary of Joshua 24.

The Israelites, having rededicated themselves to the Lord, now have a second chance to take possession of the land. Each one returns to his inheritance with renewed determination to follow the Lord. Because the sins of the inhabitants have reached their zenith, the sons of Jacob are to be the instrument God will use to remove evil from the land (cf. Gen. 15:16; Lev. 18:24–28). Significantly, they remain loyal to the Lord all the days of Joshua and the elders who survived him.

Godly Leadership (2:7–9)

We do not know how long Joshua lived after the events of 2:1–5. Like Caleb, Joshua was probably in his eighties when the people crossed the river Jordan (c. 1405 B.C.). It took seven years to occupy the land (Josh. 14:7, 10). We must also add time for the events of chapter 1. Probably Joshua continued to serve the nation for a further ten to twenty years.[2] He died at the age of 110 (1390 B.C.).

As long as there were leaders at the head of the nation whose commitment to the Lord was real, the people conformed outwardly to the conditions of the covenant. They held Joshua and the elders in esteem because of their example, and this godly leadership and right attitude brought a measure of stability to the nation (cf. Prov. 14:34).

The notable point brought out in 2:7*b* is that the knowledge of God enjoyed by Joshua and the elders was personal. They had seen the great works that the Lord had done for Israel. They had witnessed his power. They had taken notice of his miracles in the desert and had seen the parting of the waters of the river Jordan. They had been present at the overthrow of Jericho and had experienced the joy of victory when God gave the cities of the land into their hand. As a result they grew mature in the faith, and, being men of commitment, they were able to set an example to those who followed them. They founded their beliefs on God's character and the revelation of his will to them. As a consequence their values were the result of conviction and differed from those whose motives were essentially materialistic and self-centered.

The goals the people established for themselves and those for whom they were responsible reflected their knowledge of the truth and also their experience of Yahweh and his ways. They did not rule as dictators but rather exemplified the ideals of the theocracy.[3]

When Joshua dies, the Israelites bury him at Timnath-heres (2:9, a site now identified with modern Tibneh, which is about ten and a half miles northwest of Bethel and twenty miles northwest of Jerusalem).

Joshua's obituary is brief and to the point. The writer of Judges awarded Joshua the highest accolade that can be bestowed on man. The text reads so simply that we are inclined to pass over the significance of the words: "Then Joshua . . . the servant of Yahweh died." The writer did not mention Joshua's courage, his years of loyal leadership, his victories, the great events that attended his military campaigns, or even the spiritual dynamic that pervaded his life, shaped his home, and made him a devoted husband and a wise and loving father. He described him as "the servant of Yahweh."

The importance of servanthood needs to bore its way into our hearts. When we face the judgment (1 Cor. 3:13–15; 2 Cor. 5:10), our titles, degrees, fame, or honors will not be the basis of our rewards (cf. 1 Cor. 3:12, 14–15). Rather, God will judge us on the extent to which we have given of ourselves in the service of the Lord. All else will pale to insignificance before this all-important reality. How vital it is, therefore, for us to follow Joshua's example and walk day by day in reverential awe of God (Ps. 112:1; 118:6; 119:63).

Subtle Change (2:10)

The text next mentions the subtle way change took place. The Israelites see Joshua's generation of elders slowly diminish in number. One by one they die.

> And also all that generation [i.e., those living at the time of Joshua and the elders who outlived him] was gathered to [their] fathers, and there arose another generation after them who did not know Yahweh, nor yet the works which he had done for Israel.

The economic, social, and spiritual pressures remain, but a spirit of religious ignorance and indifference gradually takes over. Expediency becomes the watchword, beginning a cycle of decline

that leads to the repeated subjection of the nation by their neighbors.

THE CYCLE OF SPIRITUAL AND ECONOMIC DECLINE (2:11-23)

The Cause (2:11-19)

The writer summarized three hundred forty years of history
(1390–1049 B.C.) in verses 11 through 19. During this period Israel
endured a recurring cycle of apostasy, servitude, repentance, and
deliverance. They repeated this pattern in the remainder of the
book. The important point to remember is that those responsible
for determining national policy did not wake up suddenly one
morning and decide to rebel against the Lord. It took time for
attitudes to change. An entire generation died. During this period
spiritual apathy and indifference gradually increased.

The people of Israel ultimately showed by their actions their
disloyalty to the covenant they had entered into with Yahweh.
They ignored the beliefs, values, and goals of their fathers. Instead
the people turned to the gods[4] of the surrounding nations. We see
the irony of all this in their forsaking the fountain of all blessing to
drink from broken wells that could hold no water (cf. Jer. 2:13).

What was the nature of Israel's sin? The statement "the sons
of Israel did evil in the sight of Yahweh" is repeated seven times in
this book and describes seven apostasies of the Israelites (2:11;
3:7; 3:12; 4:1; 6:1; 10:6; 13:1). The specific nature of their "evil" was
in serving Baal (ba'al, "master," "possessor," or, depending on the
context, "husband." Ancient Near Eastern peoples used his name
with suffixes to describe places or things he supposedly exercised
power over [e.g., Baal-Peor, meaning "possessor of Peor"; Baal-
berith, "lord of the covenant," etc.]).

Baal,[5] in Canaanite mythology, was the son of El. Baal was the
god of the storm and therefore thought to be very powerful. He
was also the god of the rain and as such was responsible for fruitful
harvests (cf. Elijah's confrontation with the priests of Baal after
forty-two months of drought, 1 Kings 18:7–46; James 5:17–18).

Baal, considered a very active and powerful deity, was worshiped widely throughout the ancient Near East.

Up to the time the Babylonians took Judah into captivity (586 B.C.), the worship of Baal constituted a challenge to the worship of Yahweh. The exact nature of the worship of this pagan god is now more fully known to us as a result of archaeological research at Ras Shamra.[6] We can now understand why God indicted his people for "playing the harlot" (Jer. 2:20b; Ezek. 16:15–25) on every high hill and under every green tree. These were the favorite places of the religious prostitutes for performing their abominable rites in honor of their god.

Baal's consort was Ashtaroth[7] (or Ashtoreth), the mother goddess of love, war, and fertility. She was worshiped in Sumer as Inanna, in Babylon as Ishtar, and in northern Syria as Anath. The names of the gods and goddesses often changed with the place in which they were worshiped, taking on additional characteristics as the traditions of the people developed. Lascivious and immoral practices accompanied her worship (cf. 2:13; 10:16; 1 Sam. 7:3–4; 12:10; 1 Kings 11:5; 2 Kings 23:13) and on occasion involved child sacrifice.

Another deity, Asherah,[8] was the goddess of the sea, but in all other respects she seems to have been the same as Ashtaroth (cf. 3:7; 1 Kings 18:19; 2 Kings 23:4; 2 Chron. 15:16).

Israel's apostasy was that they forsook Yahweh, their loving, covenant-keeping God, for a different "lord." In doing so they turned their backs on their history and the scriptures that had been written up to that time. They ignored God's past faithfulness and lovingkindness and bowed down instead to representations of man made by craftsmen, who fashioned each artifact with characteristics of their own evil thought processes. It is no wonder that the Lord became angry.

To chasten Israel, God sold them into the hands of their enemies (cf. Deut. 32:21–22). The very nations whose gods they had worshiped now lorded it over them. They were powerless before their oppressors (Lev. 26:37) and could not stand before their enemies. Instead, their adversaries harassed and exploited them. No matter what strategy they developed for getting ahead, the "hand of Yahweh was against them" (cf. Lev. 26:17; Deut. 28:25, 40–42). They became frustrated and disillusioned.

Throughout his afflicting of Israel, God was revealing his displeasure at their infidelity. Physically, they felt the harshness of oppression; economically, they knew the effects of poverty; and spiritually, they came to understand the error of their ways. The cause of all their misfortunes was their rejection of the truth.

Yet out of a heart of compassion, the Lord raised up judges who delivered his people from the hand of those who oppressed them. The writer did not mention in this passage that Israel repented. From what we read in later chapters, however, we find that they did cry out to him. The writer's point here was that God graciously saved the people in spite of their proneness to sin against him.

The judges the Lord raised up served as his representatives,[9] speaking and acting on his behalf. God sovereignly chose them and worked through them. Without his aid they would have remained powerless before their inexorable foes. (In later chapters we will notice that those ruled by the judge followed the Lord all the days of that judge and only after that lapse back into idolatry.) The writer stressed the faithfulness of God and the faithlessness of those who called themselves by his name. He magnified God's grace while revealing the people's fickleness, stubbornness, vacillation, and intransigence.

Lest we be quick to point a finger at the seeming ease with which the Israelites lapsed into spiritual apathy and indifference, let us remember how often we have prayed to God in time of need only to forget our vows as soon as the urgency of the moment passes. As Arthur Cundall pointed out:

> The Israelites had short memories and when the immediate crisis was over they forgot both their earlier misery and the state of temporary repentance which it had induced. . . . How easy it is to use almighty God as a kind of emergency, crash-aid service! Gratitude for deliverance both for Israel of old and the spiritual Israel of today, ought to be expressed in lifelong dedication (cf. Rom. 12:1ff.).[10]

Those who engage in a counseling ministry within their church or community, seeking to nurture people in the faith, are able to understand more clearly what is described in verse 17. We should never underestimate the deceitfulness of sin nor its strength. It can hold people captive. They may temporarily forsake sin because of the forms of adversity that may come in its wake, but its power is so pervasive and its allurement so continuous that the temptation to revert to one's former ways is almost overpowering.

In writing of the nature of evil, the apostle Paul stated that we are "not to present the members of our body to sin as instruments of unrighteousness; but to present ourselves to God as those alive from the dead, and our members as instruments of righteousness to God" (Rom. 6:1–23; esp. verse 13).[11] Only by our union with Christ and through the inner working of the Holy Spirit can we experience deliverance from the power of evil.

The thought of God's people "going a whoring after other gods" seems unnecessarily graphic,[12] but God calls Israel his bride. The Lord has established a relationship with Israel that is as inviolable as marriage (cf. Jer. 2:20–21; 3:1, 6, 8). By worshiping other gods she had in effect forsaken him and sought other lovers. Israel violated God's covenant; and although God could have divorced her (cf. Isa. 50:1; Jer. 3:8), He justly chastised her instead.

Sin corrupts and verse 19 pictures its progressive deterioration. As each cycle repeated itself, the people sank deeper and deeper into the quagmire of their own corruption. Each chastening brought a sorer punishment. Yet Israel, like the frog in the beaker of water, neither abandoned her practices nor departed from her stubborn ways.

The Consequence (2:20–23)

The Bible teaches us that shame and guilt are to act as deterrents to further sin (Ps. 44:15; Ezek. 43:11) and to lead us to repentance (2 Cor. 7:10). When we stifle these feelings or our repentance is shallow, we soon begin to experience depression. In counseling, many clients tell me that they no longer have any awareness of God in their lives. When pressed, they will invariably describe God as "distant," "unconcerned," or "unreachable."

When depression is caused by sin it leads to a loss of a sense of esteem accompanied by a feeling of helplessness or powerlessness within. These feelings lead to dejection and a lessening ability to cope with life. The depressed are unable to handle the tensions, trials, and difficulties of life. Most psychologists agree that it is almost impossible to detect depression in its early stages. Change in attitude or the way depressed persons feel or think is gradual. They do not readily perceive what is happening until life becomes drab and lackluster. Only then do they sense that something is wrong. At that stage many will consult a physician and receive medication that temporarily lifts the spirit. In reality the cause may be traceable to having drifted away from three essentials of mental-emotional health: (1) daily, diligent Bible study, (2) a prayer life that keeps us vitally in tune with the Lord, and (3) fellowship with other believers that keeps Christ at the center of life (cf. Mal. 3:16–18; Matt. 18:20).

As with the Israelites, it is easy for us to gradually turn our backs on the Lord. It begins when we, little by little, allow a spirit of self-will to take over. It may be that we have also suffered some disappointment. Our prayers may appear to have gone unanswered, or some Christian whom we highly respected may have disappointed us. We become disillusioned, and our frustration mounts. Although we would hardly admit to another person that we are angry at God or resentful over circumstances that He has permitted to come into our lives, the fact remains that this is exactly how we feel. We conclude that if God is who He says He is, He could have done . . . And unwittingly we begin looking to other sources for the comfort, peace, and satisfaction we seek. However, only by remaining close to the Lord can we enjoy a sense of belonging, worth, and competence.

In verses 20–23, Israel's primary obligation is to the covenant they made with the Lord (Deut. 4:32–40).[13] They are his people, and they have pledged themselves to walk in his ways (cf. 2 Tim. 2:19). It is a matter of commitment. What causes confusion is God's apparent change of mind. Earlier He promised that He would drive out the inhabitants of the land; now He states that He will leave foreign powers within Israel's borders to punish and also to test the faithfulness of generations yet to be born.

The sacred historian did not share our difficulties. To him God was sovereign (cf. Ps. 106:34–46). He could do as He pleased. If He chose to change the rules, it was because of Israel's disobedience.[14] The writer was confident that the Lord would always act with his lovingkindness.

JUDGES 2:6 – 3:6

THE PURPOSE OF THE TEST (3:1-6)

As we look back over Judges 2:6–23, we see Israel's cycle of decline and departure from the Lord. This scenario also reveals to us God's reason for leaving certain nations in the land.

Judges 3:1–6 gives another reason for the presence of alien elements in the land.[15] It was to give future generations of Israelites experience in the art of warfare.[16] The Israelites lived in a hostile environment, and petty kingdoms and powerful nations constantly threatened their well-being. Military skill was a necessity. Although the people could rely on the Lord, this did not absolve them of the responsibility to train and develop the skills necessary for warfare. The nations the Lord specifically selected to discipline Israel were the Philistines,[17] the Sidonians,[18] and the Hivites[19] (sometimes identified as Horites) who lived in the Lebanon mountains.

Israel's slow response to God's warnings resulted in their (1) living with the inhabitants of the land, (2) intermarrying them, and (3) serving their gods. So the cycle of decline repeated itself in each generation.

IN RETROSPECT

In Judges 2:6–3:6 we learn the importance of being aware of our heritage. Israel repeated the cycle of defection because the people failed to profit from their past (cf. Amos 8:11). Each new generation made the same mistakes. They permitted their knowledge of God to become obscured by other considerations. When this happened, temporal advantages became of greater importance to them than spiritual realities. Unfortunately for them, each time they failed to learn the lessons of history, the price went up. The oppression became more severe (cf. Hos. 4:6*a*).

Lack of Personal Conviction

We can trace the root cause of Israel's waywardness to a lack of personal conviction. It began with the leaders who succeeded Joshua and spread to the people. They had no knowledge of God either by experience or by observation. They did not know him personally nor had they witnessed any of his mighty works. It was easy for them to adopt policies based on expediency. Compromise slowly permeated every area of their lives. Because pagan beliefs offered them the promise of prosperity, they readily adopted these practices. In doing so they "forsook the Lord" and, as a consequence, incurred his wrath.

The same trend may be true of us and our children. It happens when we permit worldly pleasures, secular pressures, or selfish ambitions to obscure the real issues of life. This leads to tension between us and the one whom we serve. Although the change may be gradual at first, the results are disastrous for us and those we are responsible for rearing in the "nurture and admonition of the Lord."

Preventing Spiritual "Dry Rot"

Wendell Phillips said, "Eternal vigilance is the price of liberty." When Israel became slack in observing the words of the Lord that Moses had given them, they soon found themselves enslaved by the surrounding nations. Later, after further disobedience and rebellion, God stated that He would leave those people in the land as a thorn in Israel's side.

We do not strain the interpretation of the passage (particularly 2:21–3:4) when we compare Israel's moral and physical battles with our own spiritual warfare. The apostle Paul provided justification for this approach in his own use of the Old Testament (cf. 1 Cor. 10:1–11). In Ephesians 6:10–18 he encouraged believers to arm themselves for the spiritual battle common to all Christians. In 2 Corinthians 10:4 he affirmed that the weapons of our warfare are not of the flesh but are divinely powerful, to the pulling down of strongholds. And toward the end of his life, he wrote to Timothy and exhorted him to fight the good fight (1 Tim. 6:12) and to be prepared to suffer hardship as a good soldier of Jesus Christ (2 Tim. 2:3).

This reminder of the inevitability of spiritual conflict casts fresh light on God's decision to allow certain nations to remain in the land (3:1–3). As Matthew Henry pointed out, God's decision was

> an act of wisdom . . . [and was designed] for Israel's advantage. Without the presence of these nations, Israel would become

complacent. . . . Canaan was *exceedingly rich and fruitful,* and
abounded with dainties of all sorts, which, if [Israel] were not
sometimes made to know hardship, would be in danger of sinking
them into the utmost degree of luxury and effeminacy.[20]

Without a constant challenge before us, we would not have the
opportunity to develop the tenacity of purpose required of a good
servant of Jesus Christ (cf. 2 Tim. 2:3).

A Prevalent Weakness

We all struggle with whether our senses convey all of reality.
We act on our senses and human reason, swayed by secular
opinions that seem to promise what we most desire. Israel's
choices, as well as ours, illustrate the natural susceptibility to be
swept along by expedient policies and the dictates of others. Only
decisions based on the principles or directives contained in God's
word can be lastingly effective.

Verses 5 and 6 form an apt conclusion to this cycle of repeated
failure and a transition to what follows. They bring down the
curtain on this summary of Israel's history while providing a
backdrop for the remaining chapters.

The process of change begins with disobedience to the revealed will of God. The sons of Israel lived among the people of the
land. They did not drive them out as the Lord had said. Then they
compromised with the truth. God had expressly forbidden intermarriage (Deut. 7:3–4), but this did not stop them from yielding to
their fleshly desires. They began intermarrying with the surrounding peoples. As the true God became less and less of a reality to
them, the Israelites succumbed to those systems of belief that
further appealed to their senses. They served these false deities
and brought God's glory and presence in their midst into a reproach (20:26–28; cf. 1 Sam. 1:3; Ps. 4:2).

Centuries later, after the successive apostasies had resulted in
the northern tribes being carried into captivity by the Assyrians
and the southern tribes being deported by the Babylonians, God
spoke to the remnant of his people through Jeremiah. He pointed
out that the absence of sound teaching and the failure of his
"ministers" (described as "shepherds") to "feed" his people on
"knowledge and understanding" (Jer. 3:15) had brought on this

chastening. The priesthood had become apostate, but faithful believers—those who feared Yahweh—"spoke together. . . . And Yahweh listened and heard; and a book of remembrance was written before him of those who reverenced him and esteemed his name" (Mal. 3:16).

Lest we look down on these Israelites, let us remember that a new form of paganism called humanism has effectively removed God from the curriculum of our public schools, affected the ethical decisions reached in some of our largest corporations, injected a self-centeredness into all strata of society, distorted the basic tenets of civil government, and now permeates every area of our Western society.[21] It restricts our view of reality to the point that we exclude the almighty God. As a result, a pathological desire for power characterizes many in the upper echelons of our corporations and the decision-making chambers of those charged with the well-being of our cities, counties, states, and nation. People are expendable so long as the personal goals of a few can be attained.

Hosea's description of the people of his day is true of many today. He wrote, "Their deeds will not allow them [to return to the Lord], for a spirit of harlotry is within them" (Hos. 5:4). Those who are steadfast in their walk with the Lord, however, find that in his presence there is fullness of joy, and at his right hand there are pleasures for evermore (Ps. 16:11).

3 VANDALIZING ONE'S HERITAGE

Judges
3:7–31

Pogo, the cartoon character, and his animal friends were sent on a mission to engage an enemy. Problems arose and Pogo returned from battle. He reported, "We have met the enemy, and he is us."

Like Pogo, Israel suffered from self-destruction. As they settled in the land, they were to completely drive out the inhabitants; but they lacked the kind of commitment that leads to success; and lapsing into disobedience, they resorted to compromise.

A new generation, untaught in the ways of the Lord, did not honor the covenant their fathers had entered into with Yahweh at the time of the Exodus. Lacking internalized beliefs, values, and goals, they succumbed to external pressures to conform. They readily adopted the standards of conduct of the Canaanites, including the worship of Baal and the Ashtaroth.

The people's ignorance and disobedience affected their families. Israel strengthened its ties with the Canaanites, Hittites, Amorites, Perizzites, Hivites, and Jebusites through intermarriage. "They took their daughters for themselves as wives and gave their own daughters to their sons" (3:6). So, it wasn't long before they "served their gods." Individual disobedience soon led to corporate apostasy.[1] With peaceful relations existing between themselves and the neighboring nations, Israel first became complacent, then indulgent.

Dr. Luke H. Wiseman, in his book *Practical Truths from Judges,* commented on the situation of God's people:

> If unbelief and rebellion had been permitted to run an unobstructed course, the glory would soon have departed from Israel, and their name would have perished. It was not their own salvation only, but the whole future of mankind, which was involved in the maintenance amongst them of the worship of God and the expectation of a Redeemer. It was not solely on their own account, but also because "unto them had been committed the oracles of God," and because God in his sovereign grace had chosen the seed of Abraham, and would perform his covenant (Deut 9:4–6), that so wonderful a series of providential interpositions [as we read about in the book of Judges] mark their national history.[2]

RESPONSIBLE LEADERSHIP

Commentators have often criticized Joshua for not appointing a successor. What his critics overlook is that Israel was a theocracy. God was her ruler, and He administered the affairs of the nation through his appointed representatives. These people spoke and acted on his behalf. God distributed responsibility among the different groups. Each tribe had its leaders; and with the allotment of land in twelve separate divisions, the leaders of each tribe continued their civic responsibilities. Being elected by their own people, the tribal leaders naturally had the interests of their tribe at heart. It was a good form of administration.

In addition, there were priests and Levites. They did not have a specific inheritance, but were scattered throughout the tribes (Num. 35:1–8; Josh. 21:1–41). Their responsibility was to serve the Lord in the central sanctuary. When not on duty there, they were to teach the people God's laws. As God's representatives they had a twofold task: (1) represent the people before God; and (2) represent God to the people by teaching them his word. Because of the hardness of men's hearts, periodically God would also raise up prophets, who called the nation to turn back to the Lord.

All who served in leadership capacities—the civil rulers, the priests, and the prophets—acted on God's behalf. They were divinely appointed leaders. Their ministry continued long after Joshua had died.

RESPONSIBLE SERVICE

Israel had agreed to serve the Lord. He was their suzerain, or feudal lord. They were his "vassals." They had agreed to the principles of his rulership at Mount Sinai (Exod. 19) and had willingly accepted his lordship over them (v. 8) by promising to adhere to his laws (Exod. 20–23).

When Israel, therefore, began to serve the Baals and the Ashtaroth (3:7), this was an act of high treason. And because the nature of their service was also religious, their actions constituted spiritual apostasy. Because the worship of these pagan deities was licentious, their conduct also involved gross immorality. All this debased the nation, removing them from the source of power and blessing and plunging them into a state of moral and spiritual lethargy.

OTHNIEL: GOD'S MAN IN JUDAH

Frustration of Israel's Plans (3:8)

Israel's evil actions cause the anger[3] of the Lord to be kindled against them. In accord with his word, the Lord frustrates their plans (cf. Deut. 28–30; noting in particular 28:15–19, 47–48; 29:24–28) and sells them into the hands of Cushan-rishathaim,[4] king of "Aram-naharaim" (the "Syria of the two rivers," i.e., the upper end of the Tigris-Euphrates river valley).

Like Alexander the Great, Frederick the Wise, Ivan the Terrible, Peter the Hermit, and others, Cushan has a nickname. It is not flattering; the word *Rishathaim* means "doubly wicked." His contemporaries had probably given him the epithet, which described his character.

Cushan oppresses the Israelites from 1381 to 1373 B.C., causing the sons of Israel to cry out to the Lord. When they do so, God hears them and raises up a deliverer.

These verses about Cushan illustrate the intent of chastening (cf. Heb. 12:5–11). Only when we persist in disobedience and do not heed the Lord's gentle warnings does He discipline us. He permits trials in our lives to bring us to repentance. When they have served their purpose, He lifts from us the source of our oppression and delivers us so that we may again serve him.

The person God chooses to liberate his people is Othniel (cf. 1:11–15). The writer introduced him incidentally in connection with the attack on Kiriath-sepher (or Debir). For Othniel's valor Caleb had given Achsah to him as his wife. The couple has been living happily in the Negev for about thirty years. They have raised their sheep and cattle, enjoyed family life, and grown old together. Now a dark cloud has come over the horizon. The rumors of war brought by traders passing through the Negev have become reality. The armies of Cushan-rishathaim have marched south. The northern tribes have suffered greatly as a result of his oppression. Their cities and villages have been plundered and their women raped. Fear has become a daily part of the people's lives. The enemy has left garrisons of armed soldiers in the land. The Israelites now feel the heavy heel of Cushan's tyranny as they have to bow before this "doubly wicked" suzerain.

The Israelites probably gather in small groups. Some express their discontent and moan that Yahweh has let them down (cf. 6:13). "Where are his mighty deeds which he did for us in the past? Why has he abandoned us now? How could he possibly allow a man like Cushan-rishathaim to take control of the land that he swore to Abraham to give us?" Others speak in subdued whispers of rebellion. The people, scattered in small villages, are powerless to oppose the crushing might of a man as ruthless and as strong as the king of Aram-naharaim. But some Israelites, committed only to themselves, readily adjust. They buy off the tax officials and military officers Cushan has left in the land. They keep the enemy from ransacking their houses and harming their families by bribing them. The poor, however, become poorer until they cry out to the Lord and ask him to take an active part in their affairs once more.

Fulfillment of God's Word (3:9–11)

Dr. Robert Watson, a famous British preacher of a generation past, described God's deliverance:

> It was from the far south that help came in response to the piteous cry of the oppressed in the north; the deliverer was Othniel. . . . After his marriage to Achsah, daughter of Caleb, we

must suppose him living as quietly as possible in his south-lying farm, there increasing in importance year by year till now he is a respected chief of the tribe of Judah. In frequent skirmishes with Arab marauders from the wilderness he has distinguished himself, maintaining the fame of his early exploit. Better still, he is one of those who have kept the great traditions of the nation, a man mindful of the law of God, deriving strength of character from fellowship with the Almighty.[5]

The Spirit of the Lord[6] comes on Othniel. Before going out to battle, "he judges Israel." He becomes God's new theocratic representative to the nation. How he discharges his responsibilities is important. First he "judges" the people; then he leads them out to battle. The Hebrew word *šāpat*,[7] "to judge," means more than deciding between opposing viewpoints. In this particular situation it meant calling the nation back to the Lord, exposing their past actions in light of God's law, and leading them in acts of repentance. This probably involved the offering of sacrifices. In Israel's impoverished condition, any sacrifices would have been costly, but only through these could God again favor his people.

With a sense of Israel's restored relationship with God, Othniel leads Israel's militia against the oppressor, attacking one garrison after another. In each encounter Othniel is successful. Finally he meets and defeats Cushan himself. "And Yahweh gives Cushan-rishathaim king of Mesopotamia into his hand." The writer passed over the entire account in less than half a verse (3:10).

When God's people are right in his eyes, He often backs their cause. The outcome here is certain. The chastening has the desired effect. And the land has rest for forty years (3:11; 1373–1334 B.C.).

Mirror of the Mind

Israel's experience with Cushan-rishathaim illustrates two important truths: (1) the means of receiving God's blessings; and (2) the man God uses to accomplish his purpose.

First, a single equation shows the secret of receiving God's blessing: commitment + obedience = blessing. Commitment to the Lord plus obedience to his revealed will results in our experiencing his blessing on our lives.

Second, the kind of leader God uses to accomplish his purpose demonstrates courage and faith. Othniel was such a leader.

A Man of Courage. Othniel was a man of courage, as revealed in the kind of task he undertook. Earlier, in company with his older brother,[8] Caleb, he had attacked Hebron and fought the feared Anakim. These were the same people who had instilled fear into the hearts of the Israelite spies nearly fifty years earlier (Num. 13:32–33). Then he attacked Debir. The task was a difficult one, but his resourcefulness and fortitude brought victory to his tribe and secured Achsah as his bride.

As one writer put it:

> The brave man is not he who feels no fear,
> For that were stupid and irrational;
> But he, whose noble soul its fear subdues,
> And bravely dares the danger nature shrinks from.

A Leader of Men. Othniel was also a leader of men. His courage inspired those under him, and they followed him with confidence. The enemy he faced was strong, but he was resourceful and wise. He must have planned his strategy skillfully, used good communication skills to sell his ideas to others, and then carried out his plan with determination, for God crowned his efforts with success.

Tacitus claimed that success was due to the reason and calm judgment of the leader. He should also have added prudence, justice, temperance, and fortitude,[9] for without them people will not follow a leader for very long. Contrary to those who think that they can "win through intimidation," the Bible shows us that we must possess intrinsically the qualities of character that will win men to our side. Moses, David, Nehemiah, and others did; and their names live on in the annals of God's people.

A God-fearing and Devout Man. Othniel had a godly heritage. He had the same parents as Caleb, and scripture says that Caleb "wholly followed the LORD his God" (Deut. 1:36; Josh. 14:8–9, 14). Dr. Leon Wood believed that the Bible student can glean evidence of Othniel's righteous character from the fact that "God imparts His Spirit for enablement to those who walk carefully before Him in a life of obedience."[10]

Othniel did not grasp after earthly honors or material wealth. He declined to ask Caleb for the upper and lower springs (Judg.

1:15). He was not selfish. His genuine humility made him usable. It was not surprising that God raised him up to deliver his people.

OF CHRONOLOGICAL IMPORTANCE

The writer of Judges recorded two incidental stories that happened following the death of Othniel and before God raised up Ehud to deliver Israel from the oppression of Moab: Micah's priest and the Danites (17:1–18:31) and the Levite and his concubine (19:1–21:25).

These described the spiritual and moral conditions of God's people. They belong chronologically between verses 11 and 12 of chapter 3, which the linking of Judges 18:1 with 1:34 and Joshua 19:47 confirms by showing that this portion of history occurred in the early period of the judges. Furthermore, mention of Aaron's grandson, Phinehas (cf. Judg. 20:28 with Josh. 22:13 and 24:33) points to a date soon after Joshua's death.

These two incidents depict the spirit of the age and connect with the events described in the book of Judges. By appending them, the writer does not interrupt the historical sequence. They have a bearing on the story of Ehud, for he summoned the tribe of Ephraim to help him against the Moabite coalition. This would be all the more likely if the rest of the nation of Israel had decimated the tribe of Benjamin (21:20–21).[11]

The small but significant book of Ruth is likewise set in the period of the judges (Ruth 1:1). Often linked with the book of Judges, it illustrates God's grace to those who keep his covenant.

EHUD: HERO OF THE PEOPLE

A New Departure (3:12–14)

God chooses different kinds of people to serve him. After Othniel, who had served his generation by the will of God, died (3:11), the Israelites soon forgot the penalty for idolatry and once more began following the devices and desires of their own hearts. So "God strengthened Eglon the king of Moab against Israel" (3:12).

This seemingly incidental reference to Eglon shows God's supremacy over the affairs of this world. He prepares the people of Moab so they can chastise his wayward people, Israel (cf. Isa. 10:5ff.). God still orders and controls the destinies of nations, as He did long ago in the days of Eglon. He rules and overrules the decisions of world leaders, raises up one nation and puts down another, and all to accomplish his purpose. History is his story. We should be mindful, therefore, of the principles of godliness and watchfulness that are a part of each nation's security (cf. Prov. 14:34).

Israel's new oppressor is from Moab, a territory situated to the east of the Dead Sea and lying between the Arnon and the Zerad rivers.[12] Approximately eighty years had passed since Israel's first encounter with the Moabites. When they were en route to the promised land, the Lord had instructed them not to attack Moab because the Moabites were related to the Israelites through Lot, Abraham's nephew (Deut. 2:19). These descendants of Lot had established themselves in the land before the events of the Exodus. The Moabites must have gained ascendancy among the nations east of the river Jordan, for soldiers from Ammon and Amalek reinforce Eglon's army.

The Ammonites[13] lived northeast of Moab. They, too, were descendants of Lot and had become quite a numerous people (Gen. 19:30–38). At an early date they had occupied the territory between the Arnon and Jabbok rivers (Deut. 2:20–21; 3:11), but they had lost several cities to the Amorites (cf. Num. 21:24; Deut. 2:37;Josh. 12:2; Judg. 11:13, 22).

The Amalekites,[14] who further increased Eglon's forces, were related to the Edomites through Eliphaz, Esau's grandson (Gen. 36:12, 16). They were a nomadic race and at this time occupied a large area south of Judah that extended all the way to Sinai. At a later period in Israel's history, the Amalekites vie with the Philistines for the honor of being Israel's bitterest enemy (cf. Exod. 17:8–16; Deut. 25:17–19; 1 Sam. 15:2–3; Ps. 83:7).

This coalition under Eglon crosses the river Jordan, defeats the Israelite militia (3:13b), and takes up residence in Jericho. There they build a palace for Eglon; and, from this advantageous position, Eglon controls the lower Jordan valley and all access roads into the interior. And the Israelites languish under Eglon's lordship for eighteen years (1334–1316 B.C.).

A Daring Plan (3:15–23)

The sons of Israel again cry out to the Lord (v. 15). He hears them and raises up a deliverer. This time his choice is Ehud,[15] the son of Gera, a Benjamite who is left-handed. Benjamin (meaning "son of my right hand") is the smallest of Israel's tribes. The men of that tribe have long been known for their ambidextrous prowess (20:16; 1 Chron. 12:2). The mention of Ehud's left-handedness may be intended to convey that he did not share the expertise of his fellow tribesmen. Dr. G. Bush believed that the Hebrew expression, (literally *'tter yad-yemînô*, "hindered in his right hand") shows that he suffered from some physical deformity.[16] If this is the case, he may have grown up enduring the taunts of children in his village and the whispers of young women his age and seen the men shake their heads and wonder what he would do to earn a living when he reached manhood. Ehud may have developed ways to compensate, as many handicapped people do, and these skills would now stand him in good stead.

Becoming irritated by Eglon's oppression, Ehud decides on a course of action. He makes a dagger with two edges,[17] just under eighteen inches in length. Then, at the time of year when Israel must present its tribute, Ehud volunteers to bear the "gift." The plan he has devised is dangerous. It is the kind of scheme men may talk about but only a man of audacity has the courage to carry out.The palace guards will search Ehud and the others, and their chances of finding the weapon are very good. If it is discovered, he can expect execution without benefit of a trial.

When Ehud and the men accompanying him present their gift, Eglon probably receives them in his throne room. It is hot and poorly ventilated. Overweight Eglon perspires profusely. He is anxious to see what the Israelites have brought him, but the oppressive heat makes him long for the coolness of the special "summer" room (*meqērā*, "cool room" open on all sides and with adjustable screen slats to exclude the direct rays of the sun while admitting even the slightest breeze) that he has had built on the roof of the palace. Ehud and his fellow Israelites follow the usual custom of prostrating themselves before their suzerain, wishing him long life and happiness, and pledging their undying loyalty to him. They then present the yearly tribute.[18]

It may have been Ehud's original intention to get close enough to Eglon to kill him before the king's bodyguards killed him. At least he would then go down in the records of his people as a valiant man. If this was his original plan, perhaps the close proximity of the guards at the foot of the steps leading up to Eglon's throne made it impossible to carry out his plan. The king's attendants probably quickly dismissed Ehud and his men, and Ehud withdrew without accomplishing his mission.

Dr. Robert G. Boling, building on the similarity of expression used here and in Genesis 12:20, believes that they were then escorted along the road leading to Gilgal.[19]

Eglon is probably glad to see them go. He knows their true feelings. Furthermore, it is hot and he can hardly wait to tell those responsible for his comfort to take him to the roof and the coolness of his summer room.

If this is what took place, Ehud may have overheard the king's words to his servants. An idea may have half-formed in his mind that only took shape when he reached the idols (*pesīlīm,* from *pāsal,* "to cut," and hence possibly the quarry where the idols were made) near Gilgal.

As the departing company draws abreast of some idols standing on public display, Ehud's thoughts come together into a plan. After speaking to the captain of the guard, he hurries back to the palace. The guard, thinking only of the urgency of Ehud's message for their king, brings Ehud up to the roof of the palace and announces Ehud's presence.

Ehud bows low before Eglon. On being told to rise and state the reason for the interruption, he replies quietly and convincingly that he has a secret message for the king. He implies the servants should not overhear lest it be gossiped throughout the palace. Eglon instructs Ehud to "keep silence" and with a word of command and a wave of his hand dismisses his retinue.

Ehud respectfully approaches the throne. "I have a message from God [Ehud uses the general word, *ᵉlōhîm* , 'God' or 'god'] for you."

As a sign of respect at receiving a message from one of the gods, Eglon rises to his feet. Because of his size, this may have been a slow and laborious process. Ehud steps forward as if to further insure confidentiality. As he does so, he reaches into his tunic with his left hand and quickly removes the dagger he has made. With a single, swift stroke he plunges it into Eglon's stomach. Because of Eglon's obesity, Ehud buries not only the blade but also the handle in his belly (3:21–22). Eglon falls dead on the floor.

A Fortuitous Delay (3:24–25)

Ehud then withdraws. He locks the doors behind him, realizing that the servants will be afraid to open them without a command from Eglon. This gives Ehud time to escape.

When the servants of Eglon see the locked doors of the summer house, they believe their lord is "covering his feet" (a euphemistic expression for defecation; cf. 1 Sam. 24:3). With the passing of time, they become embarrassed. The Hebrew reads that "they tarried to the point of confusion." They are afraid to disturb their lord and equally afraid to neglect his needs. Finally, ashamed of their dereliction of duty, they send someone to get a key.

The keys of antiquity were flat pieces of wood, fitted with pins that corresponded to holes in a hollow bolt. A keyhole in the door gave access to the bolt on the inside. The key was inserted into the bolt, pushing out the pins of the lock and forcing the bolt from its socket in the doorpost. Such doors could be locked without a key but could not be unlocked.

Imagine the surprise of Eglon's servants when they unlock the door and find their sovereign lying dead on the floor. Their delay in making the discovery has, of course, given Ehud time to escape. As soon as Ehud reaches the hill country of Ephraim, he blows a trumpet and summons the sons of Israel together. Ephraim had perhaps suffered the most as a result of the Moabite occupation of the land. He encourages them with the words, "Pursue [them], for Yahweh has given your enemies the Moabites into your hands." The men quickly take the fords of the Jordan and in this way cut off the escape route of the Moabites.

An Oppressive Yoke (3:26–30)

Being leaderless throws the Moabite garrison at Jericho into confusion. Fearing reprisal, the soldiers flee. Israel kills ten thousand strong, able-bodied men from Moab and breaks the Moabite domination. For two generations the land enjoys relative peace and security (1316–1237 B.C.).

God hears us when we call on him. No matter what sins we have committed and regardless of how long they have controlled us (cf. John 8:34), the Lord listens to our prayer. As available as He is to hear and help us, however, we should never forget the blessing we forfeit when we choose to disobey him. Comparing the oppression of Cushan-rishathaim with the one under Eglon, we find that the period of time for the second one was much longer than the first. This corresponds with our experience. Each time we sin willfully, the penalty increases either in duration (as under Eglon) or in intensity (as under the Midianites). Furthermore, our hearts become calloused, and it is harder for us to turn from our sins and respond to God's discipline (cf. Jer. 2:19).

As the songwriter put it:

> What peaceful hours I once enjoyed,
> How sweet their memories still!
> But they have left an aching void
> The world can never fill.

The Lord has the power to save us, but He requires us to own his sovereignty and submit to his rule (cf. 2 Chron. 12:8).

The peace the people enjoyed was commensurate with their repentance and commitment to him. In grace He gave them eighty years of freedom from oppression.

The Man God Uses

Though some have criticized Ehud for his actions and have pointed out that the Holy Spirit did not come on him, Ehud was nonetheless a courageous man. He conceived a daring scheme, called the people to a new commitment, and acted on his plan with composure while under enormous pressure.

Like Othniel, Ehud was a man of courage. While others were bemoaning their fate, Ehud thought through the issues, assessed what he could do, and then acted. In secret he fashioned and made a new type of weapon. He intended to assassinate Eglon, even though he thought he would probably be killed himself. At least in this way the land would be rid of an oppressive leech who had enriched himself at the expense of Ehud's people.

Ehud must have shared his thoughts with a few others. Two events support this view. First, he was elected to take the tribute to Eglon; and, second, the men of Ephraim were ready to rally behind him should he be successful. They probably felt that they had nothing to lose by allowing him to follow through on the plan he had devised. If it worked, they would be rid of a tyrant. If it failed, Ehud would be killed; and they would continue as before. The risk to them was nil, but Ehud's course of action was fraught with danger. He displayed great courage throughout the months of planning and during the execution of his carefully laid plans.

Second, Ehud was a man of self-control. He carried himself well in difficult situations. He maintained his composure in the king's presence, waiting for just the right moment to carry out his plan. He calmly left Eglon's summer room, locked the doors behind him, and walked confidently past all the guards. At no time did he give the slightest hint of nervousness, haste, or anything that would lead others to become suspicious.

As with Othniel, Ehud could persuade others to follow his plans. All this required skill, sagacity, and self-control. He had developed these traits throughout his life. Whatever his earlier experiences may have been, they all contributed to Israel's victory over the Moabites.

Finally, Ehud was a man of God. Verses 15 and 28 of Judges 3 show his spiritual sensitivity. In the former verse "Yahweh raised him up." In the latter Ehud encouraged the Ephraimites with the words, "for Yahweh has delivered your enemies the Moabites into your hand." With few exceptions, only devout men and women used the covenant name for the Lord. Whatever Ehud may have lacked, there is every indication that he was a man of God.

Ehud may have used trickery in killing Eglon, but Israel was a nation at war and the usual standards of conduct had been suspended.[20] Ehud had noble qualities, and his life illustrates the way the Lord can use the experiences of life to prepare us for the future. "And the land had rest [from war] for eighty years" (3:30).

JUDGES 3:7 – 31

SHAMGAR: CHAMPION OF THE PEOPLE

With peace established on Israel's eastern border, the Philistines, living along the narrow strip of land between the Mediterranean Sea and the mountains, flexed their muscles. The Lord raised up Shamgar,[21] the son of Anath. Dr. G. Bush conjectured that Shamgar's mother was a religious prostitute in the service of the goddess Anath. When her son was born, she dedicated him to her worship.[22]

Shamgar must have turned from all pagan practices, left home, journeyed south, and eventually found a place to live in the southern territory of Judah. During his lifetime he struck down six hundred Philistines with an oxgoad, and he also delivered the Israelites, who feared for their lives because the Philistines controlled the main roads (3:31; 5:6).

What events brought this rustic farmer into prominence? The writer sandwiched his story between the extended accounts of Ehud and Deborah/Barak. And with the main period of Philistine oppression still in the future, why should we pay too much attention to a solitary verse (3:31)?

Shamgar's home probably lay near a wadi or valley that gave relatively easy access to the highlands. The Philistines would take these wadis when they went on predatory raids, as David's later wars with the Philistines indicate. As Shamgar saw these raiding parties either going out or returning from a raid, he would accost them, armed with only an oxgoad.[23] These farming instruments, eight to ten feet in length, had a sharp metal tip at one end and a flattened blade for cleaning plows at the other. It was a humble instrument, but Shamgar used it to good effect. In the course of his life he killed six hundred of the enemy, and God's endorsement of his work is that "he also delivered his people."

That Shamgar would encounter these Philistine bands illustrates the suddenness with which the enemy may confront us. Shamgar did what he could with the resources at his disposal.

LOOKING BACK

We are often our own worst enemies. We permit ourselves to be seduced by the spirit of our age, led astray by corrupt practices, and eventually identified with the world's system of values so that we provoke Christ to jealousy (cf. 1 Cor. 10:23–11:1).

What we find recorded in the history of Israel's apostasies bears a striking similarity to the teaching of the New Testament. The apostle Paul stressed that we serve as slaves whomever we choose to obey:

> Do you not know that [the person] to whom you present yourselves [as] slaves for obedience, [his] slaves you are whom you obey, whether of sin [resulting] in death, or of obedience [resulting] in righteousness. But thanks [be] to God that you were the slaves of sin, but you obeyed from the heart [that] form of teaching [by] which you were delivered, and having been freed from sin you have become slaves [lit., "were enslaved"] to righteousness (Rom. 6:16–18).

Deliverance from sin to righteousness is only possible through identification with Christ in his death, burial, and resurrection (Rom. 6:4–15). That is why, when Paul finished his doctrinal teaching, he exhorted us to present our bodies as living sacrifices to God. So that this may become an active part of our experience, we are to "reckon ourselves dead to sin" and refuse to be "conformed to this world"; instead, we are to go through the process of being transformed into the image of Christ by the "renewing of our minds," to prove by testing what is the good and acceptable and perfect will of God (Rom. 12:1–2).

Paul described this unique biblical concept of sanctification, which results in newness of life (Rom. 6:4) and is progressive in nature (2 Cor. 4:16; notice the phrase "day by day"; cf. Col. 3:10).

Unless our growth is continuous (cf. 2 Peter 3:18), we will do individually what the Israelites did nationally. The cycle that begins with us drifting away from the Lord will then run its course with each departure being of longer duration. Only through our commitment to the Lord and obedience to his word (James 2:22) can we attain to that wisdom which is from above, which is "first pure, then peaceable, gentle, reasonable, full of mercy and good fruits, unwavering [and] without hypocrisy" (James 3:17). The result is peace—symbolized by the "rest" that the Israelites enjoyed under the gracious administration of each judge.

JUDGES 3:7 – 31

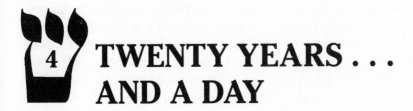

TWENTY YEARS . . . AND A DAY

Judges
4–5

When Charles Dickens began his *A Tale of Two Cities*, he wrote:

> It was the best of times, it was the worst of times, it was the age of wisdom, it was the age of foolishness, it was the epoch of belief, it was the epoch of incredulity, it was the season of Light, it was the season of Darkness, it was the spring of hope, it was the winter of despair.

The British writer was describing the differences that existed in his day between London and Paris. In the former there was gaiety and a carefree spirit. In the latter there was oppression, and people were on the threshold of revolution. He could as easily have been portraying the conditions in Canaan in 1237 B.C.

For twenty years Jabin,[1] king of Hazor, has oppressed God's people. In the Canaanite cities there is prosperity and merrymaking. The laughter of children can be heard in the streets, and even the older people go about with smiles on their faces. Jabin has succeeded in erasing the stigma of defeat inflicted on his people a hundred years earlier; but in the villages and hamlets of the sons of Israel, people feel the full yoke of bondage.

THE NEW OPPRESSOR (4:1–3)

How did this new era of bondage arise? The last report of conditions in Israel was that after Eglon's death the land enjoyed peace for eighty years.

Dr. Robert Watson supplied one answer:

During the peace that followed Ehud's triumph over Moab the Hebrews, busy with worldly affairs, failed to estimate a danger which year by year became more definite and pressing—the rise of the ancient strongholds of Canaan and their chiefs to new activity and power. Little by little the cities Joshua destroyed were rebuilt, re-fortified and made centres of warlike preparation. The old inhabitants of the land recovered spirit, while Israel lapsed into foolish confidence.

At Harosheth of the Gentiles, under the shadow of Carmel, near the mouth of the Kishon, armourers were busy forging weapons and building chariots of iron. The Hebrews did not know what was going on, or missed the purpose that should have thrust itself on their notice. Then came the sudden rush of chariots and the onset of the Canaanite troops, fierce, irresistible. Israel was subdued and bowed to the yoke; all the more galling because it was from a people they had conquered and perhaps despised that now rode over them. . . .

> Shamgar had made a clearance on the Philistine border and kept his footing as a leader, but elsewhere Canaanite spoilers so swept the land that the highways were unused and Hebrew travellers kept to the tortuous and difficult bypaths down in the glens or among the mountains.[2]

Jabin ruled from Hazor, which sat strategically four miles southwest of Lake Huleh in the territory allotted to the tribe of Naphtali. Hazor had a commanding view of the principal trade routes between Egypt and the cities at the western end of the Tigris-Euphrates river valley. Biblical writers referred to it as the "head of all those kingdoms" (Josh. 11:1, 10–11; 12:19; 19:36).[3]

The captain of Jabin's army is a general named Sisera. He lives in the cosmopolitan city of Harosheth-hagoyim (lit., Harosheth of the Gentiles; cf. Isa. 9:1, where this region is spoken of as "Galilee of the Gentiles").

Archaeologists have not positively identified Harosheth, but many scholars believe the site was about twelve miles northwest of Megiddo in a place now referred to as Tell 'Amr.

From this fortress city Sisera controlled the entire valley of the Esdraelon. The power of his army was absolute, for the Canaanites had mastered the art of iron smelting and had built nine hundred chariots that were overlaid with iron. This gave them complete mastery of the valleys and plains and enabled them to put down speedily even the slightest hint of an uprising. Against the armies of Canaan, Israel was powerless.

THE NEW JUDGE (4:4–11)

The Prophetess (4:4–6a)

During this period of spiritual apathy and economic hardship, the priests and the heads of the tribes proved unfit to lead the people (cf. 5:8). Because they, too, had participated in the general apostasy, God raised up a woman named Deborah[4] to be his representative. She was the only woman numbered among the judges.

The Hebrew text draws special attention to Deborah's unique standing by referring to her as "a woman, a prophetess" (4:4; cf. vv. 6, 9, 14). As a prophetess she was on a par with Miriam (Exod. 15:20; cf. Miriam's song of praise in v. 21 with Deborah's in Judg. 5), Huldah (2 Kings 22:14), Noadiah (Neh. 6:14), Anna (Luke 2:36), and the daughters of Philip the Evangelist (Acts 21:9).

Dr. Watson described the times:

> While she was yet young the Canaanite oppression began, and she with others felt the tyranny and the shame. The soldiers of Jabin came and lived in free quarters among the villagers, wasting their property. The crops were assessed . . . before they were reaped, and sometimes half or even more would be swept away by the remorseless collector of tribute. The people turned thriftless and sullen. They had nothing to gain by exerting themselves when the soldiers and the tax-gatherer were ready to exact so much the more, leaving them still in poverty.[5]

For twenty years Israel languishes under Jabin's harsh oppression (5:7a). Neither the Bible nor ancient Near Eastern history reveal anything about Deborah's husband, Lappidoth.[6] If children had been born into their home, they were probably grown by the time of our story.

Deborah lives such a godly and consistent life that people begin consulting her about spiritual matters. She judges them by her knowledge of the scriptures available to her and in time develops a reputation for wisdom and sagacity. As her reputation grows, she finds it necessary to spend more and more time sitting outside her humble home under a palm tree. There people come to consult her about their relationship with the Lord, his law, or anything they may have done that has caused them to experience feelings of guilt or inner misgivings.[7] It is to Deborah that the word of the Lord comes (4:6). She acts promptly and sends a messenger to summon Barak to meet with her. It is not easy for a messenger to reach Barak because the Philistines control the roadways (5:6).

Elbert Hubbard, in his famous essay "A Letter to Garcia," wrote about a faithful messenger. When war broke out between Spain and the United States, President McKinley had to communicate quickly with the leader of the insurgents in Cuba. He was a man named Garcia, who was hiding somewhere in the mountain stronghold. No one knew where, so no mail or telegraph could reach him. The president, however, needed to secure his cooperation, and speed was essential. One of President McKinley's aides told him about a resourceful soldier. This man was interviewed and commissioned to take the president's letter to Garcia. Not knowing where Garcia was and without asking any unnecessary questions, this young man swam ashore after having been dropped by night off the coast of Cuba. Within three short weeks he had traversed the hostile country on foot and delivered the letter.[8] Such a man was chosen by Deborah to take a message to Barak.

The Plan (4:6b–10)

When Barak appears before Deborah, he finds her seated on a stone under a palm tree. Here he receives a message as from God himself:

Behold, Yahweh, the God of Israel, has commanded, "Go and march to Mount Tabor, and take with you ten thousand men from the sons of Naphtali and from the sons of Zebulun.[9] And I will draw[10] out to you Sisera, the commander of Jabin's army . . . and I will give him into your hand" (4:6*b*–7).

Mount Tabor, rising from the plain of Jezreel to a height of over fifteen hundred feet above sea level, is conical in shape, with steep slopes on all sides. To this place, safe from Sisera's chariots, the Lord tells Barak to gather his men.

Barak is less than enthusiastic about the Lord's plan. He responds, "If you will go with me, then I will go; but if you will not go with me, then I will not go" (4:8).

Many believe Barak's reply revealed a lack of faith, but the writer of Hebrews numbered him among the heroes of faith.[11] He was a most capable leader who had spent twenty years trying to survive and motivate the people of his tribe to persevere. He knew how low their morale was. He also knew that he had said all to them and done all for them that he could.

As Arthur Cundall pointed out, "A great man realizes his own inadequacy when called by the Lord to some great task, but the divine call is never alone, it is accompanied by the divine provision."[12]

Dr. John Marshall Lang depicted Barak as a capable yet cautious man:

> [He was] a mighty man of valour . . . two circumstances may have increased his timidity. The one, the knowledge which, from his position he possessed, of the vast resources of the enemy, and the tremendous odds against which any uprising of Israel must contend. And the other, the isolation of his tribe from the stronger tribes. For the army of Sisera, which occupied the plain of the Esdraelon, virtually cut off all intercourse between Naphtali and the parts of the country south of the plain.[13]

Needing reassurance, therefore, Barak asks Deborah, who is stronger in faith, to go with him.

In Deborah's agreement to go with Barak, evangelicals find an ethical dilemma. Wasn't she married to Lappidoth? Would not she and Barak cause a scandal going off together and spending so much time in each other's company? Would not this place their testimonies in jeopardy? Would not the purity and consistency of their lives be held in contempt by those who delight in pointing out the moral infractions of those who claim to walk with the Lord? And what of their respective families? What would their spouses and children think?

What Deborah and Barak did was not inconsistent with the conduct of mature men and women of God in that day. Ruth spent a night with Boaz on the threshing floor (Ruth 3:6–18),[14] Elijah spent three years living in the home of a widow of Zarephath (1 Kings 17:8–16), the apostle Paul did not hesitate to accept the hospitality of a single woman from Thyatira (Acts 16:14–15), and even the Lord Jesus journeyed around Galilee and slept in the fields or in caves with his disciples and those women who followed him (Mark 15:40–41).

Although many prefer rigid guidelines for themselves and others, mature people[15] do not need such limitations. Governed by their reverential relationship to God (Prov. 14:26–27; 15:33; 16:6b; 19:23), such people can avoid the pitfalls of temptation.

Deborah and Barak were both godly individuals. The risk of impropriety on their part was minimal. Today we lack models like Deborah and Barak to guide us in our relationships. Bad examples, not scripture, have cast aspersion on male-female relationships.

Deborah's response to Barak gives a hint of her disappointment over his lack of faith. Having walked closely with the Lord for many years, she possesses keen spiritual discernment. She is confident of the outcome. She refers to the perilous war Barak is about to engage in by the simple term of "a way" or "a journey." Her reply is short and to the point.

> I will surely go with you; notwithstanding, the way that you take will not be for your own honor, for God will give Sisera into the hand of a woman (4:9).

The text of verse 10a implies that Barak may have returned to his tribe ahead of Deborah. Deborah, however, has time to tell her husband what the Lord has communicated to her. Over the years he has grown to trust her. Perhaps because of danger, as described in Deborah's song (cf. 5:6), Deborah and Barak journey northward to Naphtali, about fifty miles from Deborah's home. Part or all of the journey may have been at night.

Deborah and Barak tell the leaders of Naphtali about the Lord's command. They need encouragement (cf. 5:9). These men then send emissaries throughout the villages and hamlets encouraging young men to come and meet with Deborah and Barak (cf. 5:10–11). Secrecy is necessary because someone may betray their cause (4:12).

Naphtali, Zebulun, Ephraim, Benjamin, and Issachar respond favorably with their ablest men (5:13–15a). Some of the tribes, however, decline to help their brethren. The leaders of Reuben spend so long discussing the viability of Deborah's plan that the battle is won before they can reach a decision (5:15b–16). Gilead has not suffered under Jabin's iron hand and so prefers the safety of its inheritance across the Jordan (5:17a). Dan[16] has just begun to enjoy a settled existence and is intent on making up for its years of hardship and deprivation (5:17b). These tribes are of no help.

Parenthetically Speaking (4:11)

The writer suddenly interrupted the story and mentions Heber the Kenite. We have read of the Kenites before (1:16). Politically, Heber is a liberal. His wife, Jael, is conservative. The Kenites had associated themselves with the tribe of Judah and had settled in the Negev.

We have no means of knowing how old Heber was by now. He had been born in Judah and later chose to move northward.[17] Whether he had a falling out with certain leaders of his people or felt that the area in which they were living offered too little to him, we do not know. He chose to relocate and settled near Zaanannim (Josh. 19:33) on the border of Naphtali. Here he traded with the Canaanites and, in time, established friendly relationships with Jabin, king of Hazor. Heber was also on intimate terms with Sisera. Materially and politically, the move of this sheik and his family to northern Canaan appeared to have been a good one.

Heber and Barak were opposites. The former was a man of the world; the latter was devout and God-fearing. Heber's interests were in trade and the accumulation of wealth. He was almost certainly a shrewd and crafty businessman and quite willing to compromise if he could thereby gain an advantage. Barak, on the other hand, was a man of strong convictions. He loved righteousness, hated iniquity, and had earned the respect of his fellow-tribesmen for his leadership skills and military prowess.

THE NEW STRATEGY (4:12–16)

From the slopes of Mount Tabor, on the eve of the battle, Deborah and Barak look out over the valley and see the tents and fires of Sisera's vast army. Their chariots glisten in the flickering light.Camped along the banks of the river Kishon, the army has positioned itself between Mount Tabor and Harosheth-hagoyim.

With prophetic foresight, Deborah says to Barak, "Rise up, for this is the day in which Yahweh has given Sisera into your hand; has not Yahweh gone out before you?" (4:14).

From what we are able to deduce from 5:4b–5 and 20–22, there must have been an unseasonal downpour of rain in the highlands. Such storms are not expected until April or early May. On that night the little stream in the wadi of the Kishon begins to fill. The soldiers are lulled to sleep by the sound of the water running over the rocks. The tributaries that flow into the Kishon swell the river so that it begins to overflow its banks. The ground eagerly soaks up the water and by morning is sodden. In a matter of hours a flash flood has swept away Sisera's unique military advantage. During the night the Israelites have descended the mountain and now stage a surprise attack (4:14b). When the army awakens the next morning expecting an easy victory over the Israelites, they find their chariots sunk by their own weight into the soft earth. The cavalry is also at a disadvantage, for their horses cannot maneuver in the mud.

Sisera's army is at a loss to know what to do. Some try to get the chariots out of the mud. Others try to reach high ground with a few chariots and horses that are usable. Instead of standing and defending themselves, they take off as fast as they can for the safety of Harosheth. Sisera's infantry, so accustomed to having the advantage of chariots and cavalry to break the ranks of an opposing army, retreats in confusion.

With a marked lack of sensationalism, the author of Judges wrote, "And Yahweh routed Sisera and all his chariots and all his army, with the edge of the sword before Barak" (4:15).

The scene before Sisera is one of chaos. The lightly armed Israelites pursue his dejected and defeated army all the way from the banks of the Kishon to his fortress city (4:16). As the valley narrows, decreasing the space available for movement, the chariots that had not become bogged down in the soil jostle one another in their haste to escape. This further clutters the valley with debris and makes it even more difficult for those who are in the rear to retreat to safety.

So it is that we read, "All the army of Sisera fell by the edge of the sword; not even one was left" (4:16*b*).

THE NEW DELIVERER (4:17–22)

While Sisera's army is heading back to Harosheth in a northwesterly direction, Sisera dismounts from his chariot and, skirting Mount Tabor to the south, heads toward the tents of his friend Heber. With Heber he believes he will find sanctuary, for Heber is a Kenite, and "there is peace between Jabin . . . and Heber" (4:17). There Sisera can hide until his troops can escort him to Hazor.

As Sisera approaches Heber's encampment, Jael comes out to meet him. She epitomizes Oriental courtesy as she says to him, "Turn aside, my lord, turn aside to me; do not fear" (4:18).

In poor physical condition and utterly exhausted from his flight from the field of battle, Sisera gladly accepts Jael's hospitality. He feels safe, for in the ancient Near East whenever a visitor crosses the threshold of his host's tent or house, his host is immediately responsible for his safety.[18]

Sisera feels even more secure when Jael invites him to "turn aside" into her quarters—a place forbidden to men. She further lulls him into a false sense of well-being by symbolically covering him with a "mantle" (or fly net).[19] Her act apparently assures him of her desire to protect him.

Finally, in answer to his request for some water to drink, Jael pours some *ḥālab*, or sour milk curds, from an animal skin. Josephus claimed that travelers highly prized this as a cool, refreshing drink and some thought it had certain sedative properties.[20] Feeling safe, Sisera soon falls asleep (4:19; 5:24–25).

Had Sisera known of Jael's strong commitment to the God of her people, he would not have accepted her hospitality. But he had had no previous dealings with Jael herself. His dealings had been with her husband, and in the pagan Canaanite culture women were to keep silent in the presence of men. Those in the harem entertained guests with songs and dances while wives were kept at a respectful distance.

As soon as Sisera is asleep, Jael takes hold of a tent peg and a wooden mallet. With pounding heart and quickened breath, she stealthily approaches the recumbent form of her guest. Then, with a few swift blows, she drives the tent peg into his temple (4:21–22; 5:26–27).

This was not as difficult a task for a woman as we may at first imagine. In these lands Bedouin women were responsible for the erecting and striking of tents. Jael was strong and adept at what we today would describe as "man's work."

Because Barak and his army had pursued Sisera's forces to Harosheth, it may have been some time before they were able to count the dead and find that Sisera was not among them. In searching for him, they come to the tents of Heber about six miles from the foot of Mount Tabor, where Jael steps out from under the awning of her tent and greets Barak, "Come and I will show you the man whom you are seeking" (4:22).

So it is that Jael fulfills Deborah's prophecy: The one who had subjugated Israel for so long had fallen prey to a woman. And while Barak may have thought that Deborah was speaking of herself in 4:9, the notable honor goes to Jael (5:24).

Although Jewish commentators[21] have no difficulty understanding the actions of a person such as Jael, many indict her for her duplicity.[22] Others conclude that we are not obliged to excuse such conduct even if it happened in primitive times.

Dr. J. C. Geikie personified the dilemma faced by modern Bible scholars with his disdain for her act:

> However we may admire the feeling from which Jael acted . . . it is impossible, with the higher morality of Jesus Christ as our standard, not to condemn the deceit and falsehood by which she effected her purpose.[23]

Unlike Meroz (5:23) Jael did not allow victory to be snatched from Israel by permitting Sisera to escape, raise a new army, and renew his oppression of God's people (cf. 5:24).

Although Jael's actions provide no excuse for taking the law into our own hands, we cannot ignore Paul's teaching in Romans 15:4 and 1 Corinthians 10:11, or his statement that "all scripture is inspired by God and is profitable" (2 Tim. 3:16). Honesty in handling the biblical text demands that we seek out some abiding principle that we can relate to those living at other times and under similar circumstances. It is unwise for those who have never known domination by another power to pass judgment.

Jael's actions parallel the deceptions of World War II's underground, Afghanistan's mujahedin, and South America's freedom fighters. Jael's people, deprived of their freedom and at the brink of economic ruin, lived in despair and daily fear. Her willingness to become involved—when she was living in peace and luxury as a result of her husband's treaty with Jabin—was most commendable.[24]

THE NEW SONG (4:23–5:31)

With victory there is also praise. Around the camp fires of the Israelites, Deborah leads the people in a new song[25] to commemorate their victory over Sisera. The might of Jabin's army has been broken. They have subdued the oppressor of Israel and vanquished the king of Canaan. Although Israel has not yet captured Hazor, Israel has turned the tables on its enemy. The hand of Israel will press heavier and heavier on Jabin until he has been utterly destroyed (4:24).

In honoring God, Deborah recounts the events that have taken place. She and Jael occupy prominent positions in this paean of praise. She commends the people who participated with Barak in routing Sisera's army and censures those who didn't.[26] She describes Israel's misfortunes (5:8*a*) and their consequences (5:8*b*; cf. Deut. 32:17–18; 1 Sam. 13:19–22). She directs the main thrust of her song toward the Lord, encouraging the people to "recount [his] righteous deeds" as well as to remember the acts of bravery on the part of those who participated in the battle.

Those who rallied around Barak came from the mountains of Ephraim and from the narrow strip of land occupied by the tribe of Benjamin. The half tribe of Manasseh, situated on the east of the Jordan and referred to as Machir (cf. Gen. 50:23; Num. 32:39–40), sent a contingent, and these joined with the men of Zebulun and Issachar.

Deborah rebukes those tribes who placed personal safety above loyalty to their brethren.[27] Reuben, also situated on the other side of the Jordan, wavered; the half tribe of Manasseh on the west of the Jordan (here called Meroz after Manasseh's son, cf. Gen. 50:23; Num. 27:1) had no stomach for conflict. The bitterness of the curse pronounced on them shows that they were under a sacred obligation to obey Barak's summons. Asher, held in check by the fortress of Hazor and the garrison at Harosheth, chose the safety of inaction, and Dan was busy trying to establish a maritime trade. By way of contrast, the tribes of Zebulun and Naphtali placed their lives in jeopardy to gain freedom from oppression.

Deborah deliberately contrasts the vacillation of the people of Meroz with the patriotic zeal of the other tribes (5:23). Their lack of support for their neighbors is not simply a failure to join forces with Barak's militia, but a failure to be identified with Yahweh. Apparently Meroz commanded the pass and could have cut off the retreat of Sisera's men. The tribe did not do so, and Deborah rightly indicts them for their cowardice.

"And the land enjoyed peace for forty years!" (5:31).

ABIDING TRUTHS

We see once again how God uses a variety of people to accomplish his purposes.

Deborah, a prophetess, had faith in Yahweh, her God, and saw clearly the outcome of what God desired to accomplish. She supported and strengthened the man of God's choosing. Many women down through the years have been used as was Deborah. In this noble company of great women, we think of Sarah Edwards, Rosalind Goforth, Ann Judson, Mary Moffat, and others.

An unknown messenger carried a message to Barak. He represents all who faithfully take on and discharge difficult tasks. They are the tireless doers of good works, the faithful Sunday school teachers, those who regularly visit the sick in hospital, clean house for someone who is bedridden, or read to those whose eyesight will no longer permit such a luxury. Their efforts do not pass unnoticed by God.

Barak, a courageous man of God, had lived so long under the heel of oppression that he had lost his vision of what God could do. But when his faith was rekindled, he inspired others to follow him. His zeal for the Lord led to a remarkable victory, and the book of Hebrews lists him as one of the heroes of the faith.

Jael, a woman of courage and daring, was living comfortably, but she did not hesitate to become personally involved in the liberation of her people. Many brave and resourceful women, such as Edith Cavell, a World War I heroine, and Corrie ten Boom, have performed similar courageous acts.

Lastly, people from various tribes, in a time of crisis, risked their lives for liberty, freedom, and justice.

Opportunities to serve the Lord present themselves in a variety of ways. Not all are called to do the same task. What we need is a vision of what God wants done and a realization that He is working behind the scenes to accomplish his purpose through us.

Unfortunately, there are some who, for one reason or another, fail to advance the cause of righteousness. Their opportunity for service and its reward will forever pass them by. In eternity they will find themselves among "Reuben, Gilead, Dan, Asher, and Meroz." There, in the intense light of God's righteous presence, their excuses for failing to help the needy will be found to have been a cloak for their own selfishness.

By way of contrast, those who zealously engage in the work of the Lord will receive their just reward.

JUDGES 4 – 5

5 THINGS THOUGHT IMPOSSIBLE

Judges
6

Some years ago, while browsing through a secondhand bookstore in England, I came across a rare find. It was Dr. Alexander B. Grosart's *Representative Nonconformists*. The owner of the store had priced the ragged, timeworn piece in line with what he felt it was worth. At the rate of exchange prevailing at the time, I paid less than a dollar for it.

In *Representative Nonconformists*, Dr. Grosart took a close look at the lives of four men of God: John Howe, Richard Baxter, Samuel Rutherford, and Matthew Henry. He painted vivid word-pictures of the difficult times in which they lived and showed how their bold stand for the truth exemplified the highest ideals of the Christian faith.

Times have not changed. Society universally places a premium on conformity. Yet we are indebted to the nonconformists of all ages. Martin Luther, for example, was a maverick. He refused to follow the dictates of a decadent church and boldly nailed his "Ninety-five Theses" to the door of the castle church in Wittenberg. His protest launched the Reformation.

Golda Meir was likewise unorthodox in her approach to the problems of her people. Outspoken in her views, she not only became the first woman prime minister of Israel, but also she led her male-dominated country through a very stormy period of its history.

Jonas Salk represents another unconventional person. He disregarded the counsel of his colleagues, persevered through countless experiments, faced innumerable disappointments, and finally perfected an effective vaccine against polio.

We revere these people, but possessions, power, or prestige did not make them great. Real greatness does not depend on birth, inheritance, intelligence, beauty, or status; it grows out of the intrinsic qualities that comprise character. It is the product of beliefs, values, and goals.The ingredients for greatness are honesty, resourcefulness, humility, graciousness, devotion to principle, and courage. Great men or women have an unswerving commitment to the truth. They do not abuse their power, nor are they mean or petty. They inspire others to follow them with confidence.

Gideon, a most unconventional person, had the seeds of greatness:

THE OPPRESSION OF MIDIAN (6:1–6)

Between the closing statement of chapter 5 and the opening of chapter 6, forty years had passed (1237–1198 B.C.). A new generation had arisen in Israel. To them God's involvement in the history of their nation was but a tradition. As spiritual ignorance increased and zeal for the Lord waned, it was not long before God's people repeated the mistakes of the past; and the Lord raised up the Midianites[1] to chasten his people.

These marauding Bedouin proved to be so powerful that they oppressed God's people for seven years (1198–1191 B.C.). They even extended their control of the land down the coastline as far as Gaza.

The Midianites themselves had an interesting history. They were descended from Abraham's second wife, Keturah (Gen. 25:2). The place where they grew to be a nation was south of Edom and north of the Gulf of Aqaba. In the course of time "Midian" became the name for a desert confederation (including Ishmaelites). A division of the tribe had given Moses sanctuary when he fled from Pharaoh (Exod. 2:15–4:31; cf. 18:1–27). Subsequently Israel and

Midian became enemies. Midianite women seduced the men of Israel (Num. 25:6–18; 31:1–18; cf. Ps. 106:28; Hos. 9:10), and a religious war broke out. From then on enmity prevailed between the two races.

The renewed strength of Midian in the days of Gideon indicated that wandering tribesmen from eastern Anatolia and northern Syria had moved south. They may have brought camels with them, which gave them a decisive military advantage.[2] The Amalekites[3] and the *b^enē-qedem*, "sons of the East joined them in their predatory raids."[4] Josephus wrote:

> The Midianites [calling the Amalekites and Arabians to their assistance] made war against the Israelites, and were too hard for those who fought against them; and when they had burnt the fruits of the earth, they carried off the prey. Now when they had done this for three years, the multitude of the Israelites retired to the mountains, and forsook the plain country. They also made themselves hollows under the ground, and caverns, and preserved therein whatsoever had escaped their enemies; for the Midianites made expeditions in harvest time, but permitted them to plough the land in winter, so that when the others had taken pains, they might have fruits for them to carry away.[5]

From verse 2 it seems as if the Israelites had tried to repulse the invaders, but the "power of Midian prevailed against Israel" for a full seven years. So numerous were these nomadic people that the biblical writer likened their invasion to a swarm of locusts[6] that ravaged the land (6:5). This brought Israel, an agrarian people, to the brink of economic ruin.[7] They had to retreat annually into the mountains and ravines and make their homes in caves and defiles hollowed out by river erosion.[8]

THE APPEARANCE OF A PROPHET (6:7–10)

Israel's economic privation drives them to their knees, interceding for God's help. The text does not indicate any real consciousness of sin but only a general turning to the Lord because of the severity of the annual Midianite invasion. The Lord graciously sends a prophet to them. He is unnamed, but this is of little importance. God's prophets seldom achieved public acclaim.

This man of God goes from one encampment to another, uttering the same message. He reminds them of God's past faithfulness to them by emphasizing his power ("It was I who brought you up from Egypt"), his goodness ("and I delivered you . . . from the hand of your oppressors"), and his right to be worshiped ("I am Yahweh your God; you shall not fear the gods of the Amorites"). The man of God couples this with a stern rebuke from God: "But you have not obeyed me."

Several Bible scholars note that the mention of the "gods of the Amorites" underscores the point that the Canaanites inhabited the valleys and the Amorites the mountain region. In chapters 4 and 5 God gave Israel a notable victory over the Canaanites, showing how powerless the gods of Canaan really were. Now, however, having been driven up into the mountain area, they succumbed to worshiping the gods of the Amorites. As a result, the Lord indicted them for their disobedience.

The unnamed prophet was one of those men God raised up and endowed with extraordinary gifts for particular emergencies. In answer to the prayers of the people, God determined to grant them deliverance. He began by sending this prophet to them before raising up a savior. It was fitting that their sorrow over their waywardness should culminate in true repentance.[9] The work of the prophet was only a step toward eventual restoration. Perhaps that was why there was no promise of a deliverer in his message (cf. Deut. 28:15–16).

THE CALL OF GIDEON (6:11–40)

The Challenge (6:11–15)

The biblical writer shifted attention to the second phase of God's plan to liberate his people. The angel of the Lord[10] appears to a man of Ophrah[11] named Gideon. The site of Ophrah cannot be identified with certainty, but there was a sacred shrine in Ophrah where the people worshiped Baal (6:28ff.). Gideon is the youngest son of Joash and is from one of the smallest families in the tribe.[12]

At the time of our story, Joash had lost his other sons to the Midianites (cf. 8:18–19). Only the baby of the family remained. And he, unknown to his father, was to be raised up and divinely endowed to meet the great national emergency.

Judges presents Gideon's story at some length and with striking beauty. References to it in the prophecies of Isaiah (cf. "the day of Midian" and "the slaughter of Midian," Isa. 9:4; 10:26) show that centuries after the events of this chapter, Gideon's exploits were still fresh in the minds of God's people. As Dr. John Marshall Lang showed, Gideon's actions illustrated "the highest kind of manliness."[13]

The writer passed from the ministry of the unnamed prophet to a visit from the angel of the Lord (6:11–12) to Gideon, who was threshing wheat in a wine press. Unlike his father and fellow-tribesmen, Gideon had not bowed the knee to Baal. Gideon had boldly withstood the inroads of idolatry. For his courage he is honored by the Lord with the title *gibbōr ḥāyil*, "mighty [man] of valor" (or, less likely, "mighty warrior").

The visit of the angel of the Lord could hardly have come at a more distressing time. Threshing wheat was normally done near the harvest field. A stone slab drawn by a yoke of oxen was pulled over the grain, the driver sitting or standing on the huge stone, until the kernel had been separated from the ear, leaving only the straw chaff. Gideon, however, was flailing the grain with a stick in a wine press.[14] This was both time consuming and inefficient. The quantity that he could beat out in a day would be very small, barely enough to meet the needs of his household.

Judges 6:33 indicates the Midianites had not yet crossed the Jordan (cf. 6:11). Gideon has already gathered a quantity of barely ripe wheat and is separating the seed from the husk himself instead of delegating the task to others (who might succumb to the pressure of Midianite spies to reveal where Gideon has concealed his grain).

As he worked, Gideon's thoughts may well have been on God's deeds in the past; for in the discussion that follows, this thought is uppermost in his mind. He may even have recalled a time when older men of the village recounted the greatness and goodness of God on behalf of his people. This could account for his discouragement.

Though Gideon perhaps is cast down and humiliated, the Midianites have not destroyed his courage (cf. 2 Cor. 4:7–9). He does not spend his days fretting over the past or dreaming about what he would like to happen. He is busy doing what he can to meet the needs of those who depend on him. He is a realist, and his actions are tied to the present and to the dilemma facing him and his people.

Gideon does not recognize the angel of the Lord (6:14).[15] In fact, it takes him some time to appreciate who his guest is. This is not surprising, for Abraham (Gen. 18:1–21), Jacob (Gen. 32:24–32), Moses (Exod. 3:2), and Joshua (Josh. 5:13–15) had similar encounters—and difficulties. In Ophrah the worship of Baal had replaced the worship of the true God, and someone needed to sharpen Gideon's spiritual sensitivity.

Although Gideon may not have paid too much attention to the stranger's greeting, the angel's words are important: "Yahweh is with you, O mighty man [of] valor" (6:12).

Gideon's answer reveals his belief in Yahweh and also an absence of false humility. He does not decline the praise but merely says:

> "O my lord, if Yahweh is with us [note the plural], why then has all this happened to us? And where are his miracles that our fathers told us about, saying, 'Did not Yahweh bring us up from Egypt?' But now Yahweh has abandoned us" (6:13).

Gideon's words are not indignant but sad. They express his honest doubt and bewilderment. He has tried hard to reconcile his experience with the teaching he has received. His words also reveal an important quality of leadership. The stranger has said, "Yahweh is with you" (singular). Gideon's reply identifies himself with his people: "Oh my lord, if Yahweh is with us, why has all this happened to us?"

Bernard Montgomery, in *The Path to Leadership*, pointed out that an important ingredient in the eventual success of a venture is the leader's ability to identify with those whom he leads.[16]

Gideon's question, "Then why has all this befallen us" (6:13), is also a plain acknowledgement that the suffering he and his people are experiencing is a result of the withdrawal of God's blessing. He does not doubt the reports of the Lord's past dealings with his people, but questions their absence at the present time.

The stranger does not argue with Gideon. Instead the text simply reads, "And Yahweh looked at him, and said, 'Go in this your strength and deliver Israel from the hand of Midian. Have not I sent you?'"

Gideon is still unaware that it is the Lord who is speaking with him. His humility is plainly discernible. He gives evidence of being fully conscious of his own weaknesses. He is also aware of the difficulties he will have in obeying this order. In a society with an elaborate hierarchical structure, the youngest son has the least authority of any member of the family.[17] If his own family pays little attention to him, how can he expect to influence the men of the city, let alone the leaders of his tribe (cf. 6:15)?

The Sign (6:16–24)

God in his grace continues to lead Gideon into a deeper understanding of the unexpected guest. He assures Gideon that his presence will go with him and guarantees him success (6:16). These words further arouse Gideon's curiosity. The events of the last few minutes have left him confused. He asks, therefore, for a sign that will confirm what the stranger has said to him (cf. 1 Cor. 1:22). Since none is immediately forthcoming, Gideon seeks to detain his guest. He says, "Please do not depart from here, until I return to you, and bring out my present and lay it before you" (6:18).

The stranger replies, "I will remain until you return."

Verse 19 reflects the leisurely nature of Eastern culture. It must have taken Gideon more than an hour to secure a young goat from the few livestock that had escaped the Midianite scouts, slaughter it, and prepare the kind of meal described in the text. The generous portions assigned the visitor show something of Gideon's growing respect for the one who has been speaking with him.

On receiving the meal[18] the guest instructs Gideon to place everything on a rock (6:20). He obeys. The angel of the Lord then extends his staff and touches the meat and the unleavened bread. Fire immediately comes up out of the rock and consumes the offering.[19] And while Gideon gazes, his visitor vanishes from sight.

The Lord had progressively revealed himself to Gideon. At no time was He demanding or impatient. Nor was his revelation of himself overt. Rather it was subtle and persistent, accommodated to Gideon's rate of perception. This is the way He deals with us.

We want results immediately, if not sooner, and our impatience tempts us to give up on those believers who do not show the progress we expect of them. To us, therefore, comes the example of the Lord and his patience in leading those of us who are slow to learn (cf. Luke 24:25–27; John 14:9; 16:12).

Gideon responds in fear to the realization that he has been talking with the Lord face to face. "Alas! O Yahweh God! For I have seen the angel of Yahweh face to face" (6:22).

The Israelites believed that anyone who saw God face to face would die (cf. 13:22). The Lord, though no longer visible, immediately responds to Gideon and assures him that he will not die (cf. Gen. 16:13; 32:30; Exod. 20:19; 33:20). As a token of his gratitude, Gideon builds an altar[20] to the Lord and worships him there. His altar will serve as a memorial of all that has taken place that day.

The Summons (6:25–27)

Rejoicing in his newfound peace, and perhaps wondering how the words of the Lord will be fulfilled, Gideon returns home. After dining with his family, he retires for the night.

No lengthy interval of time separates Gideon's call from the first task that the Lord gives to him. That night God appears to him (perhaps in a vision) and instructs him to destroy the altar of Baal together with the wooden symbol of the Asherah that stands beside it. Then he is to build a new altar to the Lord on the wall of the village where all can see it and there offer the seven-year-old bullock[21] belonging to his father. This burnt offering will show Gideon's entire commitment to the Lord, as well as the means whereby he will consecrate himself to the task that the Lord has assigned to him.

To fulfill God's commission, Gideon takes with him ten trusted servants (cf. 6:27–28). He does this at night, for if he attempted to destroy the objects of the religious affections of the men of the city during daylight hours, he would most certainly be stopped.

God loathes idolatry, and He quickly communicates his will to Gideon. Gideon promptly obeys. He does not equivocate, ask for more time, or seek to evade responsibility. He rises up, awakens his servants, and, aided by the dim firelight cast by their torches, promptly carries out God's bidding.

In fulfilling the will of the Lord, Gideon is borne along by a sense of the reality of the presence of God. This overshadows all other considerations, even those of his father and his immediate family.

The Result (6:28–32)

The result is exactly as Gideon expects. The next morning, when the men of the city go out to offer the usual sacrifices to Baal at the beginning of a new day, they are furious when they find that someone has torn down the altar to their god and chopped it up for firewood. Whether their inquiries lead to Gideon or they come to the conclusion that he is responsible based on his previous opposition to their religious practices, we do not know. They form a lynch mob and storm Joash's home, demanding Gideon's blood.

Joash, who has lost his other sons to the Midianites, is not prepared to give up his last remaining heir. He shows his courage and his knowledge of human behavior by challenging the villagers. He points to the impotency of Baal and says, in effect, "If Baal is really a god and feels insulted by my son's actions, let him intervene in his own behalf. Why do you need to become involved? It is a matter between Baal and my son. Let Baal settle his differences with him." Then, lest some erstwhile protagonist of Baal secretly try to kill Gideon and secure favor for himself, he adds, "Instead, let the person die who attempts to set himself up above Baal and thus deny Baal the right to punish Gideon as he sees fit."

It is a shrewd move. The people cannot refute the logic of Joash's argument, and they soon disperse.

The Invasion (6:33–40)

Verse 33 implies that it is only after Gideon has offered his sacrifice that the Midianite invasion takes place.[22] The Midianites, Amalekites, and "sons of the East" congregate a little to the southeast of the Sea of Galilee. From this vantage point they cross the river Jordan at a convenient ford and camp in the valley of Jezreel on the eastern side of the Esdraelon. This section of the valley is very fertile and forms an ideal vantage point from which the Midianites can stage their raids. The writer continued his story: "And the Spirit of Yahweh came upon Gideon" (6:34).

JUDGES 6

God's timing, of course, is perfect. The ministry of the prophet
and the actions of Gideon have emboldened the men for action.
When they hear the sound of Gideon's trumpet, they respond. The
first group to rally around him are the men from his own extended
family. Gideon then sends messengers throughout the tribes of
Manasseh, Asher, Zebulun, and Naphtali. They likewise commit
themselves to ridding the land of the enemy. Traveling in pairs and
small groups, they make their way discreetly to an encampment
near the spring of Harod (7:1).

The Midianites have so dispersed the people of Issachar that
they cannot be gathered, and Gideon does not send messengers
to the tribe of Ephraim.[23] His reluctance to summon the people of
Ephraim showed his humanness. In spite of the empowering of the
Holy Spirit, Gideon still feared others. Ephraim was the largest and
most arrogant of the tribes, and he was intimidated by them. We
have all had such an experience, and we have no right to stand in
judgment of him for his timidity and fear. All the biblical writer did
was show us Gideon's true humanity.

The men must be discreet in their movement so as not to
arouse the suspicions of the Midianites, so it takes several weeks
for them to gather from the other tribes. The response is good;
more than thirty thousand men eventually rally. But even with
their precautions, the invaders become aware of what is happening (cf. 7:9–14). The delay is hard for Gideon. Feeling the mammoth
undertaking before him, his faith begins to waver. He asks God to
confirm his will to him. In what has become known proverbially as
"putting out the fleece" (6:36–40), Gideon seeks personal reassurance. In doing so he showed that his faith was not constant.[24]
God's patience and condescension were remarkable. He knew
Gideon's frailty and worked with him in spite of his faults (cf. Ps.
103:14).

The weakening of Gideon's faith reinforces the importance of
daily fellowship with the Lord. When the angel of the Lord met with
Gideon at the wine press, He strengthened Gideon's faith. That
night when God reappeared to him, his faith did not waver. He
showed himself strong under pressure. The recollection of all that
had happened during the day strengthened him, so he acted with
confidence. Later, when the Spirit of the Lord came on Gideon, he
did not vacillate even though he knew that his army would be

grossly inferior to the Midianite hordes. He acted promptly. With resolute determination he sent out messengers to summon the men of the tribes to meet with him. Then came a time of waiting.

It is always hard to wait. We prefer action. Inactivity gives us time to think. Questions arise in our minds. This questioning was probably what preceded Gideon's request for a sign. Will the Israelites support me? How many men will be enough? What type of strategy should I use? How will I communicate my plan of attack to my people? Will any plan be successful against so many people with better equipment and greater maneuverability? How can we possibly hope to overcome their superior numbers? And what about their camels? Of course, we know how the story ends, but Gideon did not. It was during this period of waiting that he felt the need for reassurance and asked the Lord for a sign. And the Lord gave him one (6:37–40).[25]

In spite of Gideon's weakness, the writer of Hebrews recorded his name in God's "Hall of Fame" (Heb. 11:32). God forged his faith in a furnace. The morale of the people was low after seven years of one of the worst economic depressions in their history, yet God eventually reduced Gideon's army from thirty–two thousand to three hundred.

BY WAY OF REVIEW

Nothing is too hard for the Lord (Gen. 18:14; Jer. 32:17, 27; Luke 1:37ff.). Consider the great accomplishments of men and women of faith. Their names come readily to mind. When God desires to use us, however, all of a sudden we become fearful. Timidity characterizes our thoughts, and vacillation our acts. As with Gideon, we may also be tempted to ask God for a sign. Unlike Gideon, we often demonstrate the weakness of our faith through our disobedience.

True greatness is found in our integrity (or honesty), resourcefulness, humility, recognition of our strengths and weaknesses, graciousness, devotion to duty, and the courage with which we set about doing what needs to be done. Furthermore, the point at which we come to doubt our sufficiency is the point at which God begins to use us.

JUDGES 6

Restoration of a Relationship

The key to greatness lies in the development of a relationship with the Lord that expands our world of reality. As with Gideon our tendency is to limit our horizons to the things that directly affect us. In Gideon's situation he focused on survival: evading the Midianites when they were on their predatory raids, preserving his meager wealth, and looking after the welfare of his family.

In our case our bosses may intimidate us, our fear of losing our jobs may unsettle us, and the pressure of unpaid bills and the anxieties of child rearing and family relationships may almost do us in. The result is that our world of reality can become constricted. We unknowingly leave God out. When this happens we limit our awareness of what is real to the horizontal dimensions of life.

What is the solution to this kind of dilemma? How may we expand our concept of reality?

The pressures we face are unquestioned. To handle them, we need to realize that the Lord is vitally involved in everything that takes place in our lives (cf. Ps. 139:1–24; Rom. 8:18–39). He is as present with us as He was with Gideon when this valiant man could not see him (cf. 6:16a).

As our relationship with the Lord develops, we will come to understand more of his lovingkindness toward us. We will draw encouragement from his acts in the past and also understand his desires for us in the present. A new sense of confidence (not self-confidence that stems from humanism) will then begin to characterize the things we say and do.

As our faith grows, we will come to a clearer understanding of God's right to be worshiped (cf. 6:18–24). This is the highest form of service. And as his abiding presence becomes more and more of a reality to us, we will perceive a hidden purpose behind the trials we face. His goal is to separate us from fleshly attachments and bring us into conformity to the image of Christ.

The secret of God's power in us lies in the quality of the relationship we develop with him. As with Gideon, we will have our moments of confidence and our periods of doubt. We are human. The encouragement from this story is that the Lord understands our frailty and graciously ministers to our need. In time we will be able to echo the words of the apostle Paul in 2 Corinthians

2:14*a*: "But thanks be to God, who always leads us in his triumph in Christ" (note the context: 2 Cor. 2:12–3:5).

Responsibilities and Rewards

With the restoration of our relationship with the Lord and an accompanying growth in our awareness of his presence, there comes a testing of our commitment. This invariably involves doing some specific task (cf. 6:25–27). Although the task may vary with our gifts and abilities, He designs the test to separate us from the things of the world and identify us more closely with him. The testing of our commitment often necessitates a decisive and irrevocable step. It causes us to take a stand for that which we believe.

Gideon was from one of the smallest villages of Israel and was the youngest of his family, which shows that God works through ordinary people to accomplish extraordinary things.

JUDGES 6

6 A QUESTION OF POWER

Judges
7 – 8

Robbie was an all-American boy. He and his parents visited his grandparents in California. On a visit to Disneyland Robbie developed a fascination for Space Mountain. His grandparents also took him to Magic Mountain, where he rode the roller-coaster, Colossus. Robbie shrieked with delight as the ride screeched up, down, and around the track. He had seen Star Wars so many times that his friends considered him an authority on Darth Vader, Obi-Wan Kenobi, and the Jedi Knights. He was fascinated by the gadgets in James Bond movies. Robbie could talk for hours of lasers, rockets, cosmic rays, and scientific gadgets.

His parents had been reared in nominally Christian homes. Ted and Rose MacFarlane had attended Sunday school in their childhood and felt that Robbie should, too. One Sunday they tidied up their son and sent him off with some neighbors. On his return, they asked him how he liked Sunday school.

"Okay, I guess."

"What did they teach you?" coaxed his mother.

"Well, there was this Israeli general. Some of his men were trapped behind enemy lines. The Egyptian army was closing in on them, and it would be only a matter of time before they would be wiped out.

"But the general got there first and had the engineers build a pontoon bridge across the water. Then his soldiers crossed in safety. A plane radioed that the Egyptians were only a few miles away. The general waited until they were crossing the bridge and then signaled for the jets to attack them. They blew up the bridge with rockets, and the general became some kind of hero."

His parents looked at each other in bewilderment. Finally Ted asked, "And what was the name of the general?"

"Moses," Robbie replied.

"Are you sure that is how your Sunday school teacher told the story?" asked his father.

"Well, not exactly," admitted Robbie. "But the way she told it, you wouldn't believe it!"

Unless we are familiar with the Bible, many of the events will seem as incredible to us as the events of the Exodus were to young Robbie. This is true whether we are reading about Moses at the Red Sea or Gideon at the spring of Harod.

Gideon was an untried soldier, ignorant of the methods of warfare. The Lord had placed tremendous responsibility in his hands. He was soon to learn that to "those who have no might, he increases power" (Isa. 40:29). Gideon admitted his own weakness. The Spirit of the Lord had "clothed" him, possessing, empowering, and equipping him for battle against the Midianites. Now, as he waited for men from the different tribes to gather, his sole reliance was on the Lord.

The Midianite campaign may be divided into three parts: (1) the elimination of the unfit (7:1–8); (2) encouragement of the fainthearted (7:9–15a); and the encounter with the enemy (7:15*3b*–8:21).

ELIMINATION OF THE UNFIT (7:1–8)

As the men of Israel assemble, they survey the cloud of human locusts that has already spread throughout the valley. Gideon[1] camps beside a spring, identified today with modern 'Ain Jalud,[2] at the foot of Mount Gilboa. Five miles to the north, across the valley of Jezreel, is the hill of Moreh. The Midianite encampment lies between, with their tents following the contour of the hill.[3]

In verse 1 Gideon leads his men along the southern branch of the plain, where they have a full view of the large force against which they will be moving. The prospect of doing battle with such a vast army causes many stout hearts to quail. They sense their insignificance when compared with such a mighty throng. But while they think of themselves as too few, God thinks of them as too many.

As Gideon reviews the thirty-two thousand who have left their families to join forces with him, God tells him to eliminate the unfit from his ranks (cf. Deut. 20:1–8).

> And Yahweh said to Gideon, "The people who [are] with you [are too] many for me to give Midian into their hands, lest Israel glorify itself against me, saying 'My hand has given deliverance to me.' And now proclaim in the ears of the people, saying, 'Whoever is fearful and trembling, let him return and go away from Mount Gilead'"[4] (7:2–3).

The reason God gives for the troop reduction is that Israel may become boastful and claim that they gained the victory by their own initiative (cf. Ps. 44:3). So Gideon obeys. Twenty-two thousand depart, leaving only ten thousand to face one hundred and thirty-five thousand swordsmen, not counting others numbered among Midian's vast host.

We might well imagine that after having eliminated those lacking courage, Gideon would then take on the forces of Midian. As with the Greeks at the Battle of Thermopylae, the English at the Battle of Hastings, and the brave U.S. Marines at Iwo Jima, we might expect courage and resourcefulness to win the day for Israel. Such was not the case.

Before the engagement Gideon receives a further word from the Lord, telling him, to his amazement, that his forces are still too many:

> And Yahweh said to Gideon, "The people [are] still [too] many; bring them down to the water, and I will try them [i.e., put them to a test] for you there" (7:4a).

The drinking test eliminates those lacking caution (7:4b–8).[5] After this, only three hundred men remain.

By way of encouraging Gideon, the Lord then says to him, "I will deliver you with three hundred men . . . and will give the Midianites into your hand" (7:7).

TIME OUT

From a human point of view, the thirty-two thousand men who rallied around Gideon were the bravest in Israel. Their hearts had been stirred by what the Lord was going to do, but the army before them was intimidating. When they saw the vast Midianite coalition, many of them began having second thoughts.

God does not often work through the fearful and those whose faith is inadequate to the demands of the hour. Even the Lord Jesus would not do his mighty works in Nazareth because of their unbelief (Matt. 13:58). Numbers, therefore, are no guarantee of success. Only the presence of the Lord can assure victory; and He can best work through a handful of dedicated, trusting men (cf. Deut. 8:17; Zech. 4:6b).

It must have been hard for Gideon to see two-thirds of his hastily recruited volunteers melt away before his eyes. It must have been even more difficult for him when God cut his remaining force from ten thousand to three hundred. Whereas Gideon may have justified the first reduction in strength on the grounds that it was good for the morale of the men, the second stripped away all reliance on human strength. And Gideon, who had twice asked God for a sign, now has no one to rely on but the Lord.

ENCOURAGEMENT OF THE FAINTHEARTED
(7:9–15a)

The day begins with the army of the Israelites hopelessly outnumbered. By nightfall Gideon has dismissed the thousands whom he had at first welcomed. Cold campfires and trampled grass are the only evidence of their brief stay by the spring of Harod. We have no means of knowing what Gideon's feelings were as evening fell. He was human, and while his confidence was in the Lord, it would have been natural for him to entertain doubts and misgivings. We do know that God was very conscious of Gideon's needs.

That same night the Lord tells him to go down to the camp of Midian and sneak past the sentries, where he will hear something that will encourage him. God tells him that if he is afraid, he should take Purah, his servant, with him.

Gideon obeys. In the dark, he and Purah descend the hill, pass the spring, and make their way silently and unnoticed across the valley separating the camps. Apparently discipline in the Midianite army is slack, for no sentinels challenge their approach, and they are able to find their way to one of the tents of armed men.[6]

Gideon and Purah hear voices coming from inside the tent. One of the soldiers has just awakened from a fearful dream, which he recounts to his companion. In the dream a small loaf of moldy barley bread[7] tumbled down the hill, rolled up against the tent of the king,[8] and caused it to topple over.

In Near Eastern lands dreams still are considered to be omens of the future, especially if the dreamer is a man of rank or authority. The people believe that pagan deities make their will or desires known by means of dreams. As a consequence, those living in these lands are superstitious and seek out people who can interpret dreams (cf. Gen. 37:5–11; 40:5–22; 41:1–32; Dan. 2:1–45; 4:4–28; 7:1–28).[9]

As Gideon and Purah listen to the conversation, the soldier's comrade interprets the dream:

> "This is nothing less than the sword of Gideon, the son of Joash, a man of Israel. God has given Midian and all the camp into his hand" (7:14).

The Midianites had apparently had time to send spies throughout the land. These spies had witnessed the gathering of the tribesmen and must have brought back word of Gideon's activities. So thorough was their espionage that they knew Gideon by name.

The word translated "loaf" (of barley bread) is found only here in scripture and graphically portrays the poverty of the Israelites. Because barley was the staple of the extremely poor, it represents the insignificance of Gideon in the eyes of his people and the Midianites. He was "the least [i.e., the youngest] in his father's house," from one of the smallest units in Israel; and he has now dared to come up against the combined might of the Midianites.

The "tent" is an interesting symbol of the nomadic Bedouin clustered with their wives and children at the base of Mount

Moreh. But even more significant is what happens to the tent. When the small barley loaf rolls up against it, it completely collapses. The biblical text multiplies descriptive terms to convey its utter destruction. The barley bread struck it so that it was turned upside down, flattened, and opened from the inside out (7:13).

On hearing this Gideon bows his head and worships the Lord. His faith has been strengthened. God is going to do a supernatural work. He knows that he is as insignificant as the stale, oval loaf of bread; yet God is going to do a mighty work through him. The power and the glory will belong to the Lord alone. The routing of the enemy will be God's doing.

ENCOUNTER WITH THE ENEMY (7:15b–8:21)

The writer told in great detail[10] how Gideon and his little band of three hundred men defeat the Midianite throng. The text may be divided as follows: the strategy used (7:15b–18); the rout of the enemy (7:19–23); the call for reinforcements (7:24–25); an unfortunate delay (8:1–3); the pursuit of the kings (8:4–12); judgment of the traitors (8:13–17); retribution in kind (8:18–21).

The Strategy Used (7:15b–18)

Gideon now acts with determination, for the conversation of the two soldiers has dispelled every doubt. His words to the three hundred motivate them to action and encourage them with the promise of victory: "Arise, for Yahweh has delivered Midian into your hand."

Gideon's strategy is very simple. He divides the men into three equal groups, one of which he commands himself. Each soldier takes a trumpet[11] and an earthenware jug with a firebrand concealed in it. Gideon's instructions are clear and direct:

> "Look on me, and do likewise. And behold, when I come to the outermost part of the camp, it shall be that, as I do, so shall you do. When I blow the trumpet, I and all that are with me, then you blow the trumpets also on every side of the camp, and say, 'For Yahweh and for Gideon'" (7:17–18).

The three platoons are to circle the Midianite camp and, at the signal, blow their trumpets, smash the water pots on the ground (which would have sounded ominous in the still night air), and hold high the flaming torches.

The Rout of the Enemy (7:19–23)

The men do as Gideon has instructed them. The time chosen for the attack is the beginning of the middle watch, or about ten P.M. Those in the Midianite camp have settled down for a night of rest. The children have been asleep for several hours, and the women have cleaned the dinner dishes and found warmth and comfort amid the rugs and pillows of their Bedouin beds.

The sounding of the trumpets awakens and bewilders the slumbering Midianites. Accustomed to signals given with a ram's horn, each man knows exactly what to listen for, but the trumpet blasts they hear are not those of fellow Midianites (cf. Exod. 19:13; Lev. 25:9; Num. 10:1–10; 1 Cor. 14:8). This only adds to the confusion within the camp. Furthermore, the echo of the breaking jugs makes the men think a battle has begun. They conclude that the enemy must even now be within their camp. As the women try to comfort crying infants, the men stagger to the doors of their tents. There, on every side, are torches, which the Midianites believe light the way for the fighting men. Fear grips the hearts of the Midianites. They reach for their weapons. In the darkness they strike out at anything that moves. The writer's repetitious expression "run and flee" reveals the general panic in the camp and each person's concern for his or her own safety.

All this time the men of Israel are stationary, blowing their trumpets, holding high their flaming torches, and uttering their battle cry. Midianites who can either run or ride take the shortest route to the Jordan River. The camp of Midian, with its spoils of war, in some small way recompenses the Israelites for the years of economic privation.

The Call for Reinforcements (7:24–25)

The Midianites flee eastward down the valley of Jezreel. Gideon realizes this and sends messengers throughout the country of Ephraim, asking the residents to come down against Midian and take the fords of the Jordan as far as Beth-barah.

The Ephraimites respond to Gideon's call and capture the two Midianite princes, Oreb and Zeeb. The annals of God's people record this as one of the mighty acts of the Lord (cf. Ps. 83:9–12). So ends the battle of Jezreel.[12] God has delivered the northern tribes from a fierce and rapacious enemy.

An Unfortunate Delay (8:1–3)

At this point, when speed is of the essence and Gideon needs to overtake the kings of Midian before they have time to regroup, the men of Ephraim confront him. Their attitude is harsh and contentious. As the largest of the tribes, they naturally enjoy supremacy over all the others. Having lived for the most part free from the hostile incursions of the Midianites, the Ephraimites have experienced more freedom than any of their neighbors. Furthermore, the religious centers of Bethel and Shiloh lie within their borders, and this has caused them to become proud. What the prophet Isaiah would later refer to as "the envy of Ephraim" (Isa. 9:9) is even now in the process of becoming a proverb. They are used to having things their own way (cf. Gen. 48:14, 17–20). Later Hosea will describe them as unfit for leadership, a people who do not know where their true loyalties lie (Hos. 7:8; 10:11).

Realizing that a "soft answer turns away wrath" (cf. Prov. 15:1; 16:32; 19:11), Gideon commends these hostile Ephraimites for their capture of Oreb and Zeeb and asks in effect, "What could we ever have done that could be compared with such a mighty deed?"

Then the writer added, "The anger [of the men of Ephraim] toward [Gideon] subsided when he said that." Gideon's tactful answer soothed their indignation and averted a potentially dangerous internal rivalry.

While others return to gather the spoils of war from the slain Midianites, Gideon and his brave three hundred pursue the kings of Midian.

The Pursuit of the Kings (8:4–12)

With the Ephraimites pacified, Gideon's small force continues after Zebah and Zalmunna. It is about fifty miles from Mount Moreh across the Jordan to the city of Succoth in the territory of Gad (cf.

Josh. 13:27). By the time Gideon and his soldiers reach the city, they are exhausted and in need of refreshment.

To Gideon's legitimate appeal, the men of Succoth reply with calloused indifference. They inform him that it is not politically expedient for them to aid him. He may be unsuccessful in capturing the Midianite kings, and they may return to wreak havoc on them and their city.

Dr. John Marshall Lang pointed out that Succoth was

> a city with an imposing organization of rulers and elders. No fewer than seventy-seven are mentioned; seventy councilors or elders, and seven princes or rulers at the head. It had not sent a contingent to the national army: surely in the hour of triumph, it would gladly contribute its abundance to the gallant band which [even now] pursued a common foe.[13]

The Gadites were descended from Jacob, and Gideon appeals to their common relationship. His words are tactful and directed to both their sense of humanity and their patriotism.

The response of the leaders of Succoth is harsh and unreasonable. External considerations alone motivate them. They have seen the imposing host of Midian many times. They have probably enjoyed the brisk trade that accompanied their annual migration into the area. In looking at Gideon's army—hungry, tired, and poorly equipped—they probably conclude that their ragtag outfit will never overtake Zebah and Zalmunna, let alone defeat or capture them in battle. They fear that these kings will then raise another army and return at the same time next year. The leaders of Succoth conclude, therefore, that it is safer to risk Gideon's wrath than to expose themselves to the vengeance of these powerful monarchs.

When God appointed Gideon over his people and commissioned him to deliver them, Gideon became God's representative under the theocracy. When he spoke, it was as if God spoke directly through him. When he requested aid from the men of Succoth, it was as if Yahweh himself was asking them for help. And when the men of Succoth refused to help Gideon, they were in reality refusing to help the Lord. The fact that they looked on outward appearances and weighed their decision on the basis of what was politically expedient did not make them less culpable. Their reply shows a haughty disdain. It was the kind of response that God abhors (cf. Prov. 15:25; 16:5; 21:4; Isa. 5:15; James 4:6; 1 Peter 5:5).

Tired and thirsty, Gideon's army continues to follow the trail of the retreating Midianites. Traveling along the route normally taken by caravans, they come on Penuel. Here they make the same request, and from the men of Penuel they receive the same kind of answer. Lacking anything to refresh their spirits, they press on.

Zebah and Zalmunna have taken refuge in a city some distance from Penuel named Karkor. They have with them fifteen thousand men, "all who are left of the entire army of the sons of the East."

Karkor,[14] near the Wadi Sirhan, is east of the Dead Sea. Here these kings of Midian believe themselves to be safe. Gideon, they reason, will have long since given up following them.

Gideon, however, circles behind Karkor (8:11) and comes on the camp from an unexpected direction. Once again, he routs the entire army, and the kings of Midian flee. Gideon pursues them and overtakes them. Then he and his band of three hundred men return home, taking Zebah and Zalmunna with them.

Judgment of the Traitors (8:13–17)

En route to the Jordan, Gideon's victorious army again passes by Penuel and Succoth. They remind the elders of their taunting refusal to help (8:6, 8) and then fulfill their promised (8:7, 9) punishment.

Some commentators have severely criticized Gideon for his handling of the Gadites who refused to help him and his men. Some writers even claim that the "demon of revenge" raged within his heart. Others dismiss his actions as primitive and savage. Yet Gideon carefully distinguished between the townspeople and their leaders. His quarrel was with the chief men who had shown no loyalty to the Lord. Both cities should have rallied to his aid. Instead, they did not show compassion and refused to help their own brethren. They preferred to play political games with the ungodly.[15] Their punishment was just.

Retribution in Kind (8:18–21)

From verses 18–21 it appears that Gideon returns to Ophrah. It has been an exciting and tiring campaign. Gideon is to be commended for having done so thoroughly what he set out to do. He did not allow his enemy to escape out of his hand. Now it is time to mete out judgment on Zebah and Zalmunna.

In confronting each of them, Gideon asks what kind of people they had put to death on the slopes of Mount Tabor. At an earlier time, the Midianites evidently had come unexpectedly on a group of unarmed Israelites. In fear of their lives, the Israelites had retreated up the side of Mount Tabor, but they could not escape. The Midianites captured and slaughtered them, apparently for the amusement of the leaders of Midian. Zebah and Zalmunna tell Gideon that the men they had killed "were like you, each one resembling the son of a king" (8:18).

Moses had instructed the Israelites how to redress wrongs, particularly the death of one of their people (Deut. 19:1–13). The "next of kin" assumed the role of the "avenger of blood." This duty Gideon now assumes. He shows his humanity in verse 19. Had his brothers been killed in the heat of battle, he would not have exacted vengeance on their murderers. Because the Midianites were guilty of wanton slaughter, however, Gideon says to Jether, his firstborn, "Rise, kill them." This young lad is afraid; so Gideon executes the kings of Midian himself.

REFLECTION ON A LONG LIFE (8:22–35)

Because of the notable victory Gideon has achieved over the Midianites, the people want to make him their king. They believe that a single ruler can coordinate the forces of the tribes and prevent any other foreign or domestic power from dominating the sons of Israel.

Gideon's response enhances our understanding of the theocracy. It shows Gideon's unselfishness and reveals the essential character of God's rule over his people through local representatives (cf. 1 Sam. 8:6; 10:19). Yahweh was Israel's king. He may not have been visible, but He was active in their affairs. They were his subjects. The government of Israel, therefore, was essentially theocratic.

"I shall not rule over you . . . Yahweh shall rule over you" (8:23),[16] is Gideon's reply.

With the victory won and Israel again established securely in the land, Gideon retires from public life. He does not use his newly acquired prestige to secure himself a place in one of the more honored cities of his tribe; he continues to live in the obscure village of Ophrah. In his retirement, he devotes himself to his family. His heroic actions have relieved the nation from oppression (8:28a). "And the land had rest for forty years" during the remainder of his life (8:28b).

Only one event mars Gideon's declining years. At the time the people come to him to make him their king, he requests that they give him the earrings from their spoil, which they gladly do (8:24–27). Gideon makes an ephod from the gold he receives, intending that it will remind the people of what God has accomplished. His action is not out of character with what others had done in establishing memorials (cf. Exod. 28:9–12; Num. 31:54; Josh. 4:7; 1 Sam. 7:12), but unfortunately this ephod, weighing between forty and seventy-five pounds, becomes an object of worship for Israel.

After Gideon's death the people also begin worshiping the Baals and make Baal-berith (lit., "Baal of the covenant") their god. The writer was preparing the reader for what was to follow by mentioning Abimelech, a son born to Gideon by his concubine in Shechem,[17] a Canaanite city that Israel may have incorporated through an alliance. Abimelech's name (*ᵃbî melek̠*) means "my father" [is] "king" (cf. Ruth 4:14). Most commentators have done Gideon an injustice by projecting their own feelings into the situation. They choose to see in the naming of the child Gideon's hankering after an honor he had earlier declined. Such a view ignores that the custom of the time was for mothers to name children.

POINTS TO PONDER

God takes delight in doing impossible things through unlikely people like Gideon, as Oscar Eliason captured in his well-known chorus:

> Got any rivers you think are uncrossable;
> Got any mountains you can't tunnel through?
> God specializes in things tho't impossible;
> He does the things others cannot do.

JUDGES 7 – 8

For our encouragement, God reminds us that He is the one who has made the heavens and the earth by his great power and his outstretched arm. Nothing is too difficult for him (cf. Jer. 32:17, 27). Furthermore, the Lord Jesus himself reminded his disciples that "the things impossible with men are possible with God" (Luke 18:27). The principles by which He operates, and the means by which we are able to accomplish things for his glory are (1) faith, (2) commitment, and (3) perseverance.

The Importance of Faith

Each time God spoke to Gideon, he responded promptly. He learned what God wanted done and he did it. The tasks assigned to him called for courage. They also led progressively to Gideon's becoming more and more closely identified with the Lord and his purposes for his people.

The same principle is true today. Whether it concerns work or home, unexpected setbacks or the loss of a relationship, unemployment or an unexpected pregnancy, the fact remains that the problems we face are God's opportunities.

The principle by which we cope with life's setbacks and surprises, as well as succeed in our God-appointed tasks, is faith. Faith differs from presumption or PMA—a "positive mental attitude." We do not have to "psych" ourselves up in order to have faith. All we have to do is believe what God has revealed about himself in his word. According to Hebrews 11:1, "faith is the assurance of things hoped for, the evidence of things not seen." By means of faith, we can commit everything in life to the Lord (cf. 1 Peter 5:7) and trust him to work out his purposes for us. We do not have to see the end from the beginning; we only have to yield ourselves in obedience to him who accomplishes all things in accordance with his will. He will then lead us forward one day at a time. The more consistently we do this, the easier it will be for us to understand the truth the apostle Paul expressed when he said that "all things work together for good to those who love God, to those who are called according to his purpose" (Rom. 8:28).

Gideon exercised faith when the angel of the Lord appeared to him and told him that Yahweh was going to deliver Israel by his hand. God both tested and strengthened Gideon's faith when He told him to break down the altar of Baal and make atonement for his own sins and those of his people. To faith Gideon added action. And through action his faith was strengthened. With his meager forces he took on the powerful Midianites. Solely by the power of the eternal, the "barley loaf" overturned the tent of Midian.

The Importance of Commitment

Gideon was irrevocably committed to doing what God wanted done. On two separate occasions God told him that the men comprising his small army were too many, finally reducing his band to no more than three hundred men. During this time of testing, Gideon's faith did not waver. He needed encouragement, however, because he was human. God knew this and gave him the confidence he needed to take decisive action.

In his leadership, Gideon illustrates an important spiritual principle. Bernard Montgomery expressed it this way: "Get your major purpose clear, take off your plate all which hinders that purpose and hold hard to all which helps it, and then go ahead with a clear conscience, courage, sincerity and selflessness."[18]

Gideon focused his attention on the routing of those who had invaded his land. He committed himself to this one thing. He faced setbacks, but he overcame them. And while others enriched themselves with the spoils of war, he and his men doggedly pursued the last remnant of the Midianite coalition. Finally, as a result of his faith and dedication to the will of God, he completely destroyed the Midianites and emerged victorious.

George MacDonald showed how well he knew the struggles of the human heart and the conflict fought between the flesh and the spirit when he wrote:

> I said—"Let me walk in the fields."
>> He said—"No, walk in the town."
> I said—"There are no flowers there."
>> He said—"No flowers, but a crown."
> I said—"But the skies are dark;
>> There is nothing but noise and din."
> And He wept as He sent me back—
>> "There is more," He said; "there is sin."

JUDGES 7 – 8

I said—"I shall miss the light
And friends will miss me, they say."
He answered, "Choose to-night
If I am to miss you, or they."
I pleaded for time to be given.
He said—"Is it hard to decide?
It will not be hard in Heaven
To have followed the steps of your Guide."
Then into His hand went mine,
And into my heart came He,
And I walked in the light Divine
The path I feared to see.

The Importance of Perseverance

The scriptures contain many stories of those who persevered
in spite of innumerable obstacles—mental, emotional, physical—
before succeeding in their life's work. We think, for example, of
Joseph who endured years in prison before he became prime
minister of all Egypt. Or Moses who journeyed on foot through the
desert for forty years, shepherding God's people as he led them
to the promised land. We share the heartache of Isaiah, Jeremiah,
Ezekiel, and other prophets whom God commissioned to preach
to a hard-hearted and self-willed people. We consider also the
sacrificial service of the apostle Paul who walked through Palestine, Asia Minor, and part of Europe to bring the gospel to those
who had never heard it.

Gideon is an example of the power of the will activated by the
word of the Lord. While tired and hungry, he followed the path of
the retreating invaders until he overtook them. The biblical text
describes him and his men as "faint, yet pursuing." They did not
lose sight of their goal until they had fought and won the last
battle.[19]

Faith, commitment, and perseverance are still the qualities of
those through whom the Lord accomplishes his will.

# THE ABUSE
OF POWER

Judges
9

In *Napoleon's Family*, Desmond Seward described Bonaparte's brothers and sisters as adept in collecting fortunes but unable to control their passions and hopelessly inadequate as leaders or rulers of the people. They were "drunk with the power bestowed upon them and ruinously unprepared to handle it." In time they destroyed everything that Napoleon had created.[1]

In *The Path to Leadership*, Bernard Montgomery provided his readers with biographical sketches of leaders and their varying styles. He did not limit himself to one family but focused on several great men of history. His goal was to uncover the secrets of sound leadership. A good leader, Montgomery affirmed, was a

> man who can be looked up to, whose personal judgment is trusted, and who can inspire and warm the hearts of those he leads—gaining their trust and confidence, and explaining what is needed in language which can be understood. It would seem, therefore, that the beginning of leadership is a battle for the hearts and minds of men, and this, I believe is the essence of the whole matter.[2]

Montgomery was equally clear as to what constituted bad leadership, and Judges 9 focuses on a man who exhibited such characteristics. He was Abimelech, one of Gideon's sons (cf. 8:30–35).

Although he was reared in Ophrah and had benefitted from all the material prosperity that his seventy half-brothers had enjoyed, Abimelech grew to adulthood with a pathological desire for power. The biblical writer described this desire, which Montgomery explained as "misleadership":

> Leadership which is evil, while it may succeed temporarily, always carries with it the seeds of its own destruction. . . . Misleadership is something false coming through a strong personality, and the stronger the personality, the worse the ultimate crash.[3]

THE CHOICE OF A LEADER (9:1–3)

Following the defeat of Midian, the people enjoyed four decades of peace and prosperity (8:28*b*). After Gideon's death, the people revert to the worship of Baal. As their allegiance to Yahweh declines, Abimelech seizes the opportunity to gain power, and his true motives become obvious. He approaches his mother's relatives in Shechem with the suggestion that they negotiate with the leaders of the people and have him appointed as their king (8:22–23).

> And Abimelech the son of Jerubbaal went to Shechem, to his mother's brothers, and spoke with them, and to all the family of the house of his mother's father, saying, "Speak, I pray you, in the ears of all the leaders of Shechem, 'Which [is] best for you, seventy men ruling over you, all sons of Jerubbaal, or one man ruling over you?' And you should remember that I am your bone and your flesh" (9:1–2).

The city of Shechem[4] lay in a fertile valley between Mounts Ebal and Gerizim. This valley was called the "navel of the land" and formed a natural link between the coastal plain and the Jordan valley. Several important trade routes converged on Shechem. It is probable that Gideon's business affairs had often taken him to the city. On one occasion he had seen a beautiful Canaanite woman there, whom he later took as his wife.[5] Their son had probably been born in Shechem, even though 9:1 implies he had been reared in Ophrah in the ways of the Lord with Gideon's other sons.

In spite of his godly upbringing, Abimelech is selfish and has no commitment to the truth. His appeal to his mother's side of the family bears this out, for his words distort the facts. He exaggerates the supposed threat by implying that the land is to be "redistricted" (i.e., divided) between Gideon's seventy sons. He also slyly arouses the prejudices of the people by referring to his father as "Jerubbaal," the one who had destroyed the altar to their god in Ophrah (6:25–27).

Abimelech's suggestion appeals to the self-interest of those in Shechem.[6] Like him, they are opportunists and see in his suggestion something that might benefit them. They show no loyalty or gratitude to Gideon who, though from the tribe of Manasseh, has been of immeasurable help to everyone living in the land (cf. 9:16–20).

Unscrupulous politicians have disregarded the truth and ignored the obligations of history for centuries.[7]

THE SEARING OF CONSCIENCE (9:4–6)

Abimelech's strategy works. His mother's relatives approach the leaders of the city and persuade them of the benefit of electing Abimelech as their king. Being Canaanites, they have no sympathy with the theocracy. It is to their advantage, they believe, to have a blood relative rule over them (cf. 9:26), especially one who owes them the favor of his appointment. In Abimelech they have someone they can manipulate to their advantage.

To accomplish his ambitions, Abimelech needs money. The people of Shechem lack scruples and take funds from the temple of Baal.[8] This they give to Abimelech (cf. 1 Kings 15:18; 2 Kings 18:15–16), and with it he hires "worthless and reckless" men who will eliminate all those who might obstruct his progress.

Gideon's sons have no political aspirations. They are still living quietly and peaceably in the village that has always been their home. They have not moved to any of the major centers of power. They have no interest in securing advancement for themselves now that their father is dead. Nevertheless, Abimelech takes his band of men to Ophrah and assassinates his half-brothers.[9]

Abimelech, believing that he has removed all opposition, returns to Shechem and proceeds with his coronation. His domain, though limited, will include Shechem and three adjacent towns: Beth-millo, Arumah, and Thebez (9:41, 50). But Abimelech's elevation to the throne encounters a setback. Gideon's youngest son, a youth named Jotham, escapes the massacre. By hiding during the carnage, he avoids detection.

A PARABLE OF POWER (9:7–21)

As Abimelech's coronation is in progress, Jotham interrupts the festivities from the slopes of Mount Gerizim. From this same mountain, in about 1405 B.C., six of the tribes had thundered their "Amens" as the Levites read the law (Deut. 27:12–28:68; Josh. 8:30–35). By using as a pulpit a level place a couple of hundred feet above the city, and by taking advantage of the natural acoustics of the valley below him, Jotham clarifies the issues for the people of Shechem by using a parable to illustrate the truth. His words are a protest against the treatment meted out to his brothers.

Each According to His Gifts (9:8–13)

The parable Jotham tells is designed to show, as Dr. G. Bush has pointed out, that the least deserving of people will sometimes thrust themselves into positions of power that the wise and good decline. It also illustrates that those who seek such advancement, as well as those who aid them, prove to be a source of misery to each other.[10]

Jotham describes clearly the people's rejection of the theocracy. He likens them to "trees" that go forth of their own accord to anoint a king over them.[11] The first tree to be approached with the offer of rulership is the olive. The olive rightly discerns that its appointed place in the economy of God is to bear fruit in accordance with its nature. If it accepts this invitation, it will "cause to cease" the very function by which God is honored and man is served. In fulfilling its role as an olive tree, it bears fruit naturally.

The olive tree, knowing its place in the plan and purpose of God, declines the invitation.

In the olive's rejection of the proffered crown, there is a subtle indication of the stress borne by leaders. Its words "go and wave over ['hover over'] the trees" is poetic. Although on the one hand it indicates the exercise of authority, on the other it describes the tensions and pressures (symbolized by external forces like the wind) that leaders have to endure.

The next tree to be approached with the invitation of headship is the fig tree. It, likewise, recognizes its place in God's creative design and asks rhetorically, "Shall I leave my sweetness and my good fruit, and go to wave over the trees?" It, too, declines.

The third tree to be tempted with a position of power and authority is the vine. Once again there is a recognition of divine appointment seen in the tree's reluctance to leave its natural function and the blessing it can bring to others. It, too, declines.

All three trees—the olive, the fig, and the vine—are perfectly content to fulfill the purpose God has ordained. None of them aspire to a position of leadership over the others. Jotham's question in the parable and directed to the men of Shechem is, "Why were the other trees so anxious to have a leader over them who would fulfill a function not in keeping with God's design?"

Their Nemesis (9:14–15)

In desperation the trees turn to the bramble. The irony behind Jotham's choice of the bramble is most interesting, for the bramble produces nothing of value and is worthless for its wood. In fact, it is a menace to farmers, who must wage a continual war against its encroachments. Wherever farmers leave it unchecked, it spreads a carpetlike growth that, in the heat of summer, is particularly susceptible to combustion. When a fire breaks out, it can spread rapidly.

The bramble is incapable of giving any protection (shade) to the trees of the forest. Yet in their desire to have a leader, the trees choose the bramble, the least worthy of their members, and give it the emblems of power.

The poetry in Jotham's parable heightens the unworthiness of the bramble for leadership. It underscores the unworthy motive of the trees and emphasizes the character of those who frequently seek public office.

The Importance of Integrity (9:16–21)[12]

Jotham proceeds with the interpretation of his parable.[13] In doing so he strongly appeals to his hearers' consciences (9:16). He also reminds them of past favors (9:17), rebukes them for their heartless ingratitude (9:18), and emphasizes the result of their rebellion (9:20). He then flees for his life (9:21).

Jotham drew a deliberate contrast between Abimelech and his father. He described the worthlessness of Abimelech, whom the men of Shechem had willingly appointed as their king. He also tacitly hinted at their rejection of Yahweh as the one who should rule over them. Jotham also charged the people with their shameful treatment of the family of his father, who had earned their devotion and respect. Then, instead of looking to the Lord for a leader like Gideon, they had chosen the son of his slave-concubine[14] and for the sake of personal gain had acknowledged him as "their brother."

This reference to Abimelech's mother as a "slave-concubine" was a deliberate slur, for Gideon's concubine was a free-woman, not a slave. She was probably from one of the prominent families in the city (cf. 9:1–2).

Finally, with words that bear a strong resemblance to Paul's warning in the New Testament (cf. Gal. 6:7), Jotham states that time will reveal the wisdom or folly of their actions. He predicts that "fire will come out from Abimelech and consume the men of Shechem" (9:20).

Certain men must have tried to climb to Jotham's vantage point, for the text says that Gideon's son hastily retreated (9:21).

THE FRUSTRATION OF HUMAN PLANS (9:22–49)

Jotham's parable constitutes the central truth of Judges 9. What follows underscores the veracity of his words. Abimelech rules over the people of Shechem for three years (1151–1149 B.C.). For a time all appears to go well. Those who have opposed his elevation to power are probably told how wrong they have been. Supporters of the monarchy possibly point to the beneficial aspects of Abimelech's administration. The God-fearing few must have shaken their heads and wondered about the future, but those swayed by outward appearances outnumber them.

Shechem's prosperity may have had its origin in the forty years of peace under Gideon, but no one gave credit to Gideon.

Source of Tension (9:23–25)

Abimelech founds his rise to power on corruption. Instead of enjoying peace as Gideon had done, Abimelech soon finds tension, divisiveness, treachery, and rebellion in the ranks of those who formerly supported him.[15] The first to turn against him are his "brothers," the men of Shechem. The biblical writer described this as retribution in kind (cf. 8:3–5). As Abimelech had planned the death of Gideon's sons, so now the men of Shechem plot to assassinate him.

Leader of the Opposition (9:26–29)

As anarchy becomes more and more common in the land (9:25b), a man named Gaal comes to Shechem.[16] He has with him a band of armed men. Although originally from that region, he has become a "soldier of fortune." He has gathered about him a group of mercenaries, and he and his men now take up residence in Shechem. Their numbers and combined strength are probably more than a match for the token force Abimelech has left in the city.

Gaal is shrewd enough to realize that there is a political interregnum. The people have no love for Abimelech, and he has deliberately chosen to live elsewhere. The men of Shechem are open to change, but they have been held in check by Zebul, the leader of Abimelech's garrison.

As soon as Gaal finds that Zebul commands only a token force and that the men of Shechem share his disdain for Abimelech, he sets out to gain their confidence. As he sows the seeds of discontent, he notes how easily his words sway the people.

At a festival commemorating the end of the summer harvest, when all the people of Shechem have imbibed freely, Gaal further fans the flames of discontent. He ridicules and maligns Abimelech and openly suggests that the people of Shechem place their confidence in him (9:27–29). His words are a direct challenge to the men of Shechem to cast off their allegiance to their king.

Gaal also reminds the people of Abimelech's heritage (as the son of Jerubbaal, v. 28; reversing Abimelech's own approach in vv. 1–3) and stimulates their national zeal by reminding them of the purity of their heritage as descendants of Hamor the father of Shechem (9:28b). He then encourages them to take independent action (9:29a; cf. Absalom's similar approach, 2 Sam. 15). The stage is set for the assertion of their independence. Gaal, however, has miscalculated Zebul's loyalty to Abimelech.

Misplaced Loyalties (9:30–33)

Every leader has his or her followers. These supporters are often very sincere in their loyalties; but because they lack true discernment, they sometimes align themselves with causes that are doomed.

It was so with Zebul. He was Abimelech's *pāqîd*, or "recruiter" (called a "lieutenant" in 9:28), a capable man who had allowed himself to become guilty of misplaced loyalties.

During the preceding few years, Zebul did well to maintain some semblance of order within the city. In the present situation, he apparently realizes his limitations. He knows that he cannot take on Gaal and his men. He therefore contains his anger and does not respond to the newcomer's derogatory remarks (9:28b, 30).

As soon as he can, Zebul sends a message to Abimelech. He tells him what Gaal has said and, at the same time, outlines a way that Abimelech may take the initiative and attack Shechem before Gaal realizes what is happening (9:32–33).

Suppression of a Coup (9:34–41)

Abimelech follows Zebul's counsel. He sends his cavalry at night to encircle the city (9:34). Apparently Zebul is aware of this move and deliberately seeks out Gaal the next morning. It is early and the rising sun casts irregular shadows on the hills and across the valley.

JUDGES 9

When Gaal thinks he sees men approaching, Zebul allays Gaal's suspicions (9:35–36) by saying it is difficult to distinguish anything clearly in the half light. This gains valuable time for Abimelech.

As Abimelech's forces approach even nearer the city, Gaal realizes that the "shadows" on the hillsides are, in reality, men from Abimelech's army (9:37). They are under attack.

In handling Gaal, Zebul has shown himself to be a master in the art of strategy. He had at first lulled Gaal and caused him to waste valuable time before summoning his men. Now he turns on him and says:

> "Where is your boasting [lit., 'your mouth'] now with which you said, 'Who is Abimelech that we should serve him?' Is this [i.e., these soldiers] not the people whom you despised? Go out now and fight with them" (9:38).

Gaal hastily marshals his forces, but Abimlech's cavalry routs them. They flee back to Shechem (9:39–40), but many are killed as they attempt to enter the city gates. Zebul has rallied those who are loyal to Abimelech, and they drive Gaal's men away, forcing them to find refuge elsewhere.

The victory does not assuage Abimelech's wrath. He is burning with indignation. Instead of consolidating his position in the city, he quarters his men in the nearby town of Arumah (9:41), identified today as Jabal al 'Urma.

Voice of the Prophet (9:42–49)

In keeping with Jotham's parable, fire is about to come out from the bramble and destroy the men of Shechem. In an act of willful vengeance, Abimelech attacks the city and breaches its walls. The men inside the city retreat into the inner chamber of the temple of El-berith (the same temple from which they had obtained money three years earlier to make Abimelech, "their brother," king [cf. 9:4ff.]).

There is something ironic about the Shechemites' retreat, for they enter (presumably with their families, cf. 9:49) the tower (or stronghold) of their god, seeking safety. It is as if they are hoping Baal will defend his honor and save their lives.

Abimelech is intent on satisfying his picayune and primitive instincts. Like Napoleon's family, he lacks all the qualities of a leader. His desire for vengeance is the outworking of his malice. Because he cannot tolerate any challenge to his authority, he abuses his power.

With the citizens of Shechem secure in the tower of the temple, Abimelech takes certain of his men up the heavily wooded Mount Zalmon.[17] There he cuts down a branch from a tree and instructs all his followers to do likewise. They take the branches into Shechem, lay them inside the temple, and set fire to the branches, causing an intense conflagration that destroys the tower and all those who seek shelter in it.

To show his contempt for the city, Abimelech "sows it with salt" (9:45),[18] thus fulfilling the first part of Jotham's parable.

DEATH OF A TYRANT (9:50–57)

Abimelech is not satisfied with the overthrow and destruction of Shechem. Apparently he believes that the people of Thebez (ten miles northeast of Shechem) have also conspired against him.

On seeing Abimelech and his soldiers approach their village, the people of Thebez flee into their city and take refuge in their tower. Because Abimelech's strategy against Shechem had worked to his advantage, he decides to do the same to Thebez. As he and his men are laying branches at the base of the tower, a woman who has fled into the tower with a small millstone[19] to use during the siege drops it on the monarch's head.

Realizing that he is dying and that future generations will ridicule him for being killed by a woman (cf. 4:21), Abimelech asks his armor-bearer to run him through with his sword. The young man does so. By noting these details, the inspired recorder of events preserved for us the true end of the man whose godlessness and avarice paved the way for his downfall. The writer showed the Lord's hand in the events at Thebez and Shechem:

> In this way God (Elohim) returned the evil of Abimelech, which he did to his father, to kill his seventy brothers; and all the evil of the men of Shechem God (Elohim) turned back on their own head; and on them came the curse of Jotham the son of Jerubbaal (9:56–57).

A TIME FOR REFLECTION

Men and women gain public office in many different ways. Some people come to power by a coup and then rule with dictatorial authority. When this happens, the people do not have the opportunity to vote for those who will be responsible for making policy, administering justice, and directing the affairs of their nation. Abimelech's rule illustrates how this kind of tyranny can replace freedom.

The Lust for Power

Even in countries where the people freely elect their rulers, the campaigns are often bitterly fought. Slander and innuendo are all too commonplace. In many cases the "behind the scenes" influence of powerful interest groups determines the political outcome. These groups divert monies from one cause to another so that a candidate favored by one of the interest groups can buy more television time or engage in more advertising. Often the politicians ignore the real issues and instead make appeals to the selfish desires of certain groups.

Abimelech was selfishly ambitious in his lust for power (cf. James 1:15). He subscribed to the expedient that "the end justifies the means." It was relatively easy, therefore, for him to have his brothers assassinated. He saw them as impediments to his rise to power. To gain his ends, he not only pretended to be concerned for his mother's brethren, but made false accusations about his brothers. His lies paved the way for his acceptance.

The Importance of Priorities

If we want to please God, we must not only avoid the lust for power but also understand his plan and purpose for our lives. We each have a function ordained by God. As with the olive, fig, and vine, God has given us gifts that we are to use for his glory. When we do this we prosper, and what we do benefits others.

All who are in leadership should take warning from what happened to Abimelech and the men of Shechem. As Bernard L. Montgomery pointed out, "Leadership which is evil, while it may succeed temporarily, always carries with it the seeds of its own destruction."[20] The events of this chapter prove the point he was making. God will punish the wicked. There is an irrevocable law imbedded in God's eternal decree. It is the law of retribution in kind. What we sow, we reap. Montgomery observed:

> Sound leadership is based upon truth and character. A leader must himself be the servant of the truth and he must make the truth the focus of a common purpose. He must then have the force of character necessary to inspire others to follow him with confidence.[21]

Without a commitment to the truth, we lack integrity and find it impossible to enthuse others with a sense of purpose.

A commitment to the truth infects us with genuine optimism. We are then able to persevere in the face of insuperable difficulties. We are also able to see problems clearly, formulate appropriate courses of action, and eventually master the circumstances that surround us.

When we live in accordance with the truth, we also become good judges of character. This helps us pick the right people for each task. The more capable our subordinates, the easier it is for us to achieve desired objectives.

The fundamental elements of leadership are found in integrity, sincerity, and selflessness.

The Place of Character

Integrity, selflessness, and sincerity also help us concentrate on essential issues. They prevent us from becoming side-tracked. We see the pros and cons clearly. We can then come to a decision and plan a course of action. Once we conceive our plan, it is easier to implement it.

All our plans must be carried out through people. People will only follow us over the long haul if they have confidence in us. Our characters form the basis of our leadership and the beliefs, values, and goals we seek to impart to others. These include the dignity of each individual, the necessity of enabling others to achieve personal and corporate objectives, and the ability to motivate others. A good leader must have an interest in, and a real knowledge of, people. He must be able to harness and use constructively the emotional forces inherent in each subordinate. When this is done, the godly leader can succeed where others succumb to personal ambition and exploitation of others.

There are times when a negative example highlights the importance of positive traits. The selfish ambition of Abimelech illustrates this point. Nothing noteworthy is recorded of him. He exists as a blemish on the pages of history.

JUDGES 9

8 PEACE ... AND HOW IT IS LOST

Judges
10:1–16

Thomas Hardy in *The Dynasts* wrote, "War makes rattling good history; but Peace is poor reading."[1]

He was right. In the history of the judges, the periods of peace are passed over with scarcely any comment. We read only that "the land had rest for . . . years" (cf. 3:11, 30; 5:31*b*; 8:28*b*). Nearly all of us, given the option, would prefer to live free from the threat of oppression and the trauma that follows hostile aggression.

To this end the apostle Paul exhorted believers to pray for those in authority so believers might be governed quietly and peaceably (1 Tim. 2:1–2). This was not a selfish request, but one that was in keeping with God's will for his people.

God's word describes what happens when evil stalks the land and the godly find themselves under the rule of a despot or a dictator. Discretion becomes the better part of valor, and they are compelled to keep a low profile (Prov. 28:12; 29:2, 16).

By contrast, when the righteous rule, there is peace, prosperity, and the possibility of happiness.

THE ENJOYMENT OF PEACE (10:1–5)

The first verse of chapter 10 provides an important link with the past: "Now after Abimelech died, Tola the son of Puah, the son of Dodo, a man of Issachar, rose up to deliver Israel."

Abimelech's brief reign had a disastrous effect on the tribes. He had suppressed the righteous (cf. Prov. 28:28), but the Lord had used the time to prepare his people for change—for a new form of leadership.

Many great people have disappeared from public view for periods of time. Moses spent forty years tending the sheep of his father-in-law, Jethro; Elijah lived beyond the borders of Ahab's domain with a widow of Zarephath; and the apostle Paul spent some four years in the deserts of Arabia. In modern times, the leaders Churchill, DeGaulle, and Ben-Gurion were either voted out of office or exiled. During these periods of isolation and seclusion, they had time to reflect on the issues facing their countries. They could formulate and try out different ideas in their minds. As they did so, the fire of conviction began to burn in their hearts. They became leaders of vision, confident of the solutions they had developed.

When these people, whom we now acknowledge as the great leaders of history, reemerged into the spotlight, there emanated from them a power that persuaded people of the veracity of their ideas as well as the viability of their plans. Their sincerity became contagious, their selflessness inspired confidence, and their years of planning and introspection helped them dominate and finally master the events that encompassed them.[2] Although we admire their greatness, we tend to forget the process by which they attained it.

The Man from Issachar (10:1–22)

It was this way with Tola (1149–1126 B.C.),[3] and only after Abimelech's death did he arise "to save" Israel.

Some modern writers have not given Tola the credit he deserves. One even called him a "very minor judge, who was such small fry after the glamorous Abimelech that nothing is said about anything he did."[4] This writer erred in his belief that Abimelech was a judge. He also failed to present any information to support his claim that Abimelech maintained an ostentatious court. But even more fundamental was his mistake in equating the benefits of a godly administration with the number of verses devoted to him. Scripture devotes many chapters to Nehemiah's rebuilding Jerusalem's walls but passes over his twelve years of administration with only an incidental comment.[5]

Tola[6] came from a notable family within his tribe, and his parents had named him after one of his great ancestors (Gen. 46:13; Num. 26:23). Men from Issachar were noted for their wisdom. They "understood the times, with knowledge of what Israel should do" (1 Chron. 12:32), and it is fair to assume that Tola possessed this tribal characteristic.

Tola was born, lived, and died in the hill country of Ephraim. He exerted his influence over Israel from a village that today archaeologists cannot identify with certainty. All the biblical text recorded was that he arose "to save" Israel.

The word *yāša'*, which originally meant "to give width and breadth" to something, eventually meant "to liberate."[7] When the Bible uses it with the word *mîyad*, it implies to save "from the hand" of someone or something (cf. 2:16; 8:22; 12:2; 13:5). When it is not used with a qualifying term, it has the sense of preserving existence.[8]

In place of spectacular deeds, Tola, a good and godly man, ruled quietly and effectively. As Dr. A. R. Fausset pointed out, Tola kept Israel from idolatry for the twenty-three years he was in office.[9] He had a profound influence on the people. We should not minimize his contribution to the well-being of the sons of Israel.

God's Man in Gilead (10:3–5)

Following Tola's death, Jair[10] the Gileadite (1126–1105 B.C.) became the leader of God's people. His home was east of the Jordan in the territory allotted to the half tribe of Manasseh (cf. Num. 32:41; Deut. 3:14). One of his ancestors had conquered certain towns in Gilead and had called them Havvoth-jair, the "villages of Jair."

Evidence of Jair's stature among the people and success in administering justice is suggested in 10:4. He had thirty sons (a mark of prestige), and each son rode on a male donkey (a sign of prosperity). According to Dr. Fausset, people used the ass in times of peace and the horse in times of war (cf. 5:10; 12:14; 1 Kings 1:33; 10:28; Zech. 9:9).[11] This, too, was significant, for it pointed to the state of affairs that Jair maintained.

Jair made each of his sons responsible for governing a city (1 Chron. 2:22; cf. Josh. 13:30; 1 Kings 4:13).[12] Although he would certainly have to answer the charge of nepotism today, this was a common policy in the Near East; and the fact remains that the people benefited from tranquility and prosperity for twenty-two years. Furthermore, there was no hint of unrighteousness in the administration of Jair's sons. When war broke out with the Ammonites, the cause was not attributed to them but rather to the apostasy of the people.

GOD'S PLAN FOR PEACE

The idea of peace in the Old Testament implied a state of wholeness. The use of the word *shalom* intimated health, prosperity, security, and the completeness of the blessings of the covenant (cf. Ps. 144:12–15). It involved relationships with God and man.

Tola and Jair were responsible for preserving peace. They "judged" Israel (cf. Exod. 18:15; 2 Chron. 19:6), applying the law (Exod. 20–23) to those who were unsure of their standing before God or concerned about their personal conduct or troubled by relationships with their fellow man. In this way they maintained harmony among the tribes and made possible a healthy form of peace. Jair's delegation of authority was to those whom he could trust to carry out the law. With their help he restrained evil.

The quest for peace today involves people of all nations and widely divergent ideologies. Yet few who clamor for peace work for it on peaceable terms (cf. 11:12–28), as Dag Hammarskjold's diary reveals.

Hammarskjold began keeping a diary when he was twenty years old. When it was found in his home after his death, the last entry was dated just three and one-half weeks before his death on a peace mission to Zaire.

As secretary general of the United Nations, Hammarskjold was not free to share his faith. Delegates to the U.N. come from all parts of the world and hold widely divergent beliefs, but they cannot discuss about their religious commitments, except in private. Hammarskjold's diary records his struggle to live out his faith in this hostile setting. He believed, as William James once pointed out, that war emanates from the human spirit. Peace and justice can be achieved only as people bring themselves under the control of the Holy Spirit (cf. Gal. 5:22; James 4:1). True peace does not come from a kind of pacifism that fails to consider the depravity of human nature,[13] but from a mature, righteous leadership that avoids legalism and makes possible the active practice of the "four cardinal virtues" of prudence, justice, temperance, and fortitude.

Prudence is the habit of referring all matters to the Lord for his guidance. On this hinge wisdom, impartiality, and tact. Justice is marked by fairness and giving to God and man what is rightfully theirs. This trait determines duties, religious beliefs, obedience to ethical norms and standards, gratitude, integrity, and goodwill toward others. Temperance is evidenced in self-control. Purity, humility, and patience stem from it. Fortitude is the spirit within us that resists, endures, and triumphs over the trials and temptations of life. This virtue produces moral courage, industry, and self-discipline.[14]

Tola and Jair must have incorporated these elements into their administrations, for the result was forty-five years of peace.

THE LOSS OF FREEDOM (10:6–16)

The Desire for Something Different (10:6)

With the passing of Jair, the sons of Israel repeat the sorrowful cycle that has brought on their past misfortunes. They demonstrate how blind a people can be to the lessons of history. The writer emphasized the word *again* (10:6):

> And again the sons of Israel did evil in the eyes of Yahweh, and served the Baals[15] and the Ashtoreths,[16] even the gods of Aram [Syria], and the gods of Sidon, and the gods of Moab, and the gods of the sons of Ammon, and the gods of the Philistines; and they forsook Yahweh and did not serve him. And the anger of Yahweh burned [lit., glowed (with heat)] against Israel, and he sold them into the hands of the Philistines and into the hand of the sons of Ammon. And they

shattered and crushed the sons of Israel in that year; [and for] eighteen years they oppressed all the sons of Israel that [were] beyond the Jordan, in the land of the Amorites, which [is] in Gilead. And the sons of Ammon crossed the Jordan to fight [against the sons of Israel], even against Judah, and against Benjamin, and against the house of Ephraim; and Israel was greatly distressed (10:6–9).

Israel's sin was found in three verbs: "served . . . deserted (or forsook) . . . did not serve." A religious pluralism prevailed. Dr. Luke Wiseman linked this apostasy with Israel's previous departures from the Lord:

> Their repentances to God, though general, and perhaps for the moment sincere, were only transient. The complaint uttered by the prophet Hosea four hundred years later might have been uttered with equal justice [at this time]. "Your goodness is as the morning cloud, and as the early dew it goeth away" (Hosea 6:4). [Israel] not merely returned to their own ways, but addicted themselves to new and various forms of idolatry. They exceeded the folly of the neighboring heathen, who were content with worshipping their own national divinities. They "*served Baalim and the Ashtaroth.*"[17]

These included the inexorable Haddad or Rimmon of Syria, the lewd Astarte of Phoenicia (Sidon), the relentless Chemosh of Moab and Milcom/Molech of Ammon, and Dagon of Philistia. They did not so much as allow the Most High a place among the other objects of worship.

The nations that surrounded Israel had similar religious beliefs and practices.[18] Although the names of the gods and goddesses changed, and some local traditions were added, basically the worship centered in a male deity and his female consort.

After the deaths of Tola and Jair, the new generation preferred a religion that appealed to the senses. They found the worship of God too limiting.

The Discipline of the People (10:7–9)

To reprove his wayward people, the Lord raises up the Philistines and the Ammonites as his rod of anger (Isa. 10:5; cf. Judg. 3:8,

12; 4:2; 6:1) to chasten Israel. With Philistia on the west and Ammon on the east, the Israelites find themselves between two "millstones." The oppression is very severe, and their enemies are slowly but steadily grinding them to pieces.[19]

The main weight of the Ammonite attack falls on Gilead in Transjordan, but there are also forays by the Ammonites against the western tribes of Judah, Benjamin, and Ephraim. Pressure is also brought to bear on Israel's western frontier, where the Philistines are harassing villages along their border. The predicament of the tribes is not hard to imagine. They are fighting a war on two fronts. The more acute pressure at this stage, however, comes from Ammon.[20] The result is that the peace and measure of prosperity Israel enjoyed under Tola and Jair become only a memory. It is a marvel that the Israelites endured the harshness of this oppression for eighteen years.

The slowness of Israel to turn to the Lord was not only the result of the evil's deceptive nature but the activeness of idolatrous priests. Acting as (false) prophets[21] and using methods of divination, they may have assured the people that the oppression was only temporary.

We also know from reading comparative Near Eastern texts that false leaders sometimes explained away times of adversity by saying that the gods were testing the people's sincerity (cf. Prov. 13:23, 25; 14:34).[22]

From scripture we know that Micaiah, Jeremiah, and Nehemiah also had to contend with false prophets (cf. 1 Kings 22:5–12; Neh. 6:10–14; and Jer. 2:8; 23:13).

Had the people of Israel been more knowledgeable of the law, they would not have been so easily duped or led astray (cf. Deut. 13:1–5; 18:20–22).

Today people follow radio and television personalities without pausing to compare the teaching of the Christian media with all of God's truth (cf. John 17:17b). The result is mental impoverishment and emotional enslavement of a significant segment of Christendom. Then, in a time of crisis, they discover that they have founded their faith on the teaching of humankind rather than on the inspired and inerrant word of God.

Fortunately for all of us, the Lord has ways of drawing us back to himself, as our text illustrates.

The Response of the Lord (10:10–16)

As the crisis facing Israel worsens, those who were instrumental in leading the people astray begin to lose their control[23] as the people begin to repent.

> And the sons of Israel cried[24] to Yahweh, saying, "We have sinned against you, for we have even forsaken our God, and have served the Baals [the 'lords' of the nations about us]" (10:10).

In their general confession, the Israelites specify two distinct types of transgression: (1) departing from following the Lord; and (2) serving false deities. This confession is the first step in their restoration.

The writer did not indicate how widespread this movement was, but as Arthur Cundall pointed out, "God required [then], and requires still, the steadfast love, loyalty, and obedience of His subjects, in which He can operate continually on their behalf, rather than a relationship, lightly severed, in which He is used in times of emergency only."[25]

The Lord must have sensed a lack of depth in the repentance of his people, for He reminds them of his past faithfulness and does not promise them a deliverer. He wanted to encourage them by reciting his past deliverances, including the victory over the Egyptians (who were destroyed at the time of the Exodus), the great victory over the Amorites (Num. 21:21–24, 33–35), and deliverances from the Ammonites and Moabites (cf. 3:13–14), the Philistines (3:31), the Zidonians (possibly a reference to Jabin and Sisera, 4:12–24), the Amalekites (cf. 3:13; 6:3), and the Maonites.[26]

The Lord then shows the Israelites the fallacy of trusting in those without the power to help them. "Go and cry to the gods whom you have chosen; let them deliver you in the time of your distress" (10:14).

The Lord's point was obvious. He desired the people's minds and emotions to work together. Their sorrow to date had been because of their suffering. They were grieved over what had happened to them. What they needed was a clear understanding of the reason for his anger toward them.

Only as they faced the powerlessness of the objects they had worshiped would they be able to respond to God appropriately. And only as they became convinced that these deities were lying vanities would they turn from worshiping them and give God the honor due his name.

The Lord often uses the same method in dealing with us. We should not lose heart, therefore, but rather do as Israel did and prove the sincerity of our words by acts of obedience.

But how are we to understand God's statement: "Wherefore, I will deliver you no more"?

Dr. G. Bush stated that the Lord's "emphatic declaration, 'I will deliver you no more,' is to be understood conditionally, if their idols were kept among them; for the divine threatenings always imply a reserve of mercy to the truly penitent."[27]

The Israelites submit to the discipline of the Lord and "remove the gods of the alien [nations] from their midst." Without any promise of deliverance, they return to his worship and service (10:16).

This section closes with a rather enigmatic statement: "And [Yahweh] was grieved with the misery of Israel."

How can God, who is infinitely happy in himself, be "grieved in his soul"?

The only explanation which appears satisfactory is that this is an anthropomorphism.[28] Elsewhere in scripture God is spoken of as having human emotions (e.g., being full of compassion). Here it implies that He felt their sufferings deeply.

As a father He was grieved over the afflictions of his children. He had pity on them. The word translated "grieved" was also used in other contexts to imply "shortened, contracted." Here it may have implied at once his sympathy with their suffering as well as his desire to bring it to an end.[29]

CONDITIONS OF PEACE

There are many discordant voices around us. People want the benefits of peace (e.g., freedom from anxiety, the enjoyment of prosperity, and the pursuit of happiness), but they are reluctant to face the central issues that are involved. Their plans for peace often vary or are contradictory. Then there are those who preach peace (cf. Jer. 6:14*b*; 8:11*b*) but are like the false prophets of whom we read in the Old Testament. Their message is a distortion of the truth.

JUDGES 10:1 – 16

The complexity of the problem may be seen from a few of the events that have taken place over the last seventy-five years. We have experienced two world wars and numerous other conflicts on a smaller scale. We have seen "peace marches" both at home and abroad erupt into violent demonstrations. We have listened to leaders from various countries loudly affirming their desire for peace while secretly training terrorists or planning to invade some neutral nation. We have observed advocates of peace being victimized, harassed, and, in some instances, thrown into prison. Unrest has marked totalitarian as well as democratic societies.

Violent crime is on the increase. Law enforcement officers are unable to halt the murders, rapes, aggravated assaults, lootings, and arsons. On every hand there is a disregard for the rights of others. People are unsafe in their own homes. Supermarkets and grocery stores are robbed. "Gang wars" break out at football games, and places of worship have been fired on or threatened with bombs.

Oliver Cromwell said, "If we will have peace without a worm in it, we must lay a foundation for it in justice and righteousness."

Columnist C. Neil Strait pointed out that "the road to peace leads through the inner avenues of the heart—avenues of forgiveness, love and mercy. When these attitudes are properly expressed, peace is in the making."[30]

Because corporate peace seems impossible to achieve in our troubled world (cf. Ps. 120:5–7), we may have to apply personally the principles found in Judges 10 (cf. Ps. 144:11). This does not mean that the teaching of the Bible about worldwide peace is an illusion. It is not. According to passages of scripture such as Isaiah 9:7, this will come about when Christ returns to establish his kingdom. Until then we are exhorted to pray for those in authority over us.

As with the Israelites in the days of Tola and Jair, periods of peace may be confined to specific areas. This does not mean that we cannot enjoy the benefits of peace in a measure of good health, the satisfaction of uplifting human relationships, and a degree of prosperity.[31]

Dr. Larry Richards used the experiences of David to illustrate the kind of peace that can be ours. In commenting on Psalm 29:11, he wrote:

JUDGES 10:1 – 16

More than national blessing is involved in the peace God gives. David, fleeing from Absalom during that son's rebellion, felt intense pressure (Ps. 4:1-2). But David fixed his thoughts on God and remembered the joy that came with trust in him. Comforted and at rest despite overwhelming danger, David concluded, "I will lie down and sleep in peace, for you alone, O LORD make me dwell in safety" (4:8). For us as for David, peace in difficult circumstances is a result of our relationship with the Lord. "Great peace," David says, "have they who love your law" (Ps. 119:165). The one whose life is in harmony with God's revealed will experiences inner harmony as well. It is not surprising, then, to find Ps. 37 contrast the wicked and ruthless with "the man of peace" (37:35-37). The man of peace lives in right relationship with God, for God alone is the source of human rest and fulfillment.[32]

As a result of an inner experience with God, believers may enjoy unity (Eph. 2:14-17) and a sense of wholeness (Col. 3:12-15).

JUDGES 10:1 – 16

9 "BY MY SPIRIT"

Judges
10:17–12:7

It is doubtful if we can experience any hurt more painful than the ache of rejection. The great Scottish preacher Dr. Alexander Whyte knew what this was like. He had been born out of wedlock, which carried a lifelong stigma in his day. The unfortunate circumstances of his birth excluded him from the company of his peers. He had to contend with the mockery of boys his age, the scorn of the girls, and the whispers of the townspeople whenever they saw him in the street. He knew from painful personal experience the agony of being made to bear the punishment of a sin not his own.

John Whyte, Alexander's father, had offered to marry Janet Thompson, Alexander's mother, but she refused. When Alexander was born, his mother gave him his father's surname. She reared him in poverty, but with deep spiritual piety. In time he became apprenticed to a shoemaker. Through hard work he was finally able to study at the universities of Aberdeen and Edinburgh.

Dr. Whyte never forgot his illegitimacy. His preaching was marked by a keen sensitivity to the evils of his day, as well as a profound identification with those who suffered. In the course of his ministry, he preached on most of the people of the Bible, and his character studies now fill two large volumes. His insights into the life and character of Jephthah paint a vivid word-portrait:

Jephthah the Gileadite was the most ill-used man in all the Old
Testament, and he continues to be the most completely mis-
understood, misrepresented, and ill-used man down to this day.
Jephthah's ill-usage began when he was born, and it has continued down to the last Old Testament commentary and last Bible
dictionary that treats of Jephthah's name. The iron had entered
Jephthah's soul while yet he lay in his mother's womb; and both
his father and his brothers and the elders of Israel helped forward Jephthah's affliction, till the Lord rose up for Jephthah and
said, "It is enough."[1]

THE SON OF A HARLOT (11:1–3)

Judges 11:1–3 is a parenthetical section between 10:17–18 and
11:4. Even though Jephthah had been reared in his father's house
(an act implying adoption and the conferring of legitimacy), when
his father died Jephthah's brothers disinherited him. Believing
that "might makes right," they banded together and threw him out.

And Jephthah the Gileadite became[2] a mighty man of valor; and
he [was] the son of a woman, a harlot,[3] and Gilead fathered
Jephthah; and the wife of Gilead bore him sons; and the sons of
the wife grew up, and threw out Jephthah, and said to him, "You
shall not inherit in the house of our father, for you [are] the son
of another [i.e., a 'foreign'] woman." And Jephthah fled from the
face of his brothers (11:1–3).

Jephthah yearned for someone to say a kind word to him, but
instead of compassion he saw stony glares on the faces of the
townspeople; and in place of an outstretched hand and a smile, he
saw backs being turned and doors being closed. Alone, and with
the taunts and jeers of the people ringing in his ears, Jephthah was
forced to leave his village. No one offered him counsel or gave him
food for his journey. He was an outcast.

Whether purposefully or by accident, Jephthah came eventually to the land of Tob (possibly el–Taiyibeh, fifteen miles northeast
of Ramoth-gilead).[4] There other outcasts and misfits[5] gathered
about him, and he became a "brigand-chief." With them he made
predatory raids on the villages of Aram (Syria) and the land of the
Amorites. In addition, he also may have organized some form of
limited reprisal against the Ammonites, who were oppressing his

people. He and his men also preyed on the caravans traveling to the Mediterranean from cities of the Tigris-Euphrates river valley.

Does such a livelihood shock us? Are we to shun this passage of God's word because Jephthah's occupation runs contrary to our Western ideals of what is acceptable? Or is this an opportunity to reflect on a similar situation in our own times when Afghans harass Russians who have invaded their land or Latin American nationals retaliate against those who have deprived them of their liberty?

Dr. G. Bush explained the cultural background of Jephthah's times:

> The mode of life here indicated, is precisely that which was followed by David, when his reputation brought around him men of similar character to these followers of Jephthah. This kind of military robbery is far from being considered dishonorable in the East. On the contrary, the fame thus acquired is thought as fair as any that can be obtained through any class of military operations. An Arab or Tartar desires no higher or brighter distinction than that of a successful military robber; and to make that fame unsullied, it is only necessary that his expedition should not be against his own nation or tribe.[6]

Arthur Cundall further enlarged on the comparison between Jephthah and David:

> There is [in the life of Jephthah] some correspondence with the factors that shaped the career of David who, driven into the wilderness by Saul's jealousy, gathered to himself those who were in distress or debt, or who were discontented (1 Sam. 22:2), and wielded them into a formidable force. At a later stage, still pursued by Saul and unsure of the loyalty of his own countrymen, David went over to the Philistines as a mercenary captain, learning the arts of warfare, which were to serve him in good stead in the course of his long reign. So Jephthah the despised, through dire misfortune, was prepared for the task of saving the very people who had thrust him out.[7]

Lest we conclude that these incidents from remote antiquity have no bearing on us today, let us remember that the Lord often uses similar means to prepare us for some unique task. The process seems harsh and unpleasant, but the events that mold our lives reveal his wisdom; and as we cooperate with him in the work He is doing in us, we are prepared for his service.

JUDGES 10:17 – 12:7

THE THREAT OF WAR (10:17–18)

As we go back to 10:17 to pick up the narrative of Judges, the Ammonites,[8] with their capital in Rabbah, have grown in strength; the Gileadites and those on the eastern bank of the Jordan have grown weaker. Sensing their need for help, God's people repented of their idolatry. They put away the strange gods and renewed their allegiance to Yahweh, their covenant-keeping God (10:16), casting themselves unreservedly on his mercy. Having done so, the last thing they expected was war with the sons of Ammon, but this was exactly what happened.

> And the sons of Ammon were mustered, and encamped in Gilead; and the sons of Israel assembled and camped in Mizpeh.[9] And the people [and] the chief men of Gilead said one to another [lit., "a man to his neighbor"], "Who [shall be] the man who will begin to fight against the sons of Ammon? He shall be head over all the inhabitants of Gilead." (10:17–18).

There are times in our lives when the Lord moves in the most unexpected ways. What takes place, from a human point of view, is completely contrary to our expectations. We may have anticipated blessing following our obedience. Instead, the very thing that we fear the most comes on us. What then are we to do?

Only by recognizing God's sovereignty over every situation can we mobilize our resources to meet the challenge (i.e., the external threat that has intruded into our lives).

Israel gathers together to face the Ammonites.[10] The Hebrew text indicates that the people realize before their leaders the need to defeat the Ammonites (10:18). This suggests a lack of suitable leadership. None of the once-powerful families are capable of welding their forces into a unit and spearheading a drive against their enemies. Worse still, the people lack confidence in their leaders. For too long those in positions of authority have furthered their own ends at the expense of lesser families in their tribes. This is borne out in the negotiations of the elders with Jephthah and in their continued opposition to him after he had won the victory for them (see 11:35, noticing the words "among those who trouble me"). Although the people have turned to the Lord, and with quickened consciences are now seeking to do his will, selfish considerations still appear to guide the leaders.

JUDGES 10:17 – 12:7

True leadership is not a matter of inheritance, prestige, wealth, or even popularity, but of proven character, hard-won experience, an infectious optimism, and a dedication to the task at hand. "When all is said and done, the true leader must be able to dominate and finally master, the events that surround him."[11]

Israel had many supposedly noble families, but they had sacrificed on the altar of self those qualities of godliness and integrity that produce good leaders. The internal decay became evident when they faced an external threat against which they were powerless. Fortunately, the Ammonite oppression erased class distinctions and gave both the princes and the people a common interest. But the burning question facing them was, Who shall be our leader?

THE SEARCH FOR A LEADER (11:4–11)

We can readily visualize the scene. As the various groups debate the issue, different names are mentioned. None has the qualifications or abilities that inspire confidence. Then someone asks if perhaps Jephthah could lead them.

The mention of his name makes certain of the elders nervous, but the people murmur their assent. Jephthah has attained the status of a "mighty man of valor." His father was one of their princes,[12] a leading man in their tribe. It is true that his mother was an Aramean prostitute, but who was really responsible for illegitimacy—the child or the parents?

Apparently such arguments do not convince the elders of Israel that Jephthah is the man to lead them against the sons of Ammon. After some time elapses, the leaders gather again within Israel's border. A new offensive compels the tribes of Gad (probably including Reuben) and Manasseh (11:4) to take action.

Leaders should act, not react. The reactive nature of Israel's princes should have disqualified them from serving as heads of the tribes, but the events pressure them into action.

In approaching Jephthah, these politically minded elders offer him command of Israel's militia (they invite him to become their "chief," 11:6), ignoring the wishes of the people that he be made their "head" or "prince"[13] over "all the people" (10:18). By offering to make him only their general, they seek to retain their positions of power, and by keeping him subordinate to themselves, they can later pay him off and send him away again. Such actions should not surprise us. Corrupt leadership invariably acts this way.

Jephthah, however, has an accurate understanding of human nature. He sees some of his brothers and certain elders of his tribe in the delegation and responds:

> "Have you not hated me? Yes, you threw me out of my father's house; why have you come to see me now, when you [are] in distress?" (11:7).

His words strike home. The elders of the people are responsible for administering the law and protecting the rights of all citizens. Failing to do so is the same as siding with those who do wrong, as Jephthah's brothers did. Hard-pressed for an answer, these politicians sidestep the cause of dissension, turn a blind eye to the past, and focus instead on the dilemma posed by the Ammonites. In doing so they improve on their earlier offer.

> "For this reason we have come back to you now; and you shall go with us and fight against the sons of Ammon; and you shall be our head,[14] [even for] all the people of Gilead (11:8).

"Gilead" was the central tribe on the west bank of the Jordan and probably had become the term used to describe the three tribes of Reuben, Gad, and Manasseh collectively.

Sensing the duplicity of the elders, Jephthah asks for confirmation of their offer. "If you take me back to fight against the sons of Ammon, and Yahweh[15] gives them up before me, shall I be your head?" (11:9).

Realizing, perhaps for the first time, that Jephthah is a man of honor who cannot be swayed by their shallow generosity, the elders become aware of his use of the covenant name for God. They try to convince him that they share the same values. If he is a God-fearing man, they will feign reverence also. "Yahweh is witness between us; we will surely do according to your word" (11:10).

The elders have not demonstrated any commitment to the Lord. As leaders of the people, they should have sought God's will concerning his choice of a leader. That they did not do so indicates that their only interest was their own well-being.

JUDGES 10:17 – 12:7

Jephthah saw through the elders' facade and did not allow their guile to control his response. Internal norms motivated him, and he had developed these standards by his reflection on and familiarity with the revealed will of God.

The negotiations over, Jephthah accompanies the elders to Mizpeh,[16] where the people appoint him their ruler. "And Jephthah rehearses all his words before Yahweh in Mizpeh" (11:11).

He leaves nothing to chance. He even calls on God to witness between him and those he cannot trust.

Although commentators and preachers have described Jephthah as a lawless renegade with human aspirations no higher than his own greed, the facts indicate that this may not have been the case. It is true that Jephthah led a band of reckless men, but this does not necessarily mean that he adopted their ways. Although his men may have plundered villages and carried off the women, Jephthah had but one wife. No concubines could claim to have borne him children. The biblical text is also emphatic in its repetition: He had but one child, an only daughter, the joy of his life and the delight of his heart.

THE ART OF DIPLOMACY (11:12–28)

Jephthah acts in agreement with God's word in his diplomacy (Deut. 20:1–18). Even though the Ammonites had already attacked Israel, Jephthah, instead of going to war against them, tries to reach a peaceable agreement with the king of Ammon. The word compromise[17] was not in his vocabulary.

Jephthah asks for an explanation of the unprovoked occupation of Israel's land. He also appeals for a peaceful restoration of the land.

Jephthah's respectful message to the king of Ammon offers him the opportunity to act prudently and equitably. Jephthah would be justified in repelling force with force without any negotiations. Instead he tries to persuade the invaders to withdraw.[18]

The Ammonite king's reply is terse and hostile. The emphasis on the word "*my* lands" indicates that he regards himself as a despotic overlord whose will is his people's supreme command (11:13).

The charges and countercharges of Jephthah and the Ammonite king were not uncommon in Near Eastern countries. In replying to the Ammonite's misstatements, Jephthah revealed his thorough knowledge of his people's history. He may have been expelled from the borders of his native land, but this did not cause him to leave his convictions behind him.

Jephthah's words and his deeds show his knowledge of and obedience to those portions of scripture written up to that time.

The king of Ammon had alluded to the territory between the Arnon and Jabbok rivers as belonging to him. Jephthah corrects this faulty assumption by pointing out that this region originally belonged to Sihon, king of the Amorites.[19] Israel had lawfully wrested it from him when they came up from Egypt (11:15–22; cf. Num. 21:23ff. Josh. 13:24–26 precludes all possibility of Israel occupying any Ammonite land).

Having appealed to history, Jephthah reinforces his argument with a reference to the religious beliefs of the Ammonites. It was a widely held conviction among the nations of that time that their local deity had given them the land where they lived.

In taking advantage of this belief, Jephthah says:

"And now, Yahweh the God of Israel, has expelled [i.e., dispossessed] the Amorites from before his people Israel; and would you take possession of it [i.e., set yourselves up against him]? Whatever Chemosh your god causes you to possess, do you not possess it? And all that which Yahweh has expelled from before us, we will possess" (11:23–24).

The issue is clear. It is Yahweh versus Chemosh. Jephthah says in effect, "Why not quit while you are ahead? Leave peaceably. Be content with what your god has given to you."

To the witness of history and the evidence of God's power, Jephthah adds the importance of precedent. He points out that, inasmuch as Balak, king of Moab, did not contest Israel's right to occupy the land, by what right do the Ammonites now lay claim to it? If Israel's title was not disputed for three hundred years, how can the Ammonites now plead the right of possession?

Having concluded his evidence with this appeal to reason, yet knowing that those who seek a pretext for a quarrel will not be denied, Jephthah turns to the Lord for vindication:

"I have not sinned against you, but you are doing me wrong to fight against me. May Yahweh the Judge, judge today between the sons of Israel and the sons of Ammon" (11:27).

In effect he asks the Lord to award victory to the side that he sees to be in the right.

THE BATTLE OF AROER (11:29–33)

The Ammonite monarch will not listen to Jephthah and prepares for battle.

The Spirit of the Lord comes on (or "clothes") Jephthah, equipping him for the task at hand. He sends messengers to the tribes on the west bank of the Jordan, inviting them to send their militia to help him (11:29), and He personally raises an army from the tribes of Gad and Manasseh. Apparently the response of the people is disheartening. As with Gideon before him (6:36–40), Jephthah realizes his vulnerability. His true humanity becomes evident as he senses the power of the opposition. Realizing that the Lord has not promised to deliver the Israelites from oppression (cf. 10:14), Jephthah makes a vow to the Lord:

> And Jephthah vowed a vow to Yahweh, and said, "If you will indeed give the Ammonites into my hand, then it shall be that whoever comes out from the doors of my house to meet me when I return in peace from the Ammonites, it shall belong to Yahweh, and it shall ascend [to the sanctuary instead of] a burnt offering" (11:30–31).

Almost without exception modern commentators have concluded that Jephthah's vow involved human sacrifice.[20] In their eagerness to preserve Christianity from such an unthinkable and unholy act, they have condemned Jephthah for being "rash" or for following heathen practices (cf. Gen. 22:1–2) or for being ignorant of the law of redemption (Lev. 27:2–25; notice v. 4). They have ignored the fact that God had encouraged his people to make vows (Ps. 76:11), while also warning them against entering into vows and then failing to fulfill them (Eccl. 5:4–5). And they have overlooked the many occasions when great men and women of God had made vows in time of personal need.[21]

The writer of Judges placed no value judgment on Jephthah's act, and because he lived closer to the time than we do, he was in a better position to know the exact nature of the vow. On other occasions God gave some intimation of his will so that his followers could regulate their lives accordingly (cf. Gen. 38:10; 1 Sam. 8:6–7; 2 Sam. 11:27b; 1 Chron. 21:7; Prov. 24:18; Isa. 59:15b). Here there is no word of his displeasure, so we should refrain from reaching unwarranted conclusions.

As a good leader of men, Jephthah took the initiative, and the Lord delivered the Ammonites into his hand. In contrast to the extensive recounting of events when Gideon attacked and pursued the Midianites, the writer gave the battle of Aroer a single verse (11:33). As Zerubbabel, speaking on God's behalf to the remnant of his people, would later point out: "It is not by might, nor by power, but *by my Spirit* [that victories are won]," saith the Lord (Zech. 4:6).

The victory over the Ammonites is complete. They are subdued. As a result of their failure to heed Jephthah's counsel and withdraw peaceably, they lose twenty of their cities.

THE FULFILLMENT OF A VOW (11:34–40)

News of Jephthah's victory precedes him to Mizpeh, where the people welcome him as a conquering hero. Eighteen years of oppression have ended. There is feasting and merriment everywhere. Children play in the streets, and the women sing as they go about their work. Husbands and fathers have returned safely, and the awful threat of war has passed.

Jephthah had moved his wife, daughter, and servants from Tob to Gilead. As Jephthah approaches his new home after his victory, the first person to come out to greet him is his daughter.

> And Jephthah came to Mizpeh, to his house; and, behold, his daughter came out to meet him with timbrels, and with choruses. And except for her [lit., she only, she alone] he had neither son nor daughter. And it came to pass, when he saw her, that he tore his garments, and said, "Alas, my daughter! You have brought me very low, and you are among those troubling me;[22] and surely I have opened my mouth to Yahweh, and I am not able to go back" (11:34–35).

Those who are quick to indict Jephthah for being the product of a pagan culture would do well to weigh his words and consider his daughter's response. After his daughter's birth, Jephthah's wife was unable to bear him other children. Instead of following the culture of his day and taking other wives or concubines to eventually have a male heir (or, as in the case of Gideon, Tola, and Jair, many sons), he contented himself with his little family. It is true that he had become wealthy and had a large number of servants, but this does not indicate a decadent life-style.

The response of Jephthah's daughter reveals the kind of home in which she had been reared.

> And she said to him, "My father, you have opened your mouth to Yahweh; do to me whatever has gone forth out of your mouth; since Yahweh has executed vengeance for you on your enemies" (11:36).

Her use of the covenant name for God, *Yahweh,* instead of *El* or *Elohim*, implies that she, too, considered herself a child of God.

On learning more of her father's vow, Jephthah's daughter requests permission to be allowed two months so that she and her companions may spend the time alone, and she may express her sorrow over never being able to give her father a grandson. At the end of this period, Jephthah fulfills his vow.

Did Jephthah sacrifice his daughter after the manner of the heathen (cf. 2 Kings 3:27; 16:3; 21:6)?

Jephthah knew the law of God. Reflection on his discussion with the delegation who came to him in Tob, together with a careful reading of verses 12–28, gives evidence of this knowledge. It is reasonable to assume that he knew about God's law of redemption (cf. Exod. 13:11–13; Lev. 27:2–5) and his prohibition against human sacrifice (cf. Deut. 12:29–31; 18:9–14).

Nothing in the passage indicates that Jephthah sacrificed his daughter on an altar. The origin of the Hebrew word *'ōlāh* meant "to ascend." It signified the smoke that ascended from the altar. In time it became the word used to describe a burnt sacrifice.

There is nothing in the narrative to prevent us from concluding that Jephthah's daughter went across the Jordan Valley and ascended the other side where she spent her life serving the Lord in the temple.

Places of religious significance were often located in some "high place" (cf. 1 Sam. 10:5). Furthermore, there is evidence of female attendants such as weavers, singers, and prophetesses at the temple (not only at this time, but throughout Israel's history; cf. 2 Chron. 34:22; 35:25; Neh. 7:67; Luke 2:37–39).

After learning of her father's vow, Jephthah's daughter asks for time to "bewail her virginity," not her loss of life. That is why the emphasis of verse 39 is that "she never knew a man." If she was to die, she would have wanted to spend time with her parents. Never being able to bear children would leave her father without a family in Israel. This, according to Leviticus 20:2 and Psalm 78:63, was a supreme tragedy.

If Jephthah sacrificed his daughter, it is difficult to understand why it became a fixed custom in Israel that every year the young girls would "rehearse" her act for four days.

Depending on the context, this word is also translated "to talk with, to praise, to celebrate, or even to commemorate."[23] The only logical explanation seems to be that they went to Shiloh and spent time with Jephthah's daughter, talking with her and praising her for her dedication to a life of celibacy and service.

Verses 39b–40 do not contain any censure on the part of the biblical writer. Furthermore, Jephthah is mentioned in 1 Samuel 12:11 and Hebrews 11:32 along with Gideon, Samuel, David, and the other heroes of the faith.[24]

It is difficult to imagine the Holy Spirit using Jephthah as an example of faith if his act was so contrary to God's revealed will.

The abiding principle of Judges 11:34–40 seems to be that Jephthah was a man who kept his vow.[25]

THE ENVY OF EPHRAIM (12:1–6)

While Jephthah's daughter is away with her maidens mourning her childlessness, another burden is thrust unheralded and unwanted on Jephthah. The people of Ephraim, as proud and as fierce as ever (now that the real danger is passed), confront Jephthah, probably outside his home (cf. 12:1b). They had refused to join him when he attacked the Ammonites but now are indignant about not having a share in the honor.

John Marshall Lang described the scene:

> Ephraim, the central tribe, had acquired a position in Israel which encouraged an overbearing spirit; and this spirit was manifest in an offensive attitude towards Jephthah. . . . [Their tone in

approaching him was one of hostility] and he had not deserved such reproach.

"Why have you crossed over to fight with the sons of Ammon, and you have not called on us to go with you? We will burn your house over you with fire" (12:1).

[Jephthah's] answer, though sharp, is marked by dignity. He had given the haughty Ephraimites the opportunity of helping in the war. They had declined it, leaving him and his people to do battle alone. He correctly picked up on the attitude of the men of Ephraim, and asks,

"Why have you come to me today to fight against me?" (12:3).

But remonstrance is in vain, and for the most miserable of causes, there ensues a fierce contention. The statement of the historian is that "there fell forty-two thousand Ephraimites at the passage of the Jordan."[26]

This large number gives evidence of the harm they intended when they crossed over the river to attack Jephthah.

After routing the men of Ephraim, the men of Gilead take the fords of the Jordan. When an escaping Ephraimite comes down to the river, he is asked to pronounce the word "Shibboleth." In the course of time the Ephraimites had dropped the *h* and pronounced certain *sh* words with only an *s*. Their "Sibboleth" gives them away.[27] So those who intended doing harm to Jephthah find their retreat effectively cut off.

Many condemn Jephthah for not preventing this war, but the fact remains that the people of Ephraim approached him intent on bloodshed. Their spirit was such that Jephthah could not placate them. He had become God's representative to the people as a whole; and to fight against him was tantamount to fighting against the Lord. That the Ephraimites did not recognize this indicates their spiritual insensitivity.

THE POSTSCRIPT (12:7)

Evidence of God's hand on Jephthah is found in verse 7, where it says that he "judged" Israel for six years (1087–1081 B.C.).

Although the elders had offered Jephthah the position of "commander" and the people had made him "head" or "prince" of the tribes on the east bank, only God could appoint him a "judge." His inclusion in the annals of God's people alongside Othniel,

Deborah and Barak, Gideon, and Samuel (cf. 1 Sam. 12:11) adds the weight of divine approval to his life and work. Jephthah was a leader of men.

A LEADER OF MEN

Thomas Carlyle, in *Heroes and Hero Worship,* emphasized the "great man" theory of leadership. Basing his study on history, he concluded that leadership was explicitly associated with the exercise of special powers. An outstanding leader was one who possessed the ability to grasp the dynamics of a given situation, choose the right course of action, and, using coercion if necessary, compel others to accomplish that which would ultimately be of benefit to them.

The counterpart of Carlyle's "great man" theory is today's "strong natural leader" (or SNL). Recent history has shown that an SNL may get an organization started; but as it grows, it soon exceeds his ability to control it. When this happens, the organization invariably goes into a period of decline.[28]

Realizing the weakness of the SNL theory, Dr. Douglas MacGregor, in *The Human Side of Enterprise,* propounded two separate styles of leadership. These he called "Theory X" and "Theory Y." (Although MacGregor's ideas have since undergone refinement, his basic thesis remains the same.) The failure of his theory may be traced to the fact that he believed the average worker to be externally motivated, and he made no allowance for those who are motivated from within. He worked from a premise similar to the ones adopted by Max Weber (that man is essentially an irrational component within the organization, has to be told what to do, and has to be supervised closely to ensure that the job is done correctly) and Frederick W. Taylor (who instituted methods to ensure "cost efficiency," thereby paving the way for the present depersonalization in such areas as commerce, industry, government, and education). As a result, Dr. MacGregor believed that man has an inherent dislike for work and will avoid it if he can. He excluded from his considerations those people who enjoy their work and derive fulfillment from it.

Other students of leadership have alternately focused on the functions or skills of noted leaders. After spending an entire lifetime examining different theories, Dr. Ralph Stogdill, in his *Handbook of Leadership,* concluded that because there are so many different functions of leadership, there has consequently arisen an almost equal number of definitions. He also pointed out that research has failed to describe for us the traits of a good leader or describe for us what leadership is.

In light of this, it is important to consider the biblical criteria of a good leader. Like Gilead, we are faced with a chronic shortage of good leaders. Those in positions of authority are often improperly equipped for the task. Self-seeking, exploitation, and abuse of power abound. (Christian organizations are by no means exempt from these traits; in fact, sometimes "Christian" organizations are the worst offenders.)

Jephthah illustrated the leadership principles of godliness, proven ability, wisdom, discernment, a knowledge of people, tact, courage, and determination to follow through on difficult or unpleasant tasks. These characteristics can be summarized in five statements.

First, a good leader must be a person of integrity who can be looked up to, whose personal judgment is trusted, and who can inspire others to follow him with confidence. He must gain the trust of those he leads, outline for them a plan of action, and motivate them to succeed.

Second, a good leader must have a thorough knowledge of human nature. He must be a good judge of character. He must be able to separate those who are reliable from those who are not. Those he picks for different positions or tasks must be able to accomplish their assigned duties efficiently and in keeping with established goals.[29]

Third, a good leader must be able to win the hearts of the men and women under his control. He must be able to unite them behind a common purpose and infuse them with confidence. He must be able to foresee problems and warn his followers. He must also give them some assurance of tangible rewards.

Fourth, a good leader must be able to handle opposition wisely and act decisively. Jephthah took the initiative. He did not wait for the king of Ammon to choose the battlefield that most suited him. Instead he rallied what men he could and pressed the attack. After the initial engaging and routing of the enemy, he pursued them until they were subdued. These enemies of Israel did not have the military strength to oppose God's people again until the time of David.

Finally, and most important of all, a good leader must be a man of impeccable honesty. His personal life must be above reproach. Jephthah was such a man. He fulfilled the vow he had made to the Lord. His sincerity and selflessness were not substitutes for an unfeeling and implacable spirit. In his heart was all the tenderness and compassion of a great man. His integrity was matched by his daughter's commitment to principle, and they subordinated their personal hopes and aspirations to their devotion to God.

Jephthah was a wise and versatile leader. He was resourceful in battle and just in administering the peace. Though he began life as the son of a prostitute, his name is enshrined with the noblest of God's people. At his death the people accorded him the honors of a true Gileadite and buried him in one of the cities of his people. In the providence of God, all the things denied him by his half-brothers and the elders of the people were restored to him during his lifetime.

Jephthah's perseverance in doing what was right sets him apart as a leader whose example is worthy of emulation.

10 USES OF THE PAST

Judges
12:8–13:25

Samson has suffered as much as Jephthah at the hands of biblical commentators. Some have treated his story as an excellent piece of Hebrew folklore, similar to the ancient writings of the Greeks. From Hellenistic mythology these writers have culled accounts that appear to parallel the feats of strength and victories won by Samson. Then, to add the finishing touches to their analogy, they have shown how there is also a likeness to these legendary figures in Samson's love affairs with different women. Having dismissed the biblical account as mythological, they rest in comfortable neglect of this portion of God's word.[1]

Another group has gone to the opposite extreme. In Samson's unique birth they see a parallel to the prediction of Christ's conception. Then, by using selective texts from Samson's life, they extend their typology as far as human ingenuity can go. Having "Christianized" this portion of God's word, they rest content in their mysticism, never pausing to ask if they have based their deductions on sound inductive evidence and a proper understanding of the biblical writer's theme.

A third approach is particularly common among evangelical preachers. With humor reminiscent of the fifth grade, they remind us that Samson was a "he-man" with a "she-weakness." They use

Samson's marriage to the Philistine from Timnah to denounce any union between believers and unbelievers and engage in a harangue against immorality based on Samson's visit to the prostitute in Gaza and his friendship with Delilah.

Certainly God's word warns us against becoming "unequally yoked" with unbelievers, and no one should condone acts of sexual impropriety. But to bypass the purpose of the biblical writer in favor of wearisome moralizations from the pulpit leaves those who have come for worship worse off for the experience.

A more balanced approach is to interpret the incidents in light of the theme of the book. Keeping in mind that this is a selective account of Samson's twenty-year judgeship, we should try to determine the principles God would have us learn from his own summation of Samson's exploits (cf. 15:20; 16:31*b*). By linking scripture with scripture, we can piece together a clearer, more consistent picture. The Lord's specific statement that Samson would "*begin* to deliver Israel" can then be matched with the fact that he is numbered among the great men and women of the faith (Heb. 11:32). This done, we can profit from John Milton's insights on personal accountability, when he had Samson say:

> "Nothing of all those evils hath befall'n me
> But justly; I myself have brought them on."[2]

Even in Samson's downfall, God continued to be gracious. Where sin abounded, grace did much more abound (Rom. 5:20); and the Lord even turned the wrath of men to his praise (Ps. 76:10).

We must interpret Samson's life in the context of the times in which he lived and in keeping with the purpose behind this portion of God's self-revelation. Samson "judged Israel in the days of the Philistines," and this was no easy task.

A PERIOD OF UNEVENTFUL TRANSITION
(12:8–15)

Following Jephthah's victory over the Ammonites and his subsequent judgeship, we do not read that the land had rest for a specified number of years. This constitutes a definite change in the pattern of the past and indicates a transition. True godliness was not widespread. Then, as now, the pressures of rearing a family, the uncertainties of balancing one's income against expenses, and the lack of the positive teaching of God's word caused the people to take their eyes off the Lord. As God became less and less of a reality to them, they looked to human resources for the support and help they needed.[3]

The writer mentioned three leaders in this period of transition between Jephthah and Samson and between Ammon's eighteen-year domination in the east and the Philistine threat in the west. These are Ibzan (1081–1075 B.C.) the Bethlehemite from the land of Zebulun; Elon (1075–1065 B.C.), perhaps also from Zebulun, judging from the place of his burial; and Abdon (1065–1058 B.C.) the Pirathonite (from a city in the territory of Manasseh that at this stage in Israel's history was looked on as being a part of the tribe of Ephraim). These judges[4] were wealthy individuals and stand in contrast to Samson's father, Manoah.

Ibzan (12:8–10) was obviously a polygamist, for he had thirty sons and thirty daughters. There can be little doubt of the happiness his children brought him, and he took special care that they, in turn, would be happy. He arranged the marriage of each of his daughters to the sons of prominent families outside his own clan and also selected desirable wives for his sons.[5] When he died, his people gave him an honorable burial.

Elon (12:11–12) succeeded Ibzan as God's theocratic representative and governed the people for ten years. When he died he was buried at Aijalon near Rimmon in the land of Zebulun.

Finally, Abdon (12:13–15), who likewise had a large family and saw his "children's children" (Ps. 128:6), judged God's people in Ephraim, in the hill country occupied by the Amalekites. Having a large family and having all of one's male children (including grandchildren) ride on donkeys signified wealth. Josephus recorded that Abdon spent his days peaceably, and that at his death the people gave him a magnificent funeral.[6]

During this period of growing Philistine domination to the south and west of Zebulun and Ephraim, Eli was high priest (1107–1067 B.C.). He and the women who had devoted themselves to the service of the Lord at Shiloh cared for Samuel (born about 1105 B.C.). As Dr. Robert Boling pointed out, "It was an uncertain peace that Jephthah willed to Israel, yet three judges (twenty-five years) came and went before any strife occurred that was serious enough to be recorded."[7]

JUDGES 12:8 – 13:25

With the close of Abdon's judgeship, the writer directs our attention to the preparation of a powerful leader.

THE PREPARATION OF A POWERFUL LEADER
(13:1–25)

Samson's parents were from the tribe of Dan. Their families had not migrated north to Laish with the other members of their tribe (cf. ch. 18) but had apparently preferred to stay in the portion of land allotted to them by the Lord (1:34–36). They had never been able to establish themselves in any city and had been forced to live in small, scattered tent-villages in the hill country.

Over the years the Philistines had been settling in large numbers along the coastal plain.[8] In contrast to the unsettled nature of the Danites, they had established a powerful pentapolis—a five-city confederacy consisting of Gaza, Ashkelon, Ashdod, Ekron, and Gath.[9] As they gained in strength, they began to penetrate the interior, gradually taking over the land. At first they had assimilated the land and cities of the Amorites.

Shamgar had kept raiding parties from Israel's borders during his lifetime (3:31). More recently, the Philistines and Amorites had become anxious to avail themselves of arable land. As a result, the Danites were caught in the squeeze. Whoever had the "might" was able to assert his "right" to wells and also pasture (cf. Gen. 21:25ff.; 26:20–22; Exod. 2:16–19; Deut. 6:11). It became harder and harder for the sons of Israel to find adequate grazing land for their diminishing flocks and herds. Each year others encroached on their borders. Worse still, they felt powerless to resist (14:4b).

Most of the Danites who remained in the portion allotted to them, as well as the people along Judah's western border, apparently accepted Philistine domination with some degree of docility (cf. 15:11). It is not surprising that amid such spiritual apathy they regarded intermarriage as "politically expedient." Furthermore, with the Philistines attributing their success to the power of their gods, many Israelites had been seduced into worshiping these pagan deities for the sake of survival. So it is that we read:

> And again the sons of Israel did evil in the eyes of Yahweh, and Yahweh gave them into the hand of the Philistines [for] forty years (13:1).

JUDGES 12:8 – 13:25

Because Philistine domination was broken at the Battle of Ebenezer (1047 B.C.), the oppression of this warlike nation must have begun around 1087 B.C. when Samuel was about eighteen years of age.

We may divide the beginning of God's process of deliverance as follows: (1) the announcement of an unexpected birth (13:2–7); (2) the prayer of a believing father (13:8–14); (3) the worship of a heavenly guest (13:15–23); and (4) the fulfillment of a gracious promise (13:24–25).[10]

The Announcement of an Unexpected Birth (13:2–7)

Visitors to Israel are surprised at how close one city is to another. Unlike the United States, where we find public transportation or the use of a car necessary to take us to and from work, or where relatives and friends may live at a considerable distance from our homes, Palestine is very compact. From Beersheba in the south to Dan (Laish) in the north is about 160 miles. From the Mediterranean in the west to the river Jordan, the land averages a width of only fifty miles.

Samson's parents lived in Zorah[11] (cf. Josh. 15:21, 33), a small border town between Dan and Judah in the Shephelah or lowland,[12] about fourteen miles west of Jerusalem. It sat about 1,170 feet above sea level on the brow of a sharp hill on the northern side of the valley of Sorek (now known as Wadi es-Sarar), immediately opposite the town of Beth-shemesh ("house of the sun").[13] Timnah was located about four miles southwest of Zorah at the mouth of the valley.[14]

Now there was a man [i.e., a certain man] of Zorah, of the family of the Danites, and his name [was] Manoah. And his wife [was] barren, and had not borne [children]. And the Angel of Yahweh appeared to the woman, and said to her, "Behold, now, you [are] barren and have not borne [children]; but you shall conceive and bear a son. And now, be careful; please do not drink [any] wine or strong drink, and do not eat any unclean [thing]. For behold you [are] pregnant and bearing a son, and a razor shall not go up upon his head, for the boy shall be a Nazirite to God from the womb; and he shall begin to deliver Israel from the hand of the Philistines." And the woman came and spoke with her husband,

JUDGES 12:8 – 13:25

saying, "A man of God came to me and his appearance [was] like
the appearance of an angel of God, very awesome" (13:2–6).

Joseph Hall, in his *Contemplations on the Historic Passages of
the Old and New Testaments,* took note of the emphatic repetition
of the words "was barren and bore not" and said, "If Manoah's wife
had not been barren, the angel had not been sent to her. Afflictions
have the advantage, that they occasion God to show that mercy
to us, whereof the prosperous are [ignorant]. . . . God addresses
His comforts to those hearts that have the most need."[15]

In much the same way that a physician tells us first of the
nature of our illness before assuring us of the remedy, so the Lord
reminded Manoah's wife of her condition before promising her a
son.[16] By showing his knowledge of her condition, He prepared her
heart to accept by faith his assurance that she would bear a child.

Infertility was not uncommon in Bible times. Both Sarah (Gen.
18:9–15) and Elizabeth (Luke 1:5–25) were told of their expectant
motherhood when all hope of conceiving a child was gone. Hannah, too, shared something in common with Manoah's wife, for her
son would likewise be a Nazirite from the time of his birth (1 Sam.
1:10–11). Samson's mother, however, shared the restrictions of a
Nazirite with her unborn son.[17]

The conditions of the Nazirite vow are found in Numbers 6 (cf.
Amos 2:11–12; Acts 21:23ff.). There were three stipulations: (1)
abstain from all products of the vine;[18] (2) leave the hair uncut for
the duration of the vow; and (3) do not defile oneself with a dead
body. Any breach of these conditions nullified the vow.

Arthur Cundall echoed the criticisms of many as they approach these chapters of the Bible. He wrote:

> It is clear from the Samson stories that he concerned himself only
> with the regulation concerning his hair. He is often found in
> contact with the dead, and not accidentally (cf. 14:8, 9); and his
> presence at the carousal of 14:10, 17 hardly suggests abstinence
> from strong drink.[19]

Although such comments reinforce the disgrace that some
have heaped on Samson's head, the sentiments expressed are not
necessarily accurate, nor do they bear up under scrutiny. God
appointed Samson a Nazirite as well as a deliverer of his people.
He knew that Samson would have to fight against the Philistines.

That is why the only condition explicitly laid on him was that "no razor will come upon his head" (13:5). The other prohibitions were not a part of the angel of the Lord's stipulations.

But even if this were not so, the criticisms of Samson cannot be substantiated without contradicting what God specifically ordained. The central issues lie in our interpretation of the text.

First Samuel 15:32–33 sheds light on Samson's actions. There we read that Samuel killed Agag, king of the Amalekites. This act did not negate or nullify Samuel's vow. If we don't take exception to Samuel's execution of Agag, why should we indict Samson for fulfilling God's will and delivering his people from Philistine oppression? There appears to be a difference between acts committed at God's specific behest and the ceremonial defilement that occurs when one comes into contact with a decaying body. It is the latter that is the subject of Numbers 6, not the former.

It 's true that Samson was often found in the "wrong company," but this does not automatically mean that he imbibed the same intoxicating liquor as his companions did. It is hard to imagine anyone inducing some muscular strongman to drink something he did not wish to drink. It is true that circumstantial evidence implies that Samson engaged in drinking with his friends, but a person cannot be convicted on such slender evidence. The text implies that this kind of celebration was customary, and Samson was complying with the custom. His strength was sufficient to guarantee him respect, and he may well have done as many Christians do today when they have to attend certain functions, namely, refrain from consuming anything with alcohol in it.

A person normally took the Nazirite vow for a limited period of time. The permanent state into which God placed Samson and Samuel set them apart as unique.

The text of 13:5 appears to conclusively answer Samson's critics. The angel of the Lord specified only the importance of Samson not cutting his hair. This, and this alone, was to be the sign that he was set apart to the Lord.

Samson's mother also was to observe the restrictions of a Nazirite during her pregnancy. She was not to drink anything made from grapes, or any strong drink made from fruits, honey, or grain. She was also to avoid contact with dead things. Thomas Kirk pointed out that "in this injunction to the mother we may see a recognition of the now well known law of heredity, according to which the habits and tendencies, especially of mothers, are transmitted to their offspring."[20]

Some commentators believe the statement that Samson would "begin to deliver" his people points to the "incompleteness of his life's work,"[21] and many writers and preachers have read into these words Samson's weaknesses. They have been quick to indict him for his failures. But the angel of the Lord said this before Samson's birth (when he had done none of the things that are described later in the text), and Luke made a similar remark, without moral overtones, about the Lord Jesus Christ (Acts 1:1). God is kinder to Samson than his critics. All this phrase does is show the nature of Samson's work. Israel's sins were such that only after twenty years of a "Bible teaching" ministry could Samuel lead the people in repentance (cf. 1 Sam. 7:2b). This was in 1047 B.C., two years *after* Samson's death. Only then were the Philistines driven from the land. During his lifetime, Samson had to face Israel's enemies alone (15:9–13, 20). No one stood by his side to help or encourage him. Samuel would not have been able to carry on his ministry with such relative freedom had not Samson kept the Philistines at bay.

It was the task of Samson's parents to prepare their son for the hardships he would have to endure. As a general rule, couples who enjoy a healthy relationship are able to rear healthy children. There is enough evidence in the text for us to conclude that the marriage of Manoah and his wife was a good one. They enjoyed open and honest communication. They shared common beliefs, values, and goals. Everything in the text indicates that they had not taken part in the general apostasy.

The Prayer of a Believing Father (13:8–14)

On receiving the message from the angel of the Lord, Manoah's wife immediately goes in search of her husband. Not having asked the messenger for his name or his place of origin, she presumes him to be a "man of God" who travels from one place to another. She recounts these facts to Manoah as fully as her excitement will allow.

JUDGES 12:8 – 13:25

In contrast to the disbelief of Zacharias at news of the unexpected pregnancy of his wife, Elizabeth (Luke 1:11–20), Manoah immediately believes the information relayed to him. He has not seen the angel of the Lord; yet his response is one of believing prayer:

> Then Manoah prayed to Yahweh, and said, "O my Lord, the man of God whom you sent, let him come, I pray, again to us and teach us what we shall do as the boy [is] being born [i.e., for the boy who shall be born]" (13:8).

As Dr. G. Bush noted:

> [Manoah's] request appears to have been prompted by a strong faith and a high esteem of the promised blessing, and a sincere desire to receive further intimations of duty. He may have thought it possible, too, that his wife's joy for the promise should have made her forget some part of the charge.[22]

This she had indeed done. Her partial lapse of memory is understandable.

Zacharias, in better circumstances, asked for a sign to confirm God's word, but Manoah quickly turns to the Lord in believing prayer, which indicates the extent to which his beliefs regulate his life. His piety is not perfunctory. His relationship with God is real. His prayer expects an affirmative answer. His petition, "Teach us what we shall do to the child that shall be born," shows his humility. It also establishes a model for present-day parents who have to face the same bewildering complexities of life.

The conversation between Manoah and his wife is important for another reason. It shows the mutual respect each has for the other. She shares with him what happens in her life, and this moves him to take spiritual leadership and pray for their needs. They enjoy equality of life and purity of motive. These are traits we should emulate. Children learn from both parents. The involvement, modeling, and instruction they receive is indispensable to their growth. From 13:24b we realize how well Samson's parents discharged their duty.[23]

In answer to Manoah's prayer, God sends his messenger a second time. Previously He may have visited Manoah's wife in her tent (13:3), but this time He appears to her while she is busy in the field.

Some preachers and teachers have discredited Manoah because the angel of the Lord did not appear to him. They portray him as a person of slow mind who stood in his wife's shadow personally, intellectually, and spiritually. They can only maintain such a view by reading into the text more than is there.

The angel of the Lord appeared to Manoah's wife to show God's recognition of her worth. She had to bear the stigma of her infertility. She was looked down on because she had not borne her husband children. At that time it was a common belief that women unable to bear children were being punished by God for committing some terrible sin. By appearing to her the second time, the Lord reaffirmed her dignity and worth. Once again Manoah's wife runs to tell her husband. The Hebrew text preserves something of her haste and excitement: "Behold, he has appeared to me [again], the man [of God] who came to me the [other] day" (13:10).

Manoah immediately leaves what he is doing and accompanies his wife to the place where the "man of God" is waiting.

Manoah is a peasant-farmer who, amid widespread spiritual decline, has retained his belief in God's involvement with his people; therefore, he shows great respect to the "man of God," not knowing that he is conversing with God manifest in a theophany.[24] He thinks the person before him is a prophet.

"Are you the man who spoke to the woman?" he asks.

"I [am]."

"Now let your words come about [as you have said]."

Manoah simply expresses an earnest wish that the promise made to his wife be fulfilled. Dr. G. Bush described it as a "pious amen."[25]

Then follows, for Manoah's benefit, a repetition of the instructions given to his wife (13:13–14). This done, and with his mission complete, the Lord is about to leave. Manoah, on seeing this, wishes to detain his guest to express his thanks in an appropriate manner.

The Worship of a Heavenly Guest (13:15–23)

Still believing that the person before them is only a "man of God," Manoah says: "Please let us detain you, and prepare before you a kid of the goats."

JUDGES 12:8 – 13:25

To which the stranger replies: "If you detain me, I will not eat of your bread [i.e., food]; but if you prepare a burnt offering, you shall offer it to Yahweh."

To this the biblical writer added an important comment: "For Manoah did not know that [his visitor] was the angel of the Lord" (13:16).

The angel of the Lord had accepted the hospitality of Abraham (Gen. 18) and made himself known to Gideon in a remarkable manner (6:17–22), but on this occasion He refuses Manoah's invitation. He does not, however, deprive Manoah and his wife of the opportunity to express their thankfulness. Instead He suggests an appropriate means.

Manoah still wishes to acknowledge God's messenger and so asks, "What is your name, so that when your words come about, we shall then honor you?"

Manoah's intention was probably to send the "man of God" a gift at the birth of their son.

The angel of the Lord declines to give Manoah and his wife his name; but when they offer their sacrifice on a humble altar, He "ascends in the flame" to the wonderment of the couple. Suddenly they realize that they have been in the presence of God, and this fills them with fear.[26] They fall to the ground with their faces between their knees (cf. Lev. 9:24; 2 Chron. 7:1–3).

Although the ascent of the Lord in the flame of the couple's sacrifice indicates the acceptance of their offering, they are nonetheless overcome with fear. As Thomas Kirk pointed out:

> The knowledge that their visitor is not a man, but the Angel of the Lord, makes a very different impression upon them. The biographer says, verses 22 and 23, "And Manoah said unto his wife, 'We shall surely die, for we have seen God [cf. Exodus 20:19; 33:20; John 1:18].' But his wife [who had seen the angel of the Lord once before, and had survived] said to him, 'If the Lord were pleased to kill us, He would not have received our burnt-offering and a meal-offering at our hand, neither would He have shewed us all these things, nor would at this time have told us such things as these.'"[27]

The Fulfillment of a Gracious Promise (13:24–25)

After these events we hear no more until Manoah's wife bears her husband a son (13:24). When Samson is born, they give him a name that means "sunny" (in much the same way that Isaac was given a name that meant "laughter," Gen. 21:3, 6). Some scholars have seen in *šimšôn* a reference to the worship of the sun god whose principal shrine was across the valley in Beth-shemesh ("house of the sun").[28] Other commentators have vigorously refuted this theory.

The reference to Samson's early years (13:24*b*) recalls a similar statement made about Samuel (1 Sam. 2:26), as well as Luke's words concerning John the Baptist and the Lord Jesus Christ (Luke 1:80; 2:40, 52). In keeping with the other judges, the Spirit of the Lord comes on him and empowers (*pā'am*, "to impel") him for special tasks. The place where he begins to exercise his strength is the "camp of Dan" between Zorah and Eshtaol.

By referring to Samson's home as "Mahaneh-dan,"[29] an encampment without walls or permanent dwellings, the writer subtly showed the plight of this tribe 320 years after the settlement of the Israelites in the land. He contrasted their weakness with Philistine strength. Furthermore, 14:4*b* and 15:11 reveal that the Israelites were conscious of their impotence.

IN RETROSPECT

The birth of Samson demonstrates two important truths: (1) the love of God for his people; and (2) the grace of God in answering prayer.[30]

The Love of God for His People

God's people did not call on him when He delivered them into the hands of the Philistines. Repeated sinning had brought about a hardening of their spiritual arteries. His love for them, however, was as much in evidence in the provision He made for their deliverance as it was in the way He chose to meet the need of Manoah and his wife. He was aware of his people's afflictions as well as the reproach that rested on the righteous and godly husband and his infertile wife. His all-seeing eye noted the impenitence of the nation as well as the grief of the couple who could not understand his apparent anger toward them in withholding what would make their lives complete. In the free exercise of his providence, He met the needs of both the nation and the humble pair who honored his name.

Although the Lord may not send an angelic messenger to us in visible form to tell us of his loving concern (cf. Heb. 1:14), He has given us his word in which He records his deep concern for us and his willingness to turn our grief into joy and our sorrow into rejoicing. His knowledge is linked with his mercy and his compassion with his power. As a result of his lovingkindness, we can commit our cares to him (Ps. 55:22a), knowing that He cares for us (1 Peter 5:7).

Furthermore, God's lavish generosity toward Manoah and his wife is evident from 16:31a. As Hannah bore her husband, Elkanah, other children following the birth of Samuel (1 Sam. 2:20–21), so apparently additional children were born to Manoah and his wife. Each child was truly an evidence of God's lovingkindness toward them. He fully compensated them for having to wait so long for the birth of Samson. In his providence their desires were met while the nation also benefited from his undeserved mercy.

God's love for us is evident in many ways. We are not always deserving of his grace and favor. He answers prayer, and this encourages us to wait on him in faith, believing the Bible's teaching about the importance of our prayers in his plan and purpose for us (cf. Heb. 11:1, 6).

The Grace of God in Answering Prayer

A careful study of the prayers of the Bible (e.g., Hannah's in 1 Sam. 1:10–11; Nehemiah's in Neh. 1:8–11 et al.; Daniel's in Dan. 2:16ff.) reveals how ready God is to hear us when we call on him.

When Manoah heard his wife recount the events of the angel of the Lord's visit, his first thought was to pray. This showed that he had not lost his acquaintance with God even though the people around him were backslidden. His request was not to gratify his idle curiosity but so he and his wife might demonstrate appropriate responsibility in rearing their son.

All of us have been given the gift of faith, but not all of us possess it in the same measure. It is our responsibility to develop our trust in the Lord through our study of what He has chosen to reveal (cf. Rom. 10:17). As Dr. Joseph Hall pointed out in his

Contemplations, a faith that is faddish is faulty and dangerous.[31] There is a difference between sound reason for our faith and a reason that sounds good. Manoah's commitment to the Lord led him to recognize the truth of his wife's words. His spirit witnessed with her spirit, and he believed her report. His response was to pray. In doing so he put in motion the greatest power available to man.

Manoah's prayer was the opportunity for God to graciously answer him by sending the angel of the Lord a second time. In this He showed his free, unmerited, spontaneous grace. From the answer Manoah received, we realize that prayer still is the nerve that moves the muscles of omnipotence.

When our prayers are answered, our most appropriate response is worship. Worship needs no justification. It is a simple act of rendering to God the praise and adoration that is due him and of which He is worthy.

Worship, or thanksgiving, does not have to take place in a building set apart for the purpose. Manoah and his wife bowed in reverential awe before God in the field where the angel of the Lord had met with the woman (13:9). Isaiah had a similar experience (Isa. 6:1–5). And the apostle John fell prostrate before the Lord while he was incarcerated on the barren island of Patmos (Rev. 1:17).

William Cowper wrote of God's availability in one of his hymns:

> Jesus, where'er Thy people meet,
> There they behold Thy mercy-seat;
> Where'er they seek Thee Thou art found,
> And every place is hallowed ground.[32]

Samson's parents prepared him for his life of service through their godly example. As a result of their faith, he developed an intimate relationship with the Lord (as was evident from his own prayers and the work that he single-handedly performed). Furthermore, his ability to cope with the rejection of the people (15:11–13) and to endure twenty years of loneliness as he served as a buffer between the sons of Israel and the Philistines (15:20) was only possible as he drew on the Lord for his strength. Having first learned of God's love and grace from his parents, he was able to endure life's vicissitudes.

JUDGES 12:8 – 13:25

11 THE STRONG AND THE WEAK: PART 1

Judges
14

Certain evils affect all of us. Slander, misunderstanding, rejection, and loneliness attack our sense of worth and make us feel isolated, vulnerable, and weak. How quickly we pass from strength to weakness, from an ability to enjoy life to the inability to overcome the power others have to affect our temporal well-being. So it was with Samson. In no other portion of the book of Judges is the tension between the strong and the weak, the powerful and the impotent, so forcefully brought before us as in chapters 14–15. Happily for us the story also holds an encouraging reminder that the power of the Holy Spirit can make all of us strong.

Swiss physician Dr. Paul Tournier drew our attention to the tension between strength and weakness:

> It is not a case of having a life with no difficulties, but of having the strength to surmount them. No one is exempt from conflict, which can strengthen a man as well as overwhelm him. There are physical combats with [those] who set upon us; moral conflicts with parents, with brothers and sisters, and with rivals; social conflicts; conflicts with one's own failings. All of them are both useful in the reactions they arouse in us, and harmful in the cowardly defeats and proud victories to which they lead. Only

the spirit which we bring to them determines whether they are good or evil.

We never find ideal conditions of life and work. We always think that if only things were different, we could really show what we are capable of. How many charitable movements there are which, in their penurious beginnings when ardent pioneers toiled in attics with packing cases for furniture, did wonders which they no longer accomplish now that they have become large and richly endowed organizations.[1]

Many commentators have focused on Samson's unhappy love affairs,[2] but Samson's marriage and the succeeding events are the backdrop against which the Spirit of God displays human frailty and his almighty power.

The events of this section may be outlined as follows: (1) the occasion by which God began to deliver his people (14:1–20); (2) the events by which the Philistine oppression was broken (15:1–20).

THE OCCASION BY WHICH GOD BEGAN TO DELIVER HIS PEOPLE (14:1–20)

Setting the Stage (14:1–24)

In the ancient Near East, fathers customarily arranged the marriages of their children (cf. 12:9). Even though Samson was in his late teens, Manoah had not yet sought a bride for his son. Apparently no young woman in the small tribe of Dan was suitable for the one the Lord had designated as a deliverer of his people.

One day while visiting Timnah, Samson notices a beautiful woman. He watches her closely and is strangely attracted to her. It is almost certain that he knew of God's prohibition against marrying Canaanite women (cf. Deut. 7:1–5), but he may have reasoned, "She is a Philistine and therefore not under the same ban." Dr. G. Bush pointed out that though the Philistines "were not indeed prohibited to the Israelites by the *letter* of the law, by its *spirit* they undoubtedly were."[3]

What follows indicates that Samson probably thought through the issues before deciding on marriage because he chose a form of marriage that would leave him free to serve his people. Young people tend to rationalize situations and to follow instructions legalistically. They have not yet matured enough to understand the wisdom behind regulations and substitute principles for precepts.[4] This appears to have been true of Samson.

Youth, however, are not the only ones to evidence immaturity. As we grow older, the same tendency persists. We may unwittingly show our immaturity by our desire to have matters clearly spelled out for us. We want to see things in black-and-white and have ambiguity removed from our lives. We also reveal our lack of readiness for responsibility by allowing the opinions of others to affect our decisions. Only by living our lives under the authority of scripture can we be really free (cf. John 8:32; 17:17b). We easily condemn Samson for his weakness. We even derive an element of comfort from the process. Finding someone whose weaknesses are more obvious than our own directs attention away from ourselves. But gaining satisfaction from such acts is ill-advised because doing so may develop a complacency that deprives us of the opportunity for further growth.

This same immaturity is the reason we have difficulty in reconciling Judges 14:4 ("[Yahweh] was seeking an occasion against the Philistines") with our understanding of God's providence (Isa. 55:8–9; cf. Prov. 20:24). Our preconceptions of what we believe should have happened often hinder our knowledge of the Lord and his ways. We have limited discernment and knowledge of the facts, so we often fail to see his plan on the broad canvas of world affairs and thereby judge situations based on our limited views of right and wrong. When we find that God does not accommodate himself to our myopic beliefs, we then retreat into the security of our traditions rather than face the hard task of developing a truly biblical philosophy of life (cf. Deut. 29:29; Rom. 15:4; 1 Cor. 10:6–11; 2 Tim. 3:16–17).

Dr. G. Bush's treatment of Samson's marriage illustrates the caution of a careful scholar. In commenting on the background of the times, he wrote:

> The danger of [Israel] being enticed into idolatry was the reason of the law as it respected alliances with the Canaanites, and this reason we cannot but suppose was equally applicable to connections with the Philistines. Still the law was merely ceremonial, and if God saw fit to dispense with it in regard to any of his

servants, he could do so unimpeached. That this was the case in the present instance, there are strong grounds from the actual event to believe. At least, we do not feel at liberty, from a view of the facts recorded, to pronounce a sentence of condemnation on this part of Samson's conduct.[5]

Moved by the Spirit of God to do something for his oppressed people, and having seen a woman—evidently from an influential family—who pleased him, Samson may have fancied that an alliance with her could secure for Israel a measure of relief from Philistine domination. If so, equitable relationships could be established without hostility or bloodshed.

Roland deVaux, who studied closely the customs and culture of the ancient Israelites, observed the similarities and differences between Samson's proposed form of marriage and a form found among Palestinian Arabs today. Among the Arabs, a woman remains the mistress of her own house, and the husband, known as "a visiting husband," comes to see her as often as his form of livelihood will allow.[6] In ancient Israel the wife remained with her father or his people.

Sidīqā marriages, such as Samson's, were arranged between the groom and the family of his wife-to-be. The transaction did not necessarily involve the groom's parents.

Samson showed filial loyalty by requesting that his parents negotiate with the father of his intended bride. Their hope, of course, had always been that he would marry someone from their tribe. Both his father and mother try to dissuade him from marrying a Philistine. This shows how much pressure they brought to bear on him.[7]

> "Is there not among the daughters of your brothers [i.e., from among your cousins] or among all my people [i.e., from the remnants of the tribe of Dan] a woman that you [are] going to take a wife from the uncircumcised Philistines?" (14:3*b*).

The argument of Manoah and his wife is weak. They probably sense that they have failed in their duty to find a wife for their son. Perhaps because of the widespread immorality, they had not found even one acceptable young woman among the remnant of their tribe.

Those who say Samson's parents could have gone to Judah or Ephraim or an adjoining tribe to secure a bride for their son need to remember that Dan stood last in tribal prominence. No father would allow his daughter to marry into a tribe that could not boast of one walled city within its borders.

Samson tactfully introduced the idea of marriage to a Philistine, recounting for his father and mother the events of his visit to Timnah (14:2), but he later became insistent (14:3b). The kind of marriage he proposed did not obligate him either by law or custom to consult with them. Their objections, therefore, only complicated matters for him.

Whatever Samson's real reasons were for wishing to marry the woman from Timnah, certain truths worth noting emerge from the passage.

First, genuine love is a well-developed emotion. The maturity level of the couple is more important than age.[8] The Bible has much to say about the honor due those whose wisdom and experience qualify them to lead people (Job 12:12; 32:7; cf. Lev. 19:32). Failure to heed the counsel of the aged is a mark of a decadent society (Isa. 3:5), provided the advice is in accord with God's word (Prov. 16:31).

God gave his people a whole body of "wisdom literature,"[9] but few have mastered these portions of inspired scripture. As a result we lack much of the necessary knowledge to guide our young people in making wise decisions. If knowledge and example do not back our words, we should not be surprised that our counsel goes unheeded.

When talking with young people about matters as important as marriage, God's model must be the basis from which we discuss the principles of true love and commitment. We must set an example or our words are empty.

We should also deal kindly and knowledgeably with their emotions before seeking to direct their wills. Only as we give them the opportunity to express their feelings openly and without censure can we understand their motives. And only when we understand their motives can we ask the kind of questions that will lead them to think through the issues.

Second, according to Dr. E. O. James in his book *Marriage and Society*, the kind of marriage Samson proposed had emerged over time. In hunting communities, as well as in pastoral societies, the husband and father had to a spend a considerable amount of time away from home. In this respect the *ṣidîqâ*[10] marriage was not unlike the relationship of married men and women today who are traveling salespersons, conference speakers, construction workers, professional athletes, evangelists, politicians, international traders, sailors, or airline personnel. Their work requires that they spend much time away from their homes. Though far from ideal, these circumstances should caution us not to condemn Samson's plans too quickly. The key to any marriage is the couple's commitment to a lasting relationship.[11] The events of Judges plainly show that Samson had this commitment.

First Display of Strength (14:5–9)

Whatever Samson's parents felt, and however long they tried to turn him from his plans, eventually they agreed to accompany him to Timnah, where they arranged for the wedding. The negotiations were carefully worked out to comply with the social customs (cf. 14:10*b*) and civil laws of both Philistines and Hebrews.

Arthur Cundall believed, based on the use of the word *'iššāh*, "woman" (instead of either *na⁽rāh*, "girl," or *b⁽tūlāh*, "virgin"), that Samson's bride was either widowed or divorced. The week-long festivities (14:12, 15, 17) argue against his view.[12]

Timnah originally was an Israelite town (Josh. 15:10; 19:43; 2 Chron. 28:18). At the time of our story, however, it was regarded as a Philistine city. Built on a ridge overlooking the Wadi es–Sarar, it was approximately three hundred and fifty feet above the valley, at an elevation of about eight hundred feet above sea level. It was about an hour's walk from Samson's home.

As Samson and his parents travel to Timnah, he leaves them to go into one of the unfenced vineyards growing on the steep slope of the hill. The text does not explain the reason for his action.[13]

In the vineyard a lion attacks Samson, who has nothing in his hands with which to defend himself. But the Spirit of the Lord comes on Samson, and he rips the lion apart. He accomplishes this feat as easily as one would tear apart a roasted lamb or a young goat.

This may have been the first time Samson experienced such phenomenal strength. It would be natural for a young man to recount to others what has happened, but Samson does not tell anyone. He even keeps it from his parents. And when he spends time with his bride-to-be, he does not mention the event. In this he shows uncommon modesty and self-control.[14] Instead, the two of them talk of other things. Samson's original favorable impression of the woman is confirmed. She pleases him. He finds in her that which answers to his own spirit.

Samson did not need to boast of his accomplishments. Perhaps his parents had given him much affirmation as a child so he did not need praise from others to reinforce his sense of worth. This humility is evidence of his growing maturity.

To Samson's humility must be added his discretion. He did not need to tell all. His inner strength freed him from the insecurities that often cause us to look to others for approval or support. This also contributed to his sense of purpose. He was strong mentally and emotionally, as well as physically.

Some Background on Local Customs (14:10)

The interval between betrothal and marriage varied from a few days to a full year. During this period the couple was considered married, even though their relationship had not yet been consummated.[15] The interval gave the groom time to pay compensation to his wife's parents for the loss of their daughter's contribution to the household. Samson's wife would continue to live with her parents, so such compensation was probably unnecessary. (This may explain why Samson, and not the bride's father, bore the expense of the week-long feast. Among the Hebrews a feast was usually given by the bride's father [cf. Gen. 29:21–28].)[16] The interval also gave the groom's parents the assurance that their future daughter-in-law was not pregnant. At the end of the betrothal period, the marriage was consummated.

In biblical times couples did not exchange vows as we do today. Their families agreed to the conditions of the union. On the first evening of the festivities, the father would lead his heavily veiled daughter to a room where the groom was waiting. Their conjugal union made them husband and wife.

JUDGES 14

The wealth and social prominence of the families determined the length of the feast. Dancing, singing, juggling, wrestling, and conundrums or banquet-riddles entertained the guests during the merrymaking.[17] These were for the amusement of the guests as well as to pass the time between feasting and resting.

During the festivities, the groom devoted himself to his bride's comfort and lavished his love on her. She responded in a warm and loving manner (cf. Song of Sol. 1:1–5:1).

The Powerful Are Powerless (14:11–14)

When Samson returns to Timnah to take his wife, curiosity causes him to turn aside and view the remains of the lion he had killed earlier. Inside the skeleton he finds a swarm of bees.[18] He takes some of the honey, and this becomes the basis of his riddle[19] during the wedding celebrations.

The Philistines, intimidated by Samson, select thirty strong men whom they designate as "friends of the bridegroom."[20] These men are to be with him at all times, except when he and his bride retire for the night. Ironically, those who ruled over Israel (14:4; 15:11) suddenly feel powerless in the presence of one man.

As the wedding feast progresses, Samson confidently challenges all thirty of his companions to compete with him in solving a riddle. Confident of their corporate wisdom, they readily accept his dare: "Out of the eater came forth food [i.e., something to eat], and out of the strong came forth [something] sweet [lit., sweetness]."

Samson's enigmatic riddle shows his quick wit and ready sense of humor. Furthermore, he is unawed by the Philistine strongmen assigned to guard him and eagerly enters into a wager with them.

Unlike his countrymen, Samson has developed a certain disdain for the Philistines. He knows the thirty "friends of the bridegroom" are actually guards, so he is probably not upset when they lose all joy in the festivities. He is not prepared, however, for the lengths to which they go to avoid humiliation.

At the end of three days (14:14*b*), the men are still baffled by the riddle. They resort to what they know best: coercion and intimidation.

The Strong Gives Way to the Weak (14:15–19)

They call Samson's wife aside and demand that she tell them the answer. "Declare to us the riddle, or else we will burn you and your father's house with fire" (14:15).

They compel her to entice Samson into explaining the solution. From this time on, in public as well as in private (cf. 14:16–17), she weeps before him and pleads with him to tell her the answer. The ambience of the happy occasion has become tense and depressing. Samson's bride is fearful, their guests are angry because they have lost face before a despised Hebrew, and Samson's expectations of happiness have been shattered.

Samson is caught between a woman afraid to tell him of the threats made on her life and his implacable enemies who are masters in the art of tyranny.

To reduce stress, Samson tells his wife the answer. The strong gives way to the weak. She immediately tells the men, who tauntingly offer Samson an explanation. They do not solve the riddle nor properly understand it, but Samson is too angry to protest. He merely responds, "Unless you had plowed with my heifer, you would not have found [out] my riddle" (14:18b).

Samson then leaves town.

And the Spirit of the Yahweh came mightily upon him and he went down to Ashkelon[21] and struck thirty of the men [of that city], and took their plunder [i.e., their clothes], and gave the changes [of clothing] to those who had declared the riddle (14:19).

Samson probably selects Ashkelon, about twenty-four miles southwest of Timnah, so the Philistines will not realize where he has gotten his payment for the wager.

Samson's anger continues to burn after his return. Feeling that his wife has betrayed him, he leaves her and goes to his father's house.

Postscript (14:20)

The inspired writer added a postscript: "And his wife became his companion's, [the man] who had been his best man" (14:20).

JUDGES 14

POINTS TO CONSIDER

The interplay between strength and weakness in ourselves and others is difficult to comprehend. Those who observe this phenomenon realize how easy it is to place people into categories, subconsciously identifying them as either strong or weak. Dr. Paul Tournier wrote:

> There are those who seem doomed to be defeated and trampled upon. They have been so often beaten in this universal free-for-all that they are always expecting it to happen again, and this saps their strength. Those who know them also expect it, and gather strength and assurance for themselves from the fact. Even a stranger has an immediate intuition of their weakness, and treats them either condescendingly or aggressively—to do either is to humiliate them. On the other hand, the same intuition warns him of the strength of the strong, so that he adopts towards them an attitude of timidity or deference which confirms their strength.[22]

In the presence of Samson, the Philistines felt weak. Their fear was evident in their selection of thirty men "to be with him" and ensure that no harm came to them. Accustomed to issuing threats and engaging in acts of oppression, they coerced Samson's wife. This gave them a feeling of strength. In this they are like those who take out their frustration on a spouse or child after being threatened or humiliated by an unjust supervisor at work.

During our formative years we all learn coping techniques. Some learn to rely on physical strength to ensure safety; others develop an acquired dependency and use their weaknesses to get by.

> Many neuroses and illnesses, more or less consciously cultivated, serve as tools to bring within reach things otherwise unobtainable. Impulsiveness serves one, while tenacious obstruction serves another; interminable or eloquent speeches win for some, while others use an obstinate silence.[23]

Perhaps the greatest point of vulnerability for those who imagine themselves to be strong is the thought that they are immune to the weaknesses of others. God seems to favor them. The Philistines, for example, were accustomed to having everything their own way. They crushed all who opposed their will. This attitude became their nemesis. As the Lord Jesus would later point out, those who live by the sword die by the sword (Matt. 26:52). Their acts of oppression became habitual. After a while they could not relate to anyone (even their own kind) without resorting to threats of violence. They had lost all natural feeling.

Samson, at this stage in his experience, could have begun to take his strength for granted.[24] At this early period of his life, he was modest and unassuming (cf. 2 Cor. 12:10). That is why the Lord used him, and for twenty years Samson judged God's people.

JUDGES 14

12 THE STRONG AND THE WEAK: PART 2

Judges
15

Long before he achieved fame as a reformer, Martin Luther, as a plainly dressed monk, stood before the distinguished court of the German emperor to answer charges brought against him by leading clergymen. On display were his published writings. His bold attack on the indulgences of the established church revealed a crack in its supposedly impregnable armor.

Interrogators asked Luther whether the books were his.

"Yes, these are my books," he replied.

"Will you recant and deny their errors?" they demanded.

Martin Luther asked for time to explain his position. He then began a brilliant defense of his beliefs and ended by asking the scholars, who had gathered to try him for heresy, to point out his errors. He offered to be the first to throw his writings into the fire if they could do so. "But unless I shall be convinced by the testimonies of the scriptures, I cannot recant anything, since I cannot act against my conscience. Here I stand! I cannot do otherwise."

Martin Luther's courage shook the court. He persuaded many of the nobles of the viability of his cause, and his bold defense of the truth changed history. Only in recent years have some influential Roman Catholic leaders admitted that the medieval church erred in its treatment of this courageous monk.

Everyone admires those who are strong and accomplish great things despite overwhelming obstacles. Another person, living at another time, exhibited similar courage. Ione Reed, while a student in the Moody Bible Institute, learned of the martyrdom of John and Betty Stamm in China. She dedicated her life to the Lord and began preparing for missionary service. In time this brave woman went to the Congo (now Zaire) as a member of the Unevangelized Fields Mission.

While engaged in evangelistic work, Ione met Hector McMillan. They fell in love, were married, and had six sons.

The McMillans spent twenty-three happy years in Central Africa. In the late fifties and early sixties, when the communist-inspired Simba uprising threatened the lives of all foreigners, Hector and Ione did not retreat. They stayed to protect other missionary women and children at a bush station called Kilometer 8.

One day the Simbas came to their station and brutally murdered Hector McMillan and wounded two of their sons. Facing extreme danger, the missionary wives and children made their way to safety soon after the attack. Later, when the events of the uprising became known, the world was stunned by the women's bravery in the ordeal.

Most of us appear strong in the company of those who admire us. We are weak, however, in the presence of those whose gifts, personality, or power are superior to our own. We identify with David in his weakness and fear (cf. Pss. 3:1–8; 4:1, 6; 5:1–2, 8, 11 et al.) more than in his defeat of Goliath. So it has been with the great men and women of history.

The interplay of strength and weakness in Judges 14–15 will culminate in the breaking of the Philistine power over God's people.

THE EVENTS BY WHICH THE PHILISTINE
OPPRESSION WAS BROKEN (15:1–19)

The Philistines have become confident of their strength. They enjoy superior weaponry, are more experienced in the art of warfare, have developed greater tactical skills, and recently may have defeated the Israelites in the Battle of Aphek (1 Sam. 4:1–11, notice v. 9). Their vaunted superiority, however, proves to be their undoing. As Dr. Paul Tournier remarked:

> The strong have learned how to play their hand so as to win in the game of life, and they become prisoners of the game . . . [they develop] a systematized habit of mind as a simplistic philosophy which ends by drying them up and cutting them off from true life.
>
> Their repeated success soon leads them to believe that they are better than other people—above all, better than the weak, who think that God disapproves of them. Their success, even when it is unjust, they take to be a flattering sign of divine blessing; and this deprives them of the most fruitful experience this world affords—the experience of God's grace, to which the only road is repentance.[1]

The Israelites, by contrast to the Philistines, are at one of the lowest points of their national existence. God appointed the men of Judah to be the military leaders of his people (cf. Gen. 49:8–12), but the writer depicts them as sniveling cowards (15:9–13). Their betrayal of the one whom God appointed as their deliverer reveals the true nature of their weakness. Their weakness was attitudinal rather than numerical, and in this respect they differ little from us when we face repeated setbacks. Dr. Tournier's comments are again most apropos:

> When the weak, who [seldom] retaliate, and appear content to allow themselves to be trampled upon, come to us and open their hearts, we find there an immense accumulation of grievances encumbering and poisoning them. It is only with difficulty that they bring themselves to put these [feelings] into words. They are afraid that we too will rebuke them for keeping secret account of all the injuries, affronts and prohibitions they have suffered. They fear that we shall call them selfish and vindictive, and think them too critical of their parents, their teachers, their friends, their husbands or wives.
>
> The truth is that they are no more vindictive than anybody else. All they have done is to repress the natural reflexes of defense which come into play quite normally whenever a person is injured. Every attempt at domination of any living being arouses at once a legitimate movement of defense. In man a further movement, inspired by grace, may enable him to forgive. . . .

JUDGES 15

Genuine forgiveness is a spiritual victory that frees the heart from all resentment. Suppression is but a weak reaction, liquidating nothing, and laying up in the heart a store of fierce grievances.[2]

God had given Israel the means to enjoy lives of relative peace and tranquility. They had neglected to repair their relationship with him as their true Lord and so had to suffer under feudal lords whose implacable spirit left them feeling bereft of strength.

The Occasion of Further Aggression (15:1–28)

Samson is both strong and weak. He feels the mysterious power God has given him and realizes that he possesses awesome responsibility (cf. 15:3). His fear grows with his strength, and he senses the need for controls lest he abuse this divine gift (15:7).

Verse 1 relates to 14:19. Not long after Samson's visit to Ashkelon, and during the wheat harvest (i.e., late May or early June), Samson visits his wife. As is customary in a *ṣidīqâ* marriage, he takes with him a goat so they can have a feast and perhaps invite a few of her family's friends.

Samson's father-in-law, however, will not allow him to enter his wife's bedroom (15:2).

"Indeed, I said that you surely hated[3] her, and I gave her to your companion; [now] is not her younger sister better than she? Let her please be to you instead of [my elder daughter]."

Samson had not spent the last night of the feast with his wife. To his father-in-law this was tantamount to divorce. He ignored the precedent of the Near East by which any act of repudiation began with the husband.[4] Wishing to avoid any social stigma caused by his daughter's betrayal of her husband's confidence he probably asked the men of his village what he should do. Considering that Samson directs his retaliation against the people of the village, it is likely that they were the ones who suggested she be given to the best man. This done, they may have congratulated themselves that this episode with a despised man from a downtrodden race was now a thing of the past. No one expected to see Samson again.

We can readily imagine the father's consternation when Samson arrives and wishes to see his wife. Afraid of Samson, he tries to placate him by offering him his younger daughter. As Dr. Joseph Hall pointed out, Samson clearly acted with remarkable self-control toward his father-in-law. He who had killed a lion in the vineyards of Timnah allows himself to be restrained by one who had acted out of weakness and fear.[5] Dr. G. Bush believed that the indignities heaped on Samson were directly connected to his Hebrew heritage. Otherwise the Philistines would have tried to learn his feelings toward his bride before taking such unilateral action.[6]

Samson masters his emotions, shows respect for his wife's father—even when great wrong has been done to him—determines who corroborated in the scheme, and punishes them for the offense done to him, his wife, and his nation.

Dr. G. Bush observed:

> Had [Samson] aimed to avenge only his personal injuries, it would have been sufficient to have chastised his rival and his father-in-law only: but as the slight which excited his indignation had no doubt been put upon him because he was an Israelite, he determines as an Israelite to seek revenge.[7]

Samson then goes out into the hills and catches three hundred foxes.[8] He ties a thong around the tail of each fox, knots two together, and then attaches a firebrand to the end of the thongs. When released, they run through the ripened wheat fields, setting fire to the dry shocks of harvested grain and the standing grain yet to be gathered. The fire also spreads to the vineyards and olive groves.[9]

Barley or wheat, grapes, and olives were the three staples of Near Eastern economy (cf. Deut. 7:13; Hag. 1:11). For Samson to destroy them was to strike a serious blow at the Philistines for what they had done to him and his nation.

The Philistines, unaccustomed to such reprisals, do not know whom to punish. The lords of Ekron and Gath probably make the inquiries and soon learn that Samson is the culprit. Those sent to investigate the matter explain that the act was precipitated

> because [his father-in-law] took his wife and gave her to his companion (15:6).

JUDGES 15

The Philistines themselves judge that Samson's father-in-law acted unwisely. Without giving him the opportunity to explain his side of the story, they come to Timnah and burn his house. It is an inhuman and barbarous act. And Samson's wife is caught up in the fate she had so studiously tried to avoid by betraying her husband (14:15).

We have no way of knowing how or by what providential means Samson learned of the Philistines' intentions. Perhaps he had seen a large group of armed men leave one of the cities of the pentapolis. He apparently reaches Timnah too late to save his wife from the fire. In anger he confronts the men:

> "If you do like this [i.e., bring harm on those who are powerless to resist you], surely I shall be avenged on you, and afterwards I will cease" (15:7).

As God's theocratic representative, Samson determines the extent as well as the limitations of his actions.

Samson's love for his wife must have been real, for he suffered intensely as a result of her death. He felt obligated to uphold the ancient law of retributive justice (Gen. 9:6). On him, therefore, descended the responsibility of being her *gō'ēl haddām*, "avenger of blood" (Num. 35:19).[10] And those who had abused their power and inflicted death on the defenseless now find themselves powerless before the might of Samson.

The text reads that "he struck them ruthlessly with a great slaughter" (15:8). The lords of Ekron and Gath are shocked at Samson's brashness and fearful of his power. It does not take too great an imagination to picture the effect this second setback has on them. And while they plan their next move, Samson goes to live in a cave in the rock Etam. His presence in any of the tent-villages of his people would bring harm to those who might shelter him. The Philistines are ruthless and implacable. They can watch his movements as easily as he watches theirs. Because he can only be in one place at a time, he cannot always protect those who might show him kindness.

As his retreat Samson selects a place identified as a cleft above the Wadi Isma'in, about two and one-half miles southeast of Zorah. It is a cave that can be reached only through a passage wide enough to admit one person at a time.

The Trepidation of the People of Judah (15:9–13)

If the events of the Battle of Aphek had already taken place (with the subsequent plague on Philistia, 1 Sam. 4–6), we could understand the reluctance of both Israelites and Philistines for further hostility. The Philistines had emerged the victors, but they stood in awe of the power of Israel's God. Being in a position of advantage, they were unwilling to have anyone challenge their authority, particularly when the Israelites had accepted their lordship (15:11). Samson, however, baffled them. He had single-handedly defeated a contingent of armed men[11] who had been sent to Timnah to make an example of his rash, impetuous father-in-law. He had also shown himself to be a powerful adversary. Because the Israelites were still their vassals, they could not ignore any of Samson's actions. He must be punished.

After due consultation, the lords of the Philistines send their army to the border of Judah. Instead of perceiving how fragile this show of strength is, the Israelites think only of their own weakness. Their lack of strength is evident first in their words and later in their deeds.

"Why have you come up against us?"

To which the Philistines respond, "To bind Samson [is the reason] we have come up; to do to him as he has done to us."

The obvious question is, Why did they threaten the people of Judah if their real contention was with Samson?

It was true that the rock Etam lay in the southernmost extremity of Judah, but why didn't the Philistines go there themselves? Why did they involve Judah in a squabble that had nothing to do with them?

Apparently the Philistines believed that as long as Samson was free, he was powerful. If he was subdued (i.e., bound), they could treat him as they wished. Furthermore, if he resisted being bound they would let the losses be to the Israelites, not to themselves.

The Philistines' vaunted show of strength was a cover for their own sense of weakness. They took advantage of the people's fear.

The men of Judah know where Samson is, for the hero from Dan has made no attempt to conceal his whereabouts.[12] Three thousand strong men are sent to the rock Etam. They show no loyalty to their fellow-Israelite. Instead, their pusillanimous attitude is evident in their words: "Do you not know that the Philistines [are] ruling over us? And what [is] this you have done to us?"

Dr. G. Bush called this "a most degrading confession to come from the lips of an Israelite." He went on to show that God's people "had become contented slaves, more fearful of offending the Philistines than anxious to assert their independence."[13]

Samson acts with true magnanimity toward his countrymen. His reply is modest and temperate in tone. He does not upbraid them for their cowardice in siding with the Philistines, nor does he chide them for their ingratitude toward him for trying to ease their miseries. Instead he rests his case simply and solely on the justice of his actions: "As they did to me, so have I done to them."

Samson had been living at peace with the Philistines. He had even united himself to them by the close and tender ties of marriage. They had cruelly wronged him: first, in coercing his wife to reveal his secret; then, in giving her to another; and finally, in burning her and her father alive. As they had acted toward him, so he has dealt with them.

Samson's countrymen should have been proud of his actions. Instead, they look down on this lowly Danite, and perhaps excuse their actions by rationalizing that his impulsiveness caused this unwanted confrontation. So they coolly tell him they intend to deliver him into the hands of the Philistines.[14]

After extracting from the men of Judah a promise that they will not harm him, Samson allows himself to be bound (15:12–13). Believing that one new rope is insufficient for the task, the men of Judah use two. The securely tied bonds cut into Samson's flesh. The men approach their task with all the efficiency of people intent on a lynching.

With Samson tied up like a felon, the men of Judah lead him to the Philistine encampment. His willingness to be bound produces in these cowards the appearance of courage and contentiousness.[15] God had given them another opportunity to throw off the Philistine yoke, but they allow this fortuitous occasion to slip through their grasp.

In much the same way, we may allow God-given opportunities to pass through our fingers. As with the men of Judah, past failures or fears of what others will think of us may condition our thought processes. Then, when some unexpected (and, perhaps, unconventional) opportunity presents itself to us, our insecurities betray us. We prefer the comfort and seeming security of the status quo to boldly committing ourselves to some new venture. Only as we allow God's word to daily permeate our thought processes (cf. Ps. 119:9–11, 17–18, 38–40, 97–106) can we grow strong in the Lord and in the power of his might (Eph. 6:10).

God could have given the people a great victory if their hearts had been right before him. Instead, in a display of cowardice they deliver to death the one whom the Lord had appointed to be their deliverer. But what of Samson? How did he view such actions?

Samson had sought to do his best for his people. Now he faces further rejection and the prospect of a slow and very painful death. Thomas Kirk described the march toward Lehi, where the Philistines are waiting:

> [Samson] was no doubt, saddened and humiliated as he thought of the cowardice and treachery of his body-guard. The remembrance of the glorious days of old—the victories won by Joshua, by Deborah and Barak, by Gideon and Jephthah, and others—would only deepen the darkness of the present hour, and bring into stronger relief the utter lack of patriotic valour and faith [of the people of Judah]. He probably thought that the youthful dreams, which he had so fondly cherished, of doing great and noble deeds for his country's weal, were now blasted for ever; and as he was then, in all likelihood, not more than twenty years of age, he could hardly fail to contemplate his exit from the stage of life, on which he had begun to play his part, with something like sorrowful regret.[16]

Samson's willingness to die rather than defend himself and possibly kill his own people reveals his true heroism. There is a moral grandeur in his submission to those whose lack of courage evokes contempt.

The Destruction of the Philistines (15:14–19)

The Philistines had assembled in a broad valley called Lehi, "jawbone" in the text. On seeing Samson led as a sheep to the slaughter, they let out a shout that reverberates through the hills. They will make an example of their enemy by slowly torturing him to death. This will dissuade other would-be saviors from challenging their authority.

JUDGES 15

The triumphant shouts of the Philistine soldiers coincide with a surge of power as the Spirit of the Lord comes on Samson. The ropes with which he is bound become like burned flax (cf. 16:9, 12). Grabbing a fresh jawbone of a donkey,[17] he hacks away at the Philistine ranks. The insignificance of his weapon intensifies his victory.

When he is done, the dead lie in heaps about him. Tired and thirsty, Samson expresses his contempt for his enemies. Thinking of the instrument he has used, *ᵃmôr* (which in Hebrew means both "ass" or "donkey," as well as a "heap"), he develops a catchy rhyme:

> With the jawbone of an ass,
> [I have] piled them in a mass;
> With the jawbone of an ass
> I have killed a thousand men.

It is an elegant play on words; and while Samson's part involved tremendous physical exertion, the Philistines fell as tamely as asses.[18]

Some have criticized Samson for not attributing his success to the hand of God. These critics show little knowledge of human nature. Dr. G. Bush believed that Samson's witty comment is the happy expression of his unexpected deliverance and is "rather to be understood as an exclamation of grateful and adoring wonder [at the] overthrow of his enemies" than as a statement of selfish pride.[19]

The battle over, Samson now calls the place *Ramath-lehi,* "the height of the jawbone." Then, suffering from fatigue and dehydration (15:18), he calls on the Lord for help.

"You have given by the hand of your servant this great deliverance, and now I am dying with thirst, and will fall into the hand of the uncircumcised."

God hears his prayer and graciously breaks open (probably by an earth tremor) a hollow place. In it Samson sees clear, sparkling water. He drinks, and his spirit revives. In gratitude he calls the place "The Spring of the Caller."

Thomas Kirk reflected on the views of commentators in his day:

Some have indeed gravely questioned the genuineness of [Samson's] piety; and the serious blemishes which mar his character give some colour of reasonableness to the doubt; but it seems to me that such an incident as [his prayer], which lays bare the hidden springs of his life, ought to put the genuineness of his piety beyond suspicion.[20]

Postscript (15:20)

As chapter 14 concluded with a postscript, so does chapter 15. Samson, in all probability, returns to the rock Etam. From that humble cave he patrols the southwest. Those concerned about their relationship with God or those who need a decision concerning interpersonal conflicts come to Samson in that humble cave for his judgment (cf. Deut. 1:16–17). His administration is not over all Israel but is probably limited to the territory of Dan and the southwestern section of the land allotted by God to Judah.

Scripture does not specifically state when Samson's judgeship began. It may have started in his late teens when the Spirit of the Lord began to stir him, or in Timnah when he avenged his wife's murder, or following his victory at Lehi when he dealt a heavy blow to the Philistines. In any event, his slaughter of the army sent against the people of Judah enabled him to give his people a measure of freedom.[21]

EVENTS IN REVIEW

Samson often exemplified true meekness, or bridled strength. He restrained himself from doing any physical harm to his bride's father, even though it lay well within his power to punish him for his capricious act. Samson's loyalty to his new family matched his devotion to his own people. The events of 14:20–15:3 and 15:11–13 illustrate his mastery of his feelings and his true greatness. In the former instance, when he found that the people of the city were really at fault, he took appropriate action to punish them; and in the latter case, when he realized that he could not reason with the people of Judah, he allowed them to bind him. One was an act of retaliation to vindicate his honor and the honor of his people; the other was an act of noble self-sacrifice.

The cowardliness of the people of Judah came from their own hearts. Their lack of commitment to righteousness caused them to give way to their fears. They had forgotten the Lord's promise that when his people walk before him and are pleasing in his sight, they

> shall pursue [their] enemies . . . and five [men] shall pursue a hundred, and a hundred . . . shall pursue a thousand. And your enemies shall fall before you. . . . And I shall turn toward you and make you fruitful (Lev. 26:7–9).

Having turned their backs on the Lord, the people of Judah felt powerless to resist those who oppressed them.

The Holy Spirit still imbues men and women with power and authority. He energizes people, not methods, techniques, machinery, or organizations.

In the same way that God enabled Samson to face the fear of Judah's men, so the Spirit of God helps us cope with the caprice of those who bear the name of Christ but follow the principles of the world. And as the Holy Spirit's power delivered Samson from those who abused their power, so God's power working in us (Eph. 3:7) can help us face misunderstanding and opposition. There may be times when He delivers us as He did Samson. There may be other times when we must face the fires of affliction as Daniel's friends had to do (cf. Dan. 3:17ff.). Either way, we do so confident that our attitudes and actions bring glory to the Lord.

As we depend on the Lord, his strength can supply our physical, material, spiritual, and relational needs. Samson's experience of thirst illustrates this for us. The hot, dry climate in Israel makes a ready supply of water a necessity. Visitors to the Holy Land are reminded to drink plenty of water for their physical well-being. Archaeologists, engineers, or shepherds who spend much of their time there outdoors take an adequate supply of water with them.

Samson's thirst was extreme due to his exhaustion and dehydration. He feared that the part of the Philistine army still living might return. He also realized he could not rely on his countrymen for help. He had no one to turn to but the Lord.

The humanity and simplicity of Samson's prayer is refreshing. Some of the most inspiring prayers heard in today's church meetings come from new Christians who have not yet learned the usual cliches. Their words are sincere. They expect an answer and are confident that the Lord hears them.

JUDGES 15

Samson handled rejection well. He did not act irresponsibly (even though the cowardice of his countrymen must have hurt him deeply) but "judged Israel twenty years in the days of the Philistines" (15:20). Samson decided cases of controversy between Israelites, whether these were civil, religious, or domestic. He served as God's representative. Furthermore, Samson continued to live alone. He probably made the rough cleft in the rock Etam his "home." From there he could observe any Philistine military movements. His life, however, was a lonely one. He could not form any intimate friendships or lasting attachments for fear that the Philistines might mark those close to him for reprisal.

In spite of the unnaturalness of the life forced on him, Samson faithfully served his people. He allowed neither their timidity nor their vacillation to turn him from the path of duty. And in this unswerving course of action, he persevered for twenty years. It is no wonder, therefore, that he is numbered among the great leaders of the faith.

JUDGES 15

13 / "HOW ARE THE MIGHTY FALLEN"

Judges
16

The most touching scene in Camille Saint-Saens's operatic master-
piece "Samson and Delilah" is of Samson in the prison house in
Gaza: There is Israel's champion of liberty, bereft of sight and
strength, working as a slave. His song of penitence is deeply
moving, touching us where we live. Ours is a fallen world. Not all
who profess to be God-fearing are of like commitment. Furthermore, all of us at one time or another get caught in the conflict
between the legitimate satisfaction of our desires and what is
expedient for us in the will of God. Our spirits identify with Samson
as we see this scene from his life dramatically enacted on stage.

PRELIMINARY CONSIDERATIONS

But how did the powerful become powerless? By what process
did Samson—who had so easily broken new ropes (15:13–14;
16:12), rawhide thongs (16:7–9), and a weaver's loom (16:13–14)—
become bound by shackles of brass (16:21)? How was it that he
did not know until it was too late that "Yahweh had departed from
him"?

The purpose of Judges and the events that scripture only alludes to have a direct bearing on our understanding of what transpired.

Irresolution of the Nation

Throughout Samson's judgeship Israel remained the vassal of Philistia. God did not lack the power to deliver his people, but the people failed to repent of their sins and seek his help. In grace He gave them a measure of deliverance through Samson.

Samson was a solitary champion. His life was lonely. At best he received secret honor. He watched the military movements of the Philistines in the southwest from various rocky summits. As occasion required, he routed enemy armies and wreaked havoc on their raiding parties. When peasants were being dispossessed of their land, Samson would appear and disperse the would-be "land barons." His steadfastness and perseverance in the face of such national languor and apathy were remarkable, but toward the end of his twenty-year judgeship, his enforced isolation began to take its toll on him.

Success of the Nation's Champion

In addition to being his people's single-handed defense, Samson was uniformly successful. Throughout the twenty years of his judgeship, he apparently never experienced defeat. This was a remarkable testimony to his vigilance and God's faithfulness.

From a human point of view, each victory must have increased Samson's disdain for Israel's overlords. Their unabated hatred of him matched his growing contempt for them. As often as they tried to take over Israel's wells of water or drive off a tribesmen's few sheep, goats, and cattle, Samson intervened. His justice was harsh. The intimidators feared his name and, in the end, became the intimidated.

We err, however, if we conclude that Samson won his victories easily. He did not. The Philistines learned from their experiences and took added precautions. Each encounter became harder, and each victory cost Samson a tremendous physical and emotional price. Although God gave him the power, Samson had to exert great strength to obtain each victory. As it had been at Lehi, so it was throughout his ministry as a judge. Passivity robbed God's people of his blessing.

The Philistines tried everything within their power—ambush, entrapment, assassination—to end Samson's assaults on their incursions.[1] Samson evaded each attempt to destroy him, and this required continued watchfulness and caution. He never was free to relax. At no time could he afford to enjoy deep sleep. He constantly had to be on the *qui vive.*

Deprived of Loved Ones

The only people from whom Samson received any kind of affirmation during this long period were his parents. How often he visited them, we have no means of knowing. At some time during his judgeship they must have died (cf. 16:31).[2] Their passing surely had a profound effect on him. He now felt his aloneness even more keenly.

Whenever a loved one dies, we are susceptible to depression, anger, and loneliness.[3] In some people evidence of these emotional responses shows up in increased activity, unnecessary risk-taking, and perhaps unwise attachments as they seek a replacement for the love they have lost. For example, when her brother Lazarus died, Martha remained busy in the house while her sister Mary expressed her grief (John 11). And it was after Isaac's mother died that he found comfort in a wife (Gen. 23:1–2; 24:2–4, 67). We see similar evidences of coping with loss in Samson as well.

We can divide Judges 16 as follows: (1) defying the Philistines of Gaza (16:1–3); (2) loving a woman of Sorek (16:4–22); and (3) destroying the temple of Dagon (16:23–31).

DEFYING THE PHILISTINES OF GAZA (16:1–3)

During Samson's time, Gaza (modern Ghazzeh)[4] was the south-ernmost of the Philistine cities and was approximately forty miles from the rock Etam. It was only two and one-half miles from the sea and served as the gateway between Palestine and Egypt. The trade route to western Asia passed by the sloping hill on which the city of Gaza was built. Dr. William Thompson described its setting in *The Land and the Book*: "The entire land of Philistia down to Gaza . . . lies outspread like a variegated map, and beyond it the blue Mediterranean floats away westward to meet and mingle with the hazy horizon."[5]

There was wealth as well as decadence within ancient Gaza's strong walls, and arrogance as well as exploitation of the poor. When Dr. G. Bush visited it, the city had changed little from ancient times. He wrote:

> Environed by and interspersed with gardens and plantations of olive and date trees, the town has a picturesque appearance. . . . The buildings being mostly of stone, and the streets moderately broad, the interior answers expectation better than most other towns of Syria. . . . The suburbs, however, are composed of miserable mud huts; but all travellers concur in admiring the variety and richness of the vegetable productions, both wild and cultivated, of the environs.[6]

Judges 16 begins simply: "And Samson went to Gaza" (16:1).

The text gives no explanation for his going. In what appears to be a reckless act of daring, Samson enters the strongest city of the Philistine pentapolis, passing confidently through the massive gates[7] and mingling with the crowds in the busy streets. People identify him by his long hair and make way for him as he walks leisurely through the bazaars with their merchants, storytellers, jugglers, and snake-charmers. Perhaps he also visits the temple of Dagon.

Samson may have derived pleasure when the conversation died down as he approached a group of people on a street corner or sauntered past hagglers bargaining over the price of some recent imports from Egypt. He would also have heard a different tone in the conversation as it picked up again after he passed.

The only plausible explanation for Samson's audacious act seems to lie in a mingling of anger, frustration, and contempt that had been building inside him for many years. Perhaps the death of his parents was the catalyst that brought on his reckless move. They had been good and godly people who deserved the best that life afforded. Samson may have harbored resentment that they had spent their lives in poverty because of the Philistines. If so, it is likely that he entered the strongest of the Philistine cities for the purpose of defying their power.

JUDGES 16

Descriptions of Samson probably had circulated among the inhabitants of Philistia for many years. Mothers may have kept their children indoors at night by telling them that Samson would get them. Their description of his long hair, unkempt appearance, and terrible strength filled their impressionable offspring with fear.

The Philistines trained their youth for war from their earliest years. It is not hard to imagine their boasting as they grew older. The more aggressive ones would brag to their peers about how they would track down Samson and do to him what their leaders had so far failed to do. Others would tell how they had sighted Samson, and the legend would grow.

So when the people of Gaza recognize him in their midst (16:2), word spreads quickly. They notify the lord of the city, his council, and the military commander, who maintain careful surveillance.

Samson appears to play into the hands of his enemies when he meets a society courtesan and accompanies her to her home. Like Rahab (cf. Josh. 2:1ff.), this woman holds a notable position in the community. The fact that the Philistines place watchers *around* her house implies that she is wealthy and does not live in the poor section of the city where one hut joins another.

Although I do not condone Samson's immoral conduct, I do not believe he was motivated by lust.[8] As H. L. Mencken, the acerbic social critic of a generation past, once said, "People invariably have a simple solution to every human problem—neat, simplistic, and *wrong*."[9] A more reasonable answer may be found in the widely held belief that a person who ravished another's wife or harem showed his power over his enemy.

This is what Absalom did when he sought to usurp the throne from his father, David. His first executive decision as the new king was to publicly have sexual intercourse with his father's concubines (cf. 2 Sam. 15–17, noticing 16:21). In doing so he asserted his authority over everything that belonged to his father.

Samson's cohabitation with the popular prostitute of Gaza may fall into this category. By one bold, daring move he flaunted his power in the faces of his enemies.

But this is not the end of the story. The Gazites, imagining that they have Samson within their grasp, encircle the house and set a trap for him (16:2). Apparently some men watch the house for any attempted escape, while the main force lies in wait just outside the city gates. All they have to do is wait for Samson to leave the same way he entered. The soldiers in the barracks wait anxiously for dawn, and those stationed at the gate maintain a constant vigil.

At midnight, Samson decides it is time to go. He walks through the almost deserted streets, carefully steps over the beggars sleeping on the ground, and makes his way toward the gates, which have been closed and barred since sundown. Without attempting to open them, he rips the posts out of the ground. The noise startles people all around, and those lying in wait outside the city suddenly pretend to be asleep. No one stirs. Then Samson lifts the huge gates onto his shoulders and carries them to a hill facing Hebron.[10]

Having demonstrated the Philistines' powerlessness in the face of his supernatural strength, Samson returns to the solitary place he calls "home." But he still feels restless, tired, and lonely. His life is without satisfaction. He longs for companionship—to love and be loved. While the families of Dan sleep comfortably in their tents, he sits on a rock in the darkness and looks over the fires in the valley below.

LOVING A WOMAN OF SOREK (16:4-22)

With the Philistines more subdued than ever, Samson takes liberties he previously would not have taken. He is also more vulnerable than at any other time during his judgeship. "And it was [i.e., happened] afterward that he loved a woman in the valley of Sorek, and her name was Delilah" (16:4).

Many have concluded that because Delilah's name means "worshiper" or "devotee" she was a Philistine, but her name is actually Semitic. Furthermore, there is no evidence in the text that she had either been born a Philistine or had married one (although the latter is a possibility).[11] Scripture does not explain how she and Samson meet, but her home was only a few miles from where Samson lived. The account is brief and the writer hurriedly passed over details that would be of interest to us.

Delilah's name has become synonymous with greed, cunning, and deception. She stands on an equal footing with Jezebel for her malice, with Cleopatra for her seduction, with Katherine of Russia for her whimsical imperiousness, with Madam Pompadour for her infamy, and with Mata Hari for her perfidy. We fail to discern any notable features in her character. Why then was Samson so fascinated by her? Perhaps his inner needs, following his mother's death, made him weak.

There is no reason to conclude that Delilah was a harlot like the woman of Gaza.[12] The text implies that Samson spent considerable time in her home (16:16). But there must have been times when he was absent, for Delilah was free to make contact with the Philistines. She also knew when he would return, for she concealed soldiers in a separate room of her house.[13] Samson trusted her implicitly, which has lead some to conclude that he entered into a *sidīqā* marriage.[14] Perhaps this is why he felt free to come and go as he pleased.

Both Delilah and Samson were beyond middle age. If she had ever been married, her husband probably was dead. She had no social security, no insurance, and her people had suffered from economic depression for more than twenty years, so we can understand her desire for financial security. We see her heartless selfishness, however, in the way she sacrificed her nation's hero to their enemies for five bags of silver.

On hearing of Samson's love for Delilah, the five lords of the Philistines come up from the coastal plain to the valley of Sorek. They know of Delilah's weakness:

> "Entice him, and see in what [lies] his great strength, and by what [means] we may prevail against him that we may bind him, to afflict him; and surely we will each give to you eleven hundred [pieces of] silver" (16:5).

Being superstitious they quickly conclude that the stength Samson has must lie in some charm or amulet. They believe he will become like other men if they deprive him of the source of his strength. The money they offer Delilah is sufficient for her to live out her days in opulence and ease.

Without scruple Delilah sets out to find the source of Samson's strength. When next they are alone, she coyly asks, "Tell to me, please, in what your great strength [lies], and with what you may be bound to afflict you."

It is an unusual question to come from a lover's lips. Normally a person in love would want to know what would protect the loved one, rather than what would harm him or her. As Thomas Kirk observed, "none but a woman of the coolest and most daring effrontery" could have asked it.[15] Because she is a Hebrew, Samson does not suspect her treachery. He probably considers her query feminine curiosity inspired by the desire to keep him in her power.

Delilah's first entreaty fails (16:6), but before long she again uses her femininity to gain the ends she seeks (cf. 16:10, 13, 15). She capitalizes on her supposed weakness and accuses Samson of lying to her, mocking her, and pretending to love her when in reality he does not.

It is easy to picture each scene. Delilah's entreaties become more persuasive and her reactions more manipulative. With repeated failure she becomes fearful that the coveted money will slip from her grasp (cf. 16:18). Finally her persistence wears down Samson's resistance.[16] His days with her become a continuous cycle of scolding and complaining. She warms to his embrace only to withdraw and leave him feeling rejected. If Samson had not been married to her, it is unlikely that he would have remained with her. The biblical text shows the extent of his patience: "He was grieved in his soul to death" (16:16).

Finally Samson gives in.

> There is something noble, as well as sad, in Samson's surrender. It sprang from his large-hearted tenderness and high sense of honour. His great love for this unworthy woman and his honourable disposition blinded him to her falseness. He took her to be such a one as himself. But he soon afterwards discovered . . . that his confidence in her had been altogether misplaced.[17]

Delilah's knowledge of the customs of her people makes an explanation of the Nazirite vow unnecessary (16:17). As soon as she can, she sends a message to the lords of the Philistines: "Come up this time, for he has told to me all his heart" (16:18).

When next Samson visits her, tired and weary after traveling along Israel's southern border, she sits crosslegged on some rugs and cushions and has him lay his head on her lap. Then she gently strokes his hair, soothing him to sleep.

When Samson is sound asleep, Delilah signals for a barber to come into the room and clip off his seven locks of hair.[18] Then, in a display of sadistic anger, she tosses him roughly to the ground and begins to taunt him: "The Philistines are upon you, Samson!"

The slumbering giant awakes, intending to rout his enemies, unaware that the Lord has departed from him (16:20). But his strength is gone.

After subduing Israel's champion and the "destroyer of their people," the Philistines gouge out his eyes. Sightless and helpless, Samson is led in chains of bronze over the hot desert sands to Gaza nearly forty miles away. There his captors make him do the most menial of tasks in the prisonhouse while passersby mock him.

Unnoticed by them, however, his hair begins to grow (16:22).

DESTROYING THE TEMPLE OF DAGON
(16:23–31)

The final act in this tragic drama takes place soon after harvest when the Philistines hold a feast in honor of their god, Dagon (cf. Heb. *dāgān*, "corn" or "wheat").

> Now the lords of the Philistines gathered together [to Gaza] to offer a great sacrifice to Dagon their god, and to exult; and they said, "Our god has given Samson, our enemy, into our hand." And the people saw him, and praised their god, for they said, "Our god has delivered our enemy into our hand, even the devastator of our land and [the one] who multiplied our wounded" (16:23–24).

Wine flows freely during this time of merriment. At the height of the celebrations the people call for Samson. A servant leads him into the temple courtyard, where everyone makes sport of him. They laugh at his clumsiness, deride his God, and demand that he amuse them as a clown might do at a banquet. With a touch of irony, they have a young lad hold his chain.

The dignitaries attending the feast are sitting on the main level just under the roof. Three thousand men and women who were unable to get into the temple are leaning over the balconies above. The lords of the five cities, with their wives, want to take a closer look at Samson. The servant brings him to the middle of the temple. Samson had probably seen the temple on his first visit to Gaza, so he knows that the entire structure sits on two massive pillars in the center. Samson asks to be led to the pillars so he may rest against them (16:26*b*). Then, praying fervently, he calls on the Lord his God:

JUDGES 16

"O Lord, Yahweh, remember me, I pray, and strengthen me, I pray, only this time, O God; and let me be avenged [with] vengeance [this] once[19] on the Philistines because of my two eyes" (16:28).

The names for God that Samson uses in his prayer are important: *Adonai,* "Lord," indicates God's irresistible power and might; *Yahweh,* "LORD," is the name specifically used in relation to God's covenant; and *Elohim,* "God," likewise shows God's power.[20]

Samson recognizes his weakness. His reliance on God's grace is absolute. Believing that God has heard him, Samson pushes the pillars of the temple with phenomenal exertion, causing the upper level to crash on those below. The biblical writer did not give the exact number killed with Samson, but the account notes that it was more than all those he slew during his life.

When Samson's brothers learn what has happened, they go down to Gaza. The Philistines allow them to sort through the rubble until they find Samson's mangled corpse. They carry his remains back to the territory of Dan, where they bury him in the tomb their father had prepared as a family crypt. Their tribe has no walled cities, so Samson cannot be buried in a town, as were some of the other judges (cf. 8:32; 10:2, 5; 12:7, 10, 12, 15).

AN OBITUARY

We have been conditioned from our earliest years in Sunday school to view Samson's death as evidence of his failure to fulfill the will of God. Authors who comment on his life usually write a negative obituary. In seeking truth, however, we need to be careful not to judge Samson by our Western standards. We easily superimpose our love of life on the narrative and ignore his patriotism. Those living in Near Eastern lands would never do this. They recognize that he dedicated himself to serving his people. We must evaluate his greatness by *his* values, not our own.

The Jewish historian Josephus noted how his race had continued to honor Samson's memory:

Indeed, this man deserves to be admired for his courage and strength, and magnanimity at his death, and that his wrath upon his enemies went so far as to die himself with them. But as for his being ensnared by a woman, that is to be ascribed to human nature . . . but we ought to bear him witness, that in all other respects, [his life] was one of extraordinary virtue.[21]

A MATTER OF POWER

In her book *Religion of Power*, Cheryl Forbes provided some unique insights into the struggle for power. She called it a "religion" because those who seek respect, authority, influence, and positions of importance, the symbols of success and the recognition of their peers, do so in ways that resemble religious faith and practice. Furthermore, they do so for distinct rewards. Religion, whether Christian or pagan, has a set of beliefs that is systematically set forth or instinctively recognized and accepted by those within the "group." In much the same way, the "political power structure" in our churches, clubs, and places of employment has inherent prescribed "rituals" and an identifiable "creed."[22]

As Professor Forbes was quick to point out, this quest for power is the antithesis of *true* Christianity. Nevertheless, Christians participate in this pagan practice (cf. Luke 22:24–27)[23] because sometimes it is their only way to get ahead. As a result, there is widespread misuse of the gifts God gives us.

In the book of Judges, the Philistines are archetypical of political/organizational power. The rulers of their pentapolis exercised judicial (1 Sam. 5:8), military (1 Sam. 5:11; 29:1–7), and priestly (Judg. 16:23) authority. To receive recognition in any of these spheres, a Philistine had to show his loyalty to the system. The higher he progressed, the greater his freedom and the more tangible his rewards. Any indiscretion or failure to comply with the expectations of superiors put him in an invidious position (cf. 15:6). The importance of conformity and the symbols of success were as clearly defined in Samson's culture as they are in our own.

The adage "power corrupts, and absolute power corrupts absolutely" is still true. Those intent on their own advancement treat people as expendables and lack a commitment to truth. In the end, the struggle to maintain what they have acquired consumes them. They fear younger workers, newer technology, and the possibility of takeovers. These threats undermine their health, happiness, and relationships.

Just as the Philistines model the way men seek to dominate those about them, Delilah illustrates how women use their femininity to gain what they most desire.

A woman's sexuality powerfully influences those about her. She might use her smile, the way she dresses, her perfume, her posture, the tone of her voice, or her overall attitude (e.g., cheerful, spirited, attentive) to manipulate others to fulfill her desires. A woman's power may be subtle or overt, appropriate or inappropriate.

Delilah was well-versed in the art of using her sexuality to get what she wanted. She drew Samson to her and withdrew emotionally, as occasion required. She used her femininity to play on his emotions so he would tell her the secret of his strength.[24]

Those who misuse their God-given sexuality eventually experience leanness of their souls. They make the fatal error of treating people as things and things as people. As they grow older peace eludes them. They experience no lasting satisfaction because that comes only from healthy interpersonal relationships. In the end they lead empty, unproductive lives, which is the logical consequence of their preoccupation with themselves.

Samson exemplifies the difficulties and dangers facing those who do not resort to human methods of acquiring power. Such individuals often find themselves isolated from others, branded as "troublemakers" or "mavericks," and accused of "rocking the boat" or "upsetting the status quo." People often oppose them for their nonconformity.[25]

People like Samson interrupt the rituals others have established and by which they perpetuate their authority. Professor Forbes reminded us that this is exactly what Alexander Solzhenitsyn did. Imprisoned in a Russian *gulag* as a political dissident, he realized that as long as he tried to maintain a semblance of power—with his captors or fellow-prisoners—he was at their mercy. When he relinquished all that others found important, he became completely free. Their power over him ceased, and in one of life's strange paradoxes, he became the one who was powerful.[26]

Samson drew his strength directly from God. As long as he recognized his power as God-given, he was successful. This is the secret of real power.

JUDGES 16

The apostle Paul knew the secret of this kind of greatness as well. He, too, set aside all the symbols of success that his race considered important (Phil. 4:4–14) and allowed the power of Christ to work through him (cf. 2 Cor. 4:7; 6:7; 8:3; 12:9; 13:4). Whether for Samson, Paul, or us, the principle is the same (cf. Eph. 3:14, 16). Although we may not receive the accolades freely given those who seek prominence, we can rest content in the knowledge that we have served our generation by the will of God.

# 14 MODERN BELIEFS IN ANCIENT GARB

Judges
17–18

A talk-show host practicing his lines carefully reviewed his flip-cards and mentally checked off the topics: politics, sports, TV commercials, the latest fashions, children, the president, the economy. "There's something missing," he said to an aide.

Those around him listed several fads and fancies, foibles of the rich, and fallacies of our culture. Then someone mentioned, "What about religion?"

The host sent secretaries scurrying to the office for information. That night he added some new lines to his program.

- The religion of some people consists principally of praying that God will provide.
- Many people tailor their religious beliefs to fit the pattern of their prejudice. It's me first, and you can stand in line.
- There are still some people who think religion is like a faucet—to be turned on when needed.
- Most people have some sort of religion; at least they know what church they are staying away from.
- In our day the most popular religion is CONFUSIONISM. We want beliefs that make us feel good; and when we don't, we see a psychiatrist.

• Many people use their religion as they do a bus—they ride on
it only if it is going their way.
• A lot of people are interested in a religion that makes them look
good or whose teachings promise them health, wealth, and
happiness.

Two polls confirm the validity of these quips. George Gallup
and David Poling conducted the first survey to assess the vibrancy
of our country's spiritual life. They found that 98 percent of those
who claimed to be Christians felt that Jesus Christ was a significant
factor in their lives. Sixty-seven percent felt that God, or a universal spirit, observes our actions and rewards or punishes us accordingly.[1]

Glamour magazine conducted the second survey, to which
twenty-five thousand readers responded. The results revealed
that seventy-seven percent of those who claimed some religious
affiliation said they believed in God, and eighty-seven percent said
they had prayed in times of crisis.[2]

Under scrutiny, however, both polls revealed that the par-
ticipants were more subjective than objective in their beliefs. They
chose aspects of faith that appealed to them and ignored teachings
that ran contrary to their personal goals or felt needs. Their
religious commitments were a "convenient and comfortable form
of Christianity." Pragmatism—what fits best with what I want out
of life—was the bottom line of their faith.

Practicing homosexuals and lesbians and those who admitted
to being "sexually active" outside of marriage featured prominent-
ly in both sets of statistics. And some claimed to be "Christian"
and to believe in "God" but did not believe in the Bible at all. They,
too, had a system of beliefs, but not one based on divine revelation.
Their faith had more to do with succeeding in life than living in
reverential awe of God.

Dr. Howard G. Hendricks observed that the Christian church
in America today "is about five hundred miles long, and about
one-sixteenth of an inch thick."

A FINE LINE

We all face an important choice. We must choose between
belief on the one hand or unbelief and superstition on the other.

Belief is confidence in the truth or existence of something not immediately susceptible to rigorous proof (cf. Heb. 11:1, 3, 6). To believers, the world is a riddle and their knowledge of it is incomplete. They are convinced, however, of the existence of a supreme being who is infinite and wise in all his ways and who has revealed his will through general revelation (cf. Ps. 19) and special revelation (Christ, Heb. 1:1–3; and scripture, 2 Tim. 3:16).

To believers, the purpose of life extends beyond the limited span of years allotted to them, beyond death, into eternity. They recognize that the trials of our present life are not worthy to be compared with the glory that will be revealed to us (Rom. 8:18, 28–30).[3]

Unbelief is "a self-contained finitude" in which unbelievers manifest a state or quality of not believing the truth presented to them. Having only a limited, horizontal conception of reality, unbelievers choose to place their confidence in things they can see, explain, formulate, and prove.[4]

The Swiss psychoanalyst Dr. C. G. Jung stated that rationalism and superstition are complimentary. Wherever there is a lack of genuine belief, people are left to sort their way through life relying solely on reason.[5] This makes them susceptible to superstition and a belief in forces that wish to harm them. The more they devote their lives to a rationalistic purpose, the less they are able to stand up to life's emotional crises. When these occur, they look for something stronger than themselves to hold on to. Their spiritual faculties starved, they have neither the courage to revive their belief in the true God nor the patience to submit stoically to their fate. Feeling they must do something, they grasp at anything that promises protection or provides a semblance of meaning to the enigmas of life.

Superstition often arises because people must believe in something.[6] As a result, a large and growing number of people prey on weak people. Fortune-tellers and clairvoyants advise people about their problems. Horoscopes in daily newspapers promise a better and more fulfilling way of life if the reader will follow the "message of the stars." Young people consult Ouija boards about the future. Department stores sell astrological calendars, jewelry depicting the signs of the zodiac, and games for children that involve seances and telepathy. Charlatans claim to be able to interpret dreams or read a person's future in the lines of the person's palm. People wear amulets and talismans to ward off misfortune. And exorcists offer protection against the spells of witches, warlocks, and the influence of evil spirits.

Judges 17–21 contains teaching about belief, unbelief, and superstition as it deals with the general conditions that existed in Israel during the period of the judges. These chapters are arranged topically and may be divided as follows: (1) an illustration of idolatry and expediency (17:1–18:31); (2) an illustration of immorality and anarchy (19:1–21:25).

AN ILLUSTRATION OF IDOLATRY AND EXPEDIENCY (17:1–18:31)

The Man Who Wanted Everything (17:1–13)

The events of this chapter take place during the forty years of peace after Othniel's victory over Cushan-rishathaim (1373–1334 B.C.; cf. Josh. 19:47),[7] when a measure of prosperity has begun to return to the land.

The repeated statement that "the Israelites did what was evil in the sight of Yahweh" is missing. It is replaced by the observation that "in those days there was no king in Israel; everyone did what was right in his own eyes" (17:6; cf. 18:1; 19:1; 21:25). This serves to warn us that Israel's cycle of sin and repentance (cf. 2:1–3:6) is not the theme of the book.

Judges 17:1–18:31 is bare of true spiritual conviction. Instead, superstition and policies based on expediency frequently prevail. Judges 17:1–13 reveals the personal superstition and idolatry of the people (as illustrated in Micah, vv. 1–6) and the apostasy and idolatry of the priesthood (as described by the Levite, vv. 7–13).

Personal Superstition and Idolatry of the People (17:1–6). Micah, whose name means "Who is like God?" is living in the hill country of Ephraim. The description of him gives reason to believe that a spiritual relativism prevails.[8] Following the years of heavy taxation imposed by Cushan-rishathaim, the people are intent on securing their own prosperity. The emphasis is on making money, acquiring things, and enjoying the good life.

JUDGES 17 – 18

The story opens with Micah overhearing his mother's pronouncement of a curse on the person who has stolen some of her money. That she utters her curse in his hearing indicates that she suspects he is responsible.

But why does she resort to such an expedient?

In pagan societies the ability to put some evil threat or malediction on a person was a sign of power. It instilled fear and manipulated people into carrying out another's wishes. Only in biblical Judaism and Christianity does power lie in the ability to bless.[9] Belief in God differs from unbelief and superstition in this important specific.

Micah's mother evidently has no real faith, but her curse produces the desired result because Micah confesses to stealing the money and promptly restores what he has taken.

On receiving the money, Micah's mother states that she will "wholly dedicate the silver . . . to Yahweh" (17:3). In fulfilling her vow, however, she shows the essentially pagan nature of her beliefs. She takes only two hundred pieces to the silversmith (cf. Acts 5:1–10) and instructs him to make a graven image for her son. The usual translation, "who made *them* into a graven image and a molten idol," may better be rendered "who made it [i.e., the silver] into a graven image, even a molten [as opposed to something carved out of wood] idol." This is further supported by 18:20, 30–31, which refers to a single graven image.

The various gods of antiquity were invisible, but artists often depicted them as standing or sitting on the back of a bull. In time people forgot they were worshiping an invisible deity and began worshiping the object they could see.

On receiving the image, Micah places it in a shrine he has built. He also shows his industry by making an ephod and other household idols (or teraphim). These he also places in the shrine. All this is contrary to the teaching of God's word, for the Lord specifically forbids any form of idolatry (Exod. 20:2–5) and had stated that He was to be worshiped only in his sanctuary (cf. Deut. 12).

Micah then consecrates one of his sons as his priest (17:5; cf. Exod. 6:18, 20; 28:1; Num. 3:5ff.). This, too, is contrary to the law, for only the descendants of Aaron could serve as priests.[10]

All this led C. F. Keil and F. J. Delitzsch to conclude that Micah was motivated solely by thoughts of his own well-being. His religion was purely utilitarian. He regarded his household gods as the "givers of prosperity."[11] They were the source of his power. They ensured his success.

Apostasy and Idolatry of the Priesthood (17:7–13). Here the focus shifts to a Levite who is unable to find suitable employment. His name is Jonathan (18:30), and he is a descendant of Moses[12] (not Manasseh, as some translations imply). Again the biblical writer intended to show the prevailing spiritual apathy through the experience of a single individual.

At the time Joshua led the people into the promised land, forty-eight cities had been allocated to the Levites for their personal use (cf. Num. 35:1ff.; Josh. 21:1ff.). These cities were distributed throughout the land so the descendants of Levi would be able to reside among God's people and instruct them in his ways.

Jonathan had been living in Bethlehem-judah, which was not a Levitical city, so perhaps he had not been receiving the material support on which the Levites depended and therefore had to migrate from place to place. He journeys northward and eventually comes to the hill country of Ephraim. He is on the lookout for a wealthy patron, and he finds Micah, who is looking for anyone who will further his material prosperity.

After asking Jonathan where he comes from and learning of his quest, Micah invites the Levite to become his personal priest. "Live with me," he says, "and be to me a father and a priest, and I will give you ten silver pieces for the days [i.e., a year], a suit of garments [or clothes], and your sustenance" (17:10). Micah's son, whom Micah specially consecrated, is easily removed from office.

The terms of the agreement suit Jonathan well, and he enters Micah's employment. In fact, the arrangement is so advantageous that he becomes like one of Micah's sons (17:11).

The gradual change that takes place from "be a father to me" to becoming "like one of [Micah's] sons" is not unusual for instances where one person seeks only power and the extension of his influence and the other is intent on securing only his material well-being.

The writer concludes his account of the man who had everything by recording Micah's anticipation of further good fortune: "Now I know that Yahweh will prosper me, seeing I have a Levite as priest" (17:13).

The People Who Wanted Everything (18:1–31)

The story now switches from the hill country of Ephraim to the foothills of Philistia. The Danites, unable to dislodge the Amorites (cf. 1:34–36), cannot occupy the territory allocated to them by Joshua (Josh. 19:41–46). Pressed up into the hills, they live in a very small area between Zorah and Eshtaol. This territory also borders on the inheritance of the tribe of Judah (Josh. 15:33).

The Danites evidently live in discomfort, for their residence is spoken of as a "camp" ("Mahaneh–dan" 13:25)—an unsettled, seemingly temporary and most unsatisfactory situation, which takes on the appearance of a squatters' settlement. Though close to the tribe of Judah, they do not approach their countrymen (as Judah did to Simeon, 1:3) and ask for aid in dispelling the Amorites. Instead, they try to find contentment within an ever-shrinking area.

At this time certain Danites take advantage of the victory gained by Othniel. They send a group of men throughout the tribes to find a suitable place to settle (1370 B.C.; cf. Josh. 19:47–48).

As these warriors journey northward, they come to Mount Ephraim. En route they pass by a village and hear Jonathan going through his religious ritual.[13] Some writers have conjectured that they recognized his accent to be "southern" and, therefore, turned aside to see why he was living so far from home. Probably what attracted their attention was that he was singing or chanting some religious hymn. Being superstitious, they ask him whether their mission will meet with success (18:5).

The men from Dan strike up a conversation with Jonathan and learn that Micah has hired him in hope of ensuring his continued prosperity. In answering the question of the Danites, Jonathan says: "Go in peace; your way in which you are going is before Yahweh" (i.e., will meet with his blessing).[14]

The men depart and their wanderings bring them to Laish, where the Zidonians live. These people are isolated, prosperous, and appear to have no close allies. The biblical writer hinted at the negative effects of a dictatorship: "for there was no ruler oppressing them" (18:7).

All too often the exercise of power, even in our day, takes the form of oppression.[15] This is contrary to what God intended (cf. Mark 10:42; Luke 22:25–27).[16]

The position of the people of Laish also points to the need for strong allies—those who respect individual autonomy while sharing common concerns.

Abraham, when he entered the land of Canaan, established ties with the Amorites at Mamre (Gen. 14:13). They helped him when the kings of the East captured his nephew Lot. David, even after God had established the kingdom under him, maintained a strong defense (cf. 1 Chron. 27:1–15, with twenty-four thousand soldiers guarding Israel's borders at all times) while having strong allies. This indicates that good friends, both personal and national, are vital to our well-being.

After further investigation the Danites return to their tribe. They encourage their people: "Arise, go up against them; for we have seen the land, and behold, it is very good" (18:9).

Apparently the warriors who spied out the land encounter some reluctance from their tribesmen. Certain of their number, perhaps for spiritual reasons, are unwilling to leave their location and journey northward, but six hundred families decide to migrate. This must have considerably reduced the strength of those who remained. They would now be even more vulnerable. Samson's forebears must have been among those who continued in their God-appointed place.

With the "men of war" leading the way, the women and children follow. The pace is slow, for they have with them their cattle, sheep, and goats.

In time they come to the hill country of Ephraim, where the spies recall their encounter with Jonathan. Perhaps around a campfire that night, one of them remarks to the rest:

"Do you know that there are in these houses an ephod, household idols, and a graven image—including one made of silver? Now, therefore, consider what you should do" (18:14).

He is implying that the tribe will derive distinct benefit—power as well as protection—by possessing things that give success.

The Danites show their lawlessness and disrespect for another's property by invading Micah's home and stealing the objects of his superstitious veneration. When Jonathan reprimands them (18:18b), they invite him to join their migration northward. They promise him a promotion and say, in effect, "Why stay here and be the priest to one man when you could come with us and become the 'bishop' to an entire tribe?" (18:19).[17]

Jonathan is delighted with the offer and readily accepts. It means a significant improvement in his social standing. Hardly able to believe his good fortune, he joins the men of Dan in plundering his benefactor's house (18:20).

As the Danites leave Mount Ephraim, they place the women and children in front and have the armed men follow, as if they are expecting trouble.

When Micah returns to his home and finds out what has happened, he fears economic ruin. Summoning the men of the village, he pursues the Danites.

Because the Danites must move slowly, the men of Ephraim soon overtake them. On hearing a commotion behind them, those in the rear turn around. Perhaps Jonathan points out Micah to them. The Danites demand: "What is the matter with you, that you are assembled together?"

This devious query shows that they recognize the hostile intent of the Ephraimites but that they claim ignorance of the cause.

Micah retorts:

> "You have taken away my gods that I have made and the priest
> and have gone away, and what do I have left? So how can you say
> to me, 'What is the matter with you?'" (18:24)

Micah's words clearly reveal his superstitious nature. He is in a similar position to others who trust ideals or things (such as PMA [positive mental attitude], human relationships, a family name, natural gifts, inherited wealth) for success and as a way to ensure their standing in the community.

Micah and the men of his village believe he is at the mercy of powerful and malignant forces. His trust has been in things he had made. His confidence has been in the priest he had consecrated. The raid of the Danites has robbed him of all that he believes in. In a single day he has lost the emblems of his success, his religion, and his respectability.

Calamity strikes all of us at one time or another. For some it is the loss of a family member. For others it is the loss of a job. Some reach a point of despair when God does not answer their prayer for a mate or bring to fruition some cherished dream. Suddenly they realize that what they have believed in cannot sustain them. Although we empathize with them in their disappointment, it is our faith in the one true God that sustains us during times of adversity. Micah had no such belief. Everything he trusted went out the door of his home when the Danites walked off with the objects of his devotion.

The response of the warriors of Dan only adds to Micah's discomfort: "Do not let your voice he heard among us, lest men who are bitter of soul fall on you and you lose your life."

Realizing the hopelessness of the situation, Micah returns to his home a broken man. The respect he has enjoyed and his influence in the village are gone—all because he did not found his faith on the truth. The sanctuary of the Lord was only a few miles away, but he never went there for instruction in the law. He preferred to make his own system of beliefs. While all went well and he prospered, everyone thought highly of him. When adversity struck, he had nothing to sustain him.

The writer concludes his story by recounting the activities of the Danites. They attack the defenseless city of Laish and completely rout the inhabitants. They burn the city and erect one of their own on the ashes. This done, they establish for themselves a separate center of worship and install Jonathan, the son of Gershom (Exod. 18:3), the son of Moses (Exod. 2:22), as their priest. In this capacity Jonathan and his sons continue until the captivity of the land (cf. 1 Sam. 4:1–11; Ps. 78:60; Jer. 7:12–14).

THE IMPORTANCE OF RIGHT BELIEFS

False forms of belief recur with regularity. Solomon wisely observed, "What has been is what will be, and what has been done is what will be done" (Eccl. 1:9). Every new cult is an ancient one in modern dress.[18]

Path of Disobedience

False beliefs arise through a process. It begins with disobedience to the revealed will of God. The Lord had forbidden the making of idols.[19] Micah's mother made a graven image anyway, and Micah added to this an ephod and household teraphim. Some believe these teraphim indicated the rights of the firstborn,[20] but the text plainly states that Micah regarded them as the sources of his prosperity (cf. 17:5, 13). They were probably associated with the abominable practices of the fertility cult that had degraded the lives of the Canaanites and Amorites.

Only after the Babylonian captivity did God's ancient people give up their idols. Before that time they apparently worshiped a pantheon of false deities. Even during the reigns of David, Asa, Jehoshaphat, Joash, Uzziah, Hezekiah, and Josiah the people maintained false practices in isolated places. The worship of images was so abhorrent to the rabbis that they preserved a teaching that the three cardinal sins were idolatry, unchastity, and bloodshed.[21] Idolatry came first because it implied a denial of divine revelation. Social sins (various forms of immorality and murder), which revealed a low regard for human life, followed in the wake of this departure from the worship of the living God.

Micah was not the only one guilty of disobedience. The Danites also stood condemned. They preferred to migrate rather than to fight for their inheritance. Their military vacillation explained their inability to take possession of their inheritance. They wanted the benefits of being the children of God without the rigors that accompany obedience (cf. 1 Tim. 6:12; 2 Tim. 4:7).

An Act of Defiance

God had plainly revealed that his people were to worship him in the central sanctuary (cf. Deut. 12:4–14; 16:1–7). The tabernacle with the ark of the covenant and the Shekinah were there. Gilgal, Bethel, and Shiloh were successively the places where the sanctuary was located.

Micah, in seeking to ensure his success, ignored God's mandate and established a shrine in which he placed the objects of his veneration. He then consecrated one of his sons to serve as his priest. Priding himself on his religiosity, he proceeded to enrich himself by every means at his disposal. Wittingly or unwittingly he became the leader of a new cult, and the people of his village readily supported him (18:22).

Man-made religions abound. In fact, the apostles warned that in the last days we would see an increase in such activity (cf. 1

Tim. 4:1–5; 2 Tim. 3:1–9; 2 Peter 3:1–7; 1 John 4:1–6; Jude 4, 7–8, 19). Some of these new cults use the same terminology as the Bible, but they differ greatly in essential beliefs and practices. Their character (hedonistic and anthropocentric as opposed to Christocentric and self-sacrificing) always is contrary to the plain teaching of scripture.

Micah's idols did not bring him wealth; he only thought they did. He got himself into a frame of mind that resulted in success and then gave credit to the gods he had made.

Many in our society do the same thing. They wear lucky charms, read the daily horoscope, practice Transcendental Meditation or yoga, rely on mystics or gurus, or place their faith in some other form of superstition. Sophisticated forms of these beliefs have been associated with Hare Krishna, Christian Science, Unity, Bahai, Unification Church, Scientology, New Age, spiritism, and others.[22] Each one promises success. Whatever the practice, it amounts to appointing "improper priests" to fulfill materialistic and narcissistic goals.

The Danites were as guilty as Micah of defying God's revealed will. They showed their contempt for the rights of others by entering his home and stealing his property. Then they absconded with the Levite (cf. Num. 3:1–13; Deut. 12:4–14; 31:9–13; 33:10). Their rival sanctuary in Laish (later called Dan) did not honor the Lord but only brought disunity to God's people.

The Anatomy of Power

At the root of disobedience to the word of God and defiance of the will of God is "me-ism." We observe it first in the garden of Eden. "You shall be as God [powerful, independent, and answerable to no one]," the devil promised. Latent in "me-ism" is a desire to be self-determining. We are all born with a sense of weakness (dependence). We need someone to care for us. From our earliest years, we manifest a desire for independence. Although we do not understand the theology behind it, we long for a sense of security and self-sufficiency. Thinking that money, possessions, influence, or popularity can meet these needs, we grasp for them.

This desire begins in childhood and continues throughout our lives. Adam's sin affects us all. We spend our years fearing the things that threaten our fragile well-being. Only through a vital relationship with God can we remedy our feelings of insecurity.

At the root of Micah's supposed religiosity, as well as the Danite migration, was a sense of powerlessness. Micah sought power by placating the forces he believed opposed him. He achieved materialistic goals through acts of sacrificial worship. The Danites, like the neighborhood bully, felt powerful only when they could exert their strength against unsuspecting people who had done them no harm.

Neither Micah nor the Danites truly prospered. Micah lost everything in which he had placed his confidence. The Danites endured a while as a tribe but were never successful. After the revolt of Jeroboam I (931 B.C.), Dan and Bethel became centers of idolatry (cf. 1 Kings 12:29). Even Jehu's massacre of the priests of Baal failed to stamp out this form of paganism (2 Kings 10:28–31). In time, Ben-hadad of Syria "cut off parts of Israel" (2 Kings 10:32). Dan was captured. Jeroboam II (793–753 B.C.) recaptured the area (2 Kings 14:25), but later the Assyrian monarch Tiglath-pileser (745–727 B.C.) took the city and deported the people (2 Kings 17:6). Neither the gods of the Danites nor their sanctuary could help them. They stand on the pages of history as a byword rather than as a good example.

The stories of Micah and the Danites highlight the warning of the apostle Paul:

> The sins of some men [e.g., Micah] are clear beforehand going before [them] to judgment, but some indeed trail behind them [as in the case of the tribe of Dan].

Paul continued with positive words of assurance:

> Similarly also the good works [of some are clear] beforehand, and [even] the [ones that are not] cannot be hidden (1 Tim. 5:24–25).

He who is righteous and true will judge all of us at some future time. He will assess each of us according to our works, whether we have done good or evil (cf. 1 Cor. 3:12–15; 2 Cor. 5:10). Only by following righteousness, godliness, faith, love, perseverance, and gentleness can we demonstrate the reality of our faith (cf. 1 Tim. 6:6–12).

JUDGES 17 – 18

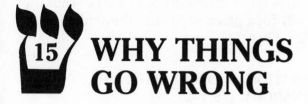

15 WHY THINGS GO WRONG

Judges
19–21

Dr. Wayne Dyer began his book *Your Erroneous Zones* with a story about a speaker who was demonstrating the evils of drinking to a group of alcoholics. On a table he placed two identical containers filled with a clear fluid. One contained water, the other pure alcohol.

The speaker placed a worm into the jar of water. The worm swam around and then headed for the side of the glass. Scooping the worm out of the water, the speaker placed it in the other container. The worm convulsed and died before it reached the bottom.

"There," said the speaker, "you have seen what happened to the worm. What does this simple illustration teach you?"

A voice from the back of the room said, "If you drink alcohol, you won't have worms."[1]

In all of life, whether personally or nationally, our beliefs, attitudes, values, and goals can so cloud the issues that we fail to recognize the truth. Personal prejudices and self-defeating forms of behavior can result in actions that rob us of the joy of living. These activities sap our strength, destroy our productivity, and deprive life of true meaning. The "appendix" to the book of Judges clearly illustrates these principles.

Soon after the death of Joshua, superstition and disrespect for the rights of others began to characterize God's chosen people (chaps. 17–18). Immorality and anarchy later brought the nation to its knees (chaps. 19–21).

The information in Judges 19–21 follows chronologically the events of Judges 17–18 (cf. 18:29 and 20:1).[2] Phinehas, the grandson of Aaron, was still alive (cf. 20:28 and Josh. 22:9–34).[3] Thus the events of chapters 17–21 took place soon after the settlement of the tribes in Canaan (c. 1370 B.C.).

AN ILLUSTRATION OF IMMORALITY AND ANARCHY (19:1–21:25)

Before God's people entered the land of Canaan, He told them how they could continue to enjoy his blessings. The final messages of Moses in Deuteronomy clearly outlined God's will. Furthermore, God's power had been evident in the overthrow of Sihon, king of the Amorites, and Og, king of Bashan, and in the crossing of the river Jordan and the capture of Jericho. With such illustrations of God's involvement with them, what could possibly make the Israelites choose willful disobedience and self-destruction?

The text reveals the process of their spiritual decline and moral disintegration: (1) a calloused disregard for human rights (19:1–30); (2) a capricious decision to right a wrong (20:1–48); and (3) a compromise that destroys family unity (21:1–25).

A Calloused Disregard for Human Rights (19:1–30)

The opening words of the chapter summarize the recurring theme: There was no king in Israel, and everyone did what was right in his own eyes (cf. 19:1; 21:25).

Our story begins with an account of a Levite who leaves his home in the hill country of Ephraim to go to Bethlehem in Judah. His wife[4] had been promiscuous and had deserted him. She went back to her father's home where she supported herself through prostitution.

The text repeatedly refers to her as a "girl" (19:3–6, 8–9), so she may have been considerably younger than her husband, resulting in a certain incompatibility. Perhaps she tired of her humdrum life in the remote parts of Ephraim. A verbal rift may have added to the emotional schism that had already occurred in their relationship. In any event, she apparently preferred the company of virile young men (19:2). She left the hills of Ephraim and journeyed alone to her father's house in Bethlehem-judah.

After four months the Levite decides, for reasons not given in the text, to go to Bethlehem-judah to persuade his wife to return home with him.

The Levite's father-in-law is delighted to meet his son-in-law. The text implies that they had not met one another before. He welcomes the Levite into his home and invites him to stay for several days (19:4–9). During this time the Levite "speaks kindly" (lit., "to the heart") of his wife. He wins her over, and she consents to accompany him back to Ephraim.

His mission accomplished, the Levite expresses his desire to leave. His father-in-law detains them, and they do not leave until mid-afternoon on the fifth day.

In journeying back to Ephraim, the Levite, his servant, and his wife decide not to spend the night in Jerusalem, six miles north of Bethlehem. This city had been retaken by the Jebusites,[5] pagans of Amoritic descent, and the Levite feels it is unsafe to lodge there. He determines to try to reach either Gibeah (modern Tell el–Ful, four miles north of Jerusalem)[6] or Ramah (later the residence of Samuel) before stopping for the night.

As the travelers enter Gibeah, the sun is setting. They sit in the open square by the well and wait for someone to offer them hospitality.[7]

Hospitality is a sacred duty in the ancient Near East. Residents of towns or villages are expected to entertain travelers in their homes (cf. Lot in Gen. 19:1–7). The Levite had straw and fodder for the donkeys and bread and wine for himself, his wife, and his servant, so their host would not be greatly inconvenienced by giving the small party shelter for the night.

No one, however, offers them accommodations. Finally an old man, originally from Ephraim, invites them to spend the night with him. After dinner the Levite and his host relax and enjoy reminiscing (19:22a). A sudden noise outside the front door[8] interrupts them. Men from the city ("toughs" or, more literally, "sons of Belial"[9]) loudly demand that the Levite be turned over to them.

JUDGES 19 – 21

They want to have sexual intercourse with him. When the old man refuses, they hurl themselves at the door in an attempt to break it down.

What perplexes us is the old man's offer to hand over instead his daughter (*bᵉtûlāh*, "virgin") and the Levite's wife (*pîleges*,[10] an unusual word implying the lowest level of wife). Many writers seize this as an indication of the low place women occupied in Hebrew society. Although I do not approve of the conduct of the men of Gibeah or of the old man's offer, it appears as if he felt himself under a sacred obligation to protect the Levite who had come under the shelter of his roof.[11] In answer to those who claim that the Bible teaches a low view of womanhood, evidence indicates that only where there is spiritual decline do men treat women as things. Scripture from Genesis 1:26–27 on portrays women as equal in worth to men, for both bear the divine image.

As the story continues, the Levite takes action inappropriate for a guest. Perhaps fearing the vacillation of the old man, he takes his wife and thrusts her through the slightly open door (19:25–26). Arthur Cundall stated, "The narrator does not dwell on the harrowing details [suffered by the young woman], but if ever a human being endured a night of utter horror it was [his] concubine on that night, which must have seemed interminable as eternity and as dark as the pit."[12]

How are we to explain the Levite's sudden change in attitude? Only five days earlier he had journeyed to Bethlehem in Judah to persuade his wife to return to Ephraim with him. Now he treats her with calloused indifference. There may be several possible reasons:

1. The Levite may have been thinking only of himself. His reputation may have suffered as a result of his wife's conduct. If so, he would have anger and resentment toward her. He may have felt that his credibility as a "man of God" was at stake. If so, his thoughts in this new crisis would have been only of himself.

2. When problems arise in any relationship, renewed contact may bring them to the surface again. In some instances "absence makes the heart grow fonder," but for the Levite and his wife the journey northward may have reopened unresolved tensions.

3. The strain resulting from their late start, their need to lengthen their journey by by-passing Jerusalem, and their fear of

the men of Gibeah may have had an unsettling effect on the Levite. Nevertheless, his conduct toward his wife is reprehensible. It indicates a deep-seated anger. He may have felt bitterness about her betrayal and, on an impulse, felt like punishing her.

Whatever his reasons, the Levite's action was unconscionable. His calloused indifference and lack of true love are most evident the next morning (19:27–28). In spite of his religious calling, he is devoid of sensitivity:

> And her master rose up in the morning, opened the door of the house, and went out to go on his way; and behold, the woman, his concubine, had fallen [at] the door of the house, and her hands [were] on the threshold. And he said to her, "Rise, and let us go." But there was no answer. And he took her [and placed her] on the donkey, and the man rose up and went to his place (19:27–28).

Only when the Levite realizes that his wife is dead does he take action. The phrase "and the man rose up" (v. 28) may also indicate that the servant, acting on his master's behalf, stooped down and lifted her body. They return to the Levite's home where he cuts his wife's body into twelve pieces (*nātah*, a "ritual dissection"; cf. Exod. 29:17; Lev. 1:6, 12; 8:20; 1 Kings 18:33; Ezek. 24:6) and sends the pieces throughout the twelve tribes of Israel (19:29–30).

Incensed by what they see and by the explanation given to them by the men who bring the woman's remains to their villages (19:30*b*), the men of Israel convene a meeting of all the tribes at Mizpah.[13]

A Capricious Decision to Right a Wrong (20:1–48)

The summons of the elders meets with an immediate response. Each tribe sends a delegation (20:1–3). With graphic brevity (20:4–7) the Levite describes what happened. Perhaps to justify himself (20:5) he adds one detail. He says that he "feared for his life." This was probably no exaggeration, but it does not exonerate him or make his conduct less despicable.

To the credit of the Israelites a sense of outrage prevails in the assembly (20:8–11). Their indignation, however, in no way excuses the oaths the men take (cf. 21:1, 5) or the actions that follow.

Although it is true that the tribe of Benjamin had not sent a delegation to Mizpah, the Israelites judge the men of Gibeah, find them guilty, and sentence them without a trial. Since Gibeah is in the tribe of Benjamin, the Israelites formally request that the Benjamites hand over the guilty men for execution (20:12–17; cf. Deut. 17:12).

The Benjamites answer by assembling for battle. They decline to investigate matters themselves and instead take action to protect the evildoers. This further heightens our understanding of the social conditions of the day. By siding with the men of Gibeah, the leaders of Benjamin effectively close the door to discussion or negotiation. They impulsively precipitate a civil war.

Realizing that "an army travels on its stomach," the Israelites wisely set aside a certain number of men to maintain provisions for those doing the fighting (20:10).

In taking on the Benjamites, the rest of the tribes face a formidable adversary. Although small in number, these descendants of Rachel are feisty. They are an ambidextrous, elite corps that can use a sling with either hand and throw a rock at a hair and not miss.[14] Each rock would weigh about a pound, and when released from the sling it would travel about ninety miles an hour (cf. 1 Sam. 17:40, 49).

The people of Benjamin will also be fighting on a hilly terrain well known to them. By hiding in the hills, their force, though small, will easily be able to hold a large army at bay. The Israelites ask the Lord who shall be the first to engage the Benjamites in battle (20:18).

God indicates that the tribe of Judah is to lead the attack. The Israelites readily engage the people of Benjamin, believing that their superior numbers will give them an easy victory (20:19–20). Instead of the anticipated triumph, they suffer an ignominious defeat (20:21–23). Completely routed, they flee in disarray.

Apparently the first attack does not last long, and the Israelites return to Bethel where they weep before the Lord.[15] Discouraged, they ask the Lord whether they are to go up against Benjamin again (20:23). They do not inquire about what their strategy should be (cf. 2 Sam. 5:18–25).

God answers affirmatively but does not volunteer any information that has not been requested.

The events of the second day are a repetition of the first (20:24–28). The Israelites again attack the people of Benjamin and are again routed. Once more they return to Bethel where they spend the day fasting[16] before the Lord. At evening they offer up burnt offerings and peace offerings, symbolizing their repentance of all known sin and their desire for reconciliation (cf. Lev. 1:4; 7:16).[17] Then they inquire of Phinehas whether they should again go out against the Benjamites (20:27–28). This time the Lord assures them of victory: "Go up, for tomorrow I will deliver them into your hand."

Apparently the defeats of the past two days have had the desired effect. The people have returned to absolute dependence on God. In the seemingly disastrous events of these two days, we see God working behind the scenes. He has been preparing Benjamin for their downfall while bringing the sons of Israel to a place where He can bless them.

The next day the Israelites set a trap (20:29–36).[18] Their strategy is similar to the one used by Joshua in taking Ai (Josh. 8:3–28). While the main force approaches Gibeah frontally, a sizeable contingent lies concealed to the north of the city. The army takes precautions not to arouse the suspicions of the Benjamites (20:30).

When Benjamin comes out to do battle, the other tribesmen retreat and soon withdraw hastily. The force from Gibeah interprets this as another rout of their enemy. As soon as the Benjamites are far from Gibeah, the troops near Geba leave their place of concealment, rush on the unprotected city, and easily subdue the token opposition. Then they set the city on fire (20:37–44). The billowing clouds of smoke signal the main force, which quickly turns against the Benjamites and inflicts heavy casualties (20:43–46).

The Benjamites flee in all directions. Many are overtaken and killed. A small force of six hundred makes its way to the rock of Rimmon (20:47).[19] They remain in this natural fortress, afraid to return to their ancestral homes (20:47b).Having gained a victory over the Benjamites, the sons of Israel are now filled with remorse. They fear their action may cause one entire tribe to perish,[20] so they contemplate a compromise. No one asks Phinehas to consult the Urim and Thummim[21] to determine the will of God. Their approach is purely pragmatic.

JUDGES 19 – 21

A Compromise That Destroys Family Unity (21:1–25)

The truth now begins to come out. The sons of Israel, in reacting to the heinous sin of the men of Gibeah, had taken an oath at Mizpah. They had sworn that none of them would give his daughter to any Benjamite in marriage (21:1–4). This now poses a threat to their nation. Without wives, the tribe of Benjamin will eventually die out. How can they provide wives for the Benjamites without breaking their vow?

As the people lament the fate of Benjamin, their theological confusion is evident by their words: "Why, Oh Yahweh, God of Israel, has this come about in Israel, so that one tribe should be missing today in Israel?"

Once again the people offer burnt offerings and peace offerings (21:4). Previously their sacrifices and prayers had resulted in success. They sense the need for God's help but do not inquire in the appropriate manner. It is as if they place a superstitious belief in the efficacy of their sacrifices rather than in personal contact with the Lord. This is evident from what follows. Someone from the crowd asks, "What one is there of the tribes of Israel who did not come up before Yahweh at Mizpah?"

The question suggests a loophole by which the people of Israel can escape from their dilemma. They make an official investigation to determine who responded to the summons and who did not (21:5–7).

The writer drew our attention to a historical fact not mentioned before. When the Israelites met at Mizpah the first time, they had bound themselves by another oath. It specified that any city or tribe which did not send a delegation against Benjamin would be put to death. Such an act was without biblical precedent.

Their investigation shows that the people of Jabesh-gilead did not come to the assembly (21:8–9). Jabesh-gilead was situated about nine miles southeast of Bethshean and about two miles east of the river Jordan.[22] The Gileadites were descendants of Manasseh, the grandson of Rachel, and therefore were related by blood to the people of Benjamin.

In developing their compromise, the sons of Israel send twelve thousand valiant warriors across the Jordan to attack Jabesh-gilead. They are to save only young women who are virgins and to kill every other man, woman, and child (21:10–12). These young women, most of them barely in their teens, are to be torn from their homes, separated forever from their parents, and given in marriage to men whose unprincipled conduct had brought on them just retribution (21:13–15).

This plan acquires only four hundred wives for the men of Benjamin. Two hundred remain without wives, so the leaders of Israel engage in a further plot. They instruct the Benjamites to go up to Shiloh (north of Bethel) and, when the daughters of the village come out of the city to take part in the festive dances, to seize two hundred young girls for themselves (21:19–24).

The delegation that discusses this strategy ignores the explicit teaching of scripture that any kidnapping deserves the death penalty. They compromise the teaching of God's word and assure the men of Benjamin that when the girls' fathers protest, the leaders of Israel will appeal to them for forbearance. Such manipulation of the Law, however, does not make right their act that so seriously violated family life. Pretending that the young girls from Shiloh were captured as an act of war merely provides the Israelites with a convenient way to remain true to their vow.

Although the compromise appeared to guarantee the Benjamites a place within the tribal structure, it violated the rights of each family involved in the loss. The men of Shiloh had little to say about the decision reached by their leaders. They were denied a voice in the proceedings. Their acquiescence to what took place was really a prudent response to coercion. They had no recourse to a higher authority (21:25). And Phineas, who had been consulted when Israel was hard pressed by repeated losses, is not mentioned in the passage.

As we review these chapters, we see that they focus on an important issue: The need for appropriate distinctions so that the rights of the family, state, and church are maintained.

THE NEED FOR APPROPRIATE DISTINCTIONS

The Israelites suffered from a lack of biblical teaching. Everyone did what was right in his own eyes. Each man was a law unto himself. Except for a few righteous individuals, the service of the Lord had become corrupt. Indifference and selfishness had replaced respect for other people's property; morality had given way to immorality; instead of freedom, there was anarchy.

As a result the men of Israel entered into oaths that were unbiblical,[23] were ignorant of the law that might commute such oaths (Lev. 27:1ff.), took unilateral action to pardon the guilty (21:6; cf. Lev. 18:22; 20:13), and on two occasions violated God's word (21:10–12, 20–23; cf. Exod. 21:16; Deut. 24:7). Their capricious civil action destroyed the homes and family lives of the innocent, and their compromises were solely for the sake of saving face and masking their pride.

From Judges 19–21 emerges a story of the abuse of power by civil leaders and a nearly total failure of the priesthood.

The root of the matter was that the leaders of the tribes failed to keep clearly in mind the Bible's teaching on the three separate, though interrelated, God-ordained institutions: the family, the state, and the sanctuary (with its religious worship, which, since Christ, has been identified with the church).[24]

The Family. The family dates back to the dawn of time. God ordained that a husband and his wife would enjoy a unique and lasting relationship.[25] They would also rear their children, taking full responsibility for their development (Deut. 6:4–7; 11:18–21). At no time was the state (i.e., the tribes) given authority over the family. Rather the state was responsible for maintaining the safety and promoting the welfare of the respective families.

In the administration of the home, the wife is to help her husband (Gen. 2:18; 3:16b), and the husband is to love, care for, and rejoice in his wife (Col. 3:18ff.). Children are the heritage of the Lord (over which neither church nor state has any jurisdiction) and are to respect their parents (Ps. 127:3; Eph. 6:1).

The family is a divinely sanctioned unit, and the elders of Israel erred in honoring their own vows at the expense of family unity and solidarity.

The State. The state consists of a body of people politically organized to form a single government. Those elected to bear civil responsibility were also entrusted with certain authority. For example, God appointed Moses to lead his people Israel. Moses had the task of providing for them and looking after their safety. He instituted laws to preserve justice (e.g., Num. 35:9–34), to protect people from danger (e.g., Deut. 22:8), to prevent accidents (e.g., Deut. 23:12–14), and to limit problems caused by ignorance (e.g., Lev. 25:1–55).

Furthermore, civil authority was to ensure the welfare of the people. Property damage, perjury or bribery, prostitution, the use of magic, the use of false weights and measures (cf. Exod. 21–23; Lev. 19), the care of the poor, laws governing inheritance, debt, clothing, and the security of loans—all fell under the jurisdiction of the state (Num. 36; Deut. 15; 22; 24).

The goal of the state was the freedom of the people and their ability to rejoice in the benefits of a righteous administration. The state did not have power over the family or the sanctuary. It was solely responsible for maintaining God's law so people might prosper under a quiet and peaceable government.

The Sanctuary. God specifically set apart Aaron and his sons to perform religious functions (Exod. 29:1ff.). Their sphere of authority differed from that of Moses and the elders of the people. Only in matters of homicide and cases involving violence did a Levitical priest participate in matters pertaining to the state (Deut. 17:8–13).

The priesthood did not have authority over the family or the state. Rather it supported both.

The Old Testament foreshadowed the teaching of the New Testament (and in particular the epistles of Paul and Hebrews). All believers now share in the privilege of the priesthood. The goal is the enhancement of the family, which consists of blood relatives and of believers.

The tragic events that close the book of Judges underscore the dangers of an imbalance in power and the ease with which either state or church can destroy family unity. The apostle Paul stated that the things which happened in Old Testament times are examples for us (cf. Rom. 15:4; 1 Cor. 10:11). Having so graphic an illustration before us, we need never be caught in this kind of predicament. The primary problem Israel faced was a lack of knowledge of God's word (cf. Hos. 4:6; Amos 8:11).

ABBREVIATIONS

Aharoni	Y. Aharoni, *The Land of the Bible,* revised ed. (Philadelphia: Westminster, 1979).
Albright	W. F. Albright, *Archaeology of Palestine* (New York: Pelican, 1962).
ANET	J. B. Pritchard, ed., *Ancient Near Eastern Texts Relating to the Old Testament,* 2d ed. (Princeton: Princeton University, 1955).
AOTS	D. W. Thomas, ed., *Archaeology and Old Testament Study* (Oxford: Clarendon, 1978).
Archer	G. L. Archer, *A Survey of Old Testament Introduction,* revised ed. (Chicago: Moody, 1974).
AV	*Authorized (King James) Version*
BA	*Biblical Archaeologist*
Baly	A. D. Baly, *The Geography of the Bible,* revised ed. (New York: Harper and Row, 1974).
BASOR	*Bulletin of the American Schools of Oriental Research*
BDB	F. Brown, S. R. Driver, and C. A. Briggs, eds., *Hebrew-English Lexicon of the Old Testament* (Oxford: Clarendon, 1907).
Boling	R. G. Boling, *Judges,* Anchor Bible (New York: Doubleday, 1975).
Bright	J. Bright, *The History of Israel,* 3d ed. (Philadelphia: Westminster, 1981).
Burney	C. F. Burney, *The Book of Judges* (London: Rivingtons, 1918).
Bush	G. Bush, *Notes Critical and Practical on the Book of Judges* (Minneapolis: Klock and Klock, 1981).
CBQ	*Catholic Biblical Quarterly*
Cundall	A. E. Cundall and L. L. Morris, *Judges and Ruth,* Tyndale Old Testament Commentaries (Downers Grove, Ill.: InterVarsity, 1968).
deVaux	R. deVaux, *Ancient Israel: Its Life and Institutions* (New York: McGraw-Hill, 1966).

EAEHL   M. Avi-Yonah and E. Stein, eds., *Encyclopedia of*
               Archaeological Excavations in the Holy Land
               (Englewood Cliffs, N.J.: Prentice-Hall, 1975–77).

EQ   *Evangelical Quarterly*

ET   *Expository Times*

Fausset   A. R. Fausset, *A Critical and Expository Commentary on*
               the Book of Judges (Minneapolis: James and Klock
               Christian Publishers, 1977).

Garstang   J. Garstang, *Joshua–Judges* (Grand Rapids: Kregel,
               1978).

Gray   J. Gray, *Joshua, Judges and Ruth,* The Century Bible
               (Greenwood, S.C.: Attic, 1967).

Harrison   R. K. Harrison, *Introduction to the Old Testament* (Grand
               Rapids: Eerdmans, 1969).

HUCA   *Hebrew Union College Annual*

IEJ   *Israel Exploration Journal*

ISBE   G. W. Bromiley, ed., *International Standard Bible*
               Encyclopedia. (Grand Rapids: Eerdmans, 1979–88).

JANES   *Journal of the Ancient Near Eastern Society* (of Columbia
               University)

JAOS   *Journal of the American Oriental Society*

JBL   *Journal of Biblical Literature*

JNES   *Journal of Near Eastern Studies*

Josephus   F. Josephus, *The Complete Works of Flavius Josephus*
               (Grand Rapids: Kregel, 1960).

JTS   *Journal of Theological Studies*

KD   C. F. Keil and F. J. Delitzsch, "Joshua, Judges, Ruth,"
               Biblical Commentary on the Old Testament (Grand
               Rapids: Eerdmans, 1968).

Lang and   J. M. Lang and T. Kirk, *Studies in the Book of Judges*
  Kirk   (Minneapolis: Klock and Klock, 1983).

LXX   Septuagint

Mayes   A. D. H. Mayes, *Israel in the Period of the Judges,* Second
               Series (Naperville: Allenson, 1974).

MBA	Y. Aharoni and M. Avi-Yonah, *Macmillan Bible Atlas,* revised ed. (New York: Macmillan, 1977).
Mishnah	H. Danby, trans., *The Mishnah* (Oxford: Oxford University Press, 1933).
Moore	G. F. Moore, *A Critical and Exegetical Commentary on Judges,* International Critical Commentary (Edinburgh: Clark, 1966).
MT	Masoretic Text
NASB	*New American Standard Bible*
NBD	J. D. Douglas, ed., *New Bible Dictionary,* 2d ed. (Wheaton, Ill.: Tyndale, 1982).
NIDBA	E. M. Blaiklock and R. K. Harrison, *New International Dictionary of Biblical Archaeology* (Grand Rapids: Zondervan, 1983).
NIV	*New International Version of the Bible*
Noth	M. Noth, *The History of Israel,* 2d ed. (London: Black, 1965).
NT	New Testament
OT	Old Testament
PEQ	*Palestine Exploration Quarterly*
POTT	D. J. Wiseman, ed., *Peoples of Old Testament Times* (Oxford: Clarendon, 1973).
Robinson	E. Robinson, *Biblical Researches in Palestine* (London: Murray, 1856).
Soggin	J. A. Soggin, *Judges, A Commentary,* Old Testament Library (Philadelphia: Westminster, 1981).
TDNT	G. Kittel and G. Frederich, eds., *Theological Dictionary of the New Testament* (Grand Rapids: Eerdmans, 1964–76).
TDOT	G. J. Botterweck and H. Ringgren, eds., *Theological Dictionary of the Old Testament,* in process (Grand Rapids: Eerdmans, 1974–).
TWOT	R. L. Harris, G. L. Archer, and B. K. Waltke, eds., *Theological Wordbook of the Old Testament* (Chicago: Moody, 1980).

VT	*Vetus Testamentum*
Watson	R. A. Watson, *The Book of Judges and Ruth,* The Expositor's Bible (New York: Armstrong, n.d.).
Weippert	M. Weippert, *The Settlement of the Israelite Tribes in Palestine,* Studies in Biblical Theology, Second Series (Naperville: Allenson, 1974).
Wood	L. J. Wood, *Distressing Days of the Judges* (Grand Rapids: Zondervan, 1975).
ZAW	*Zeitschrift für die alttestamentliche Wissenschaft*
ZPEB	M. C. Tenney, ed., *Zondervan Pictorial Encyclopedia of the Bible* (Grand Rapids: Zondervan, 1975).

NOTES

Introduction

1. *MBA.*, 52, 105; Boling, pp. 44–45.
2. Negative biblical scholarship has tried to squeeze the era of the judges into a restricted period of time. We can trace the origin of this view to a late date assigned to the Exodus. Notice, for example, the works of Boling, pp. 3–42; B. S. Childs, *Introduction to the Old Testament as Scripture* (Philadelphia: Fortress, 1979), pp. 254–62; A. S. Cooke, *The Book of Judges* (Cambridge: At the University Press, 1913), pp. xi–xlii; Cundall, pp. 15–48; R. deVaux, *The Early History of Israel,* trans. D. Smith (Philadelphia: Westminster, 1978), pp. 475–824; S. R. Driver, *Introduction to the Literature of the Old Testament* (Edinburgh: Clark, 1898), pp. 160–72; O. Eissfeldt, *Old Testament, an Introduction* (New York: Harper and Row, 1965), pp. 257–67; J. J. Lias, *Judges* (London: Cambridge University Press, 1902), pp. 9–37; A. D. H. Mayes, *VT* 23 (1973), pp. 151–70; J. L. McKenzie, *The World of the Judges* (Englewood Cliffs, N.J.: Prentice–Hall, 1966), pp. 76–119; Noth, pp. 141–63; W. E. O. Oesterley and T. H. Robinson, *Introduction to the Books of the Old Testament* (London: S.P.C.K., 1961), pp. 75–82; J. A. Soggin, pp. 173–83; S. M. Warner, *VT* 28 (1978), pp. 455–63; and M. Weinfeld, *VT* 17 (1967), pp. 93–113.

   The conservative contributions of Archer (pp. 274–79), Fausset (pp. 1–11), Harrison (pp. 680–93), and Wood (pp. 1–17) have been ignored by modern scholars.
3. R. D. Culver, *Toward a Biblical View of Civil Government* (Chicago: Moody, 1974), pp. 139–41; A. J. McClain, *The Greatness of the Kingdom* (Grand Rapids: Zondervan, 1959), pp. 91–95.
4. Culver, pp. 53, 76–77, 119, 130–34, 144–45, 202; McClain, pp. 38, 41, 86–98.
5. Cf. E. H. Sauer, *The King of the Earth* (Grand Rapids: Eerdmans, 1962), 256pp.
6. J. D. Pentecost, *Things to Come* (Grand Rapids: Zondervan, 1964), pp. 427–65, provides an excellent discussion of this theme. As with all truths, this one is subject to distortion. Examples of its abuse may be seen in the priests' and pastors' power over the people (and the misuse of passages of scripture like Matt. 18:18) and the errors inherent in the supposed "divine right of kings." A positive corrective may be found in P. Woolley's *Family, State, and Church—God's Institutions* (Grand Rapids: Baker, 1965), 48pp.

7. Cf. J. Garbett, *Christ, as Prophet, Priest, and King* (Oxford: Oxford University Press, 1842); Sauer, pp. 90–91.

8. Pentecost, p. 436; C. C. Ryrie, *Dispensationalism Today* (Chicago: Moody, 1965), 221pp.

9. Pentecost, pp. 65–94; E. W. Hengstenberg, *History of the Kingdom of God* (Edinburgh: T. & T. Clark, 1871), 1:90–469; 2:1–74.

10. Wood, p. 55; cf. E. H. Merrill, *Historical Survey of the Old Testament* (Nutley, N.J.: Craig, 1966), pp. 130–51; Noth, pp. 141–53.

11. Fausset, p. 3.

12. Archer, pp. 273–79.

13. Because the majority of scholars have allowed for numerous redactors, the authorship of the book has been unnecessarily obscured. Cf. deVaux, *The Early History of Israel,* pp. 683–93; D. M. Gunn, *VT* 24 (1974), pp. 286–317; G. T. Manley, *EQ* 31 (1959), pp. 32–37; W. L. Moran, *Biblica* 46 (1965), pp. 223–28, Y. T. Radday, D. Eickmann, and S. Talmon, *Biblica* 58 (1977), pp. 469–99; J. van Seters, *Semelia* 5 (1976), pp. 139–54.

14. A. E. Cundall, *ET* 81 (1970), pp. 178–81; E. J. Young, *Introduction to the Old Testament* (Grand Rapids: Eerdmans, 1960), p. 180.

15. V. R. Edman, "Judges," *Scripture Knowledge* (Wheaton, Ill.: Scripture Press, 1956), p. 13; cf. Z. Weisman, *ZAW* 89 (1977), pp. 399–411; M. Sekine, *Revue Biblique* 80 (1973), pp. 514–30.

16. Fausset, pp. 5–6.

17. Ibid., p. 6; Bush, pp. vi–vii.

Chapter 1

1. J. R. W. Stott made some perceptive remarks on this topic in his book *The Preacher's Portrait* (Grand Rapids: Eerdmans, 1961), pp. 11–32. His remarks, however, apply to all believers!

2. Cf. C. J. Barber and G. H. Strauss, *Leadership: The Dynamics of Success* (Greenwood, SC: Attic, 1982), 186pp., for an explanation of the biblical principles involved. For an analysis of the conquest narratives in Joshua–Judges, see W. R. Rogers, *Concordia Theological Monthly* 31 (Dec. 1961), pp. 746–60, and the extensive discussion by A. G. Auld in *VT* 25 (1975), pp. 261–85.

3. This is a Hebraism for seeking God's will. Divine guidance came through the high priest, who at this period of Israel's history inquired of the Lord by means of the Urim and Thummim (cf. *ZPEB*, 5:850–52; E. Robertson, *VT,* 14 (1964), pp. 67ff.

4. Matthew Henry, *Commentary on the Whole Bible* (Old Tappan, N.J.: Revell, n.d.), 2:121.

5. Soggin, p. 27. Information pertaining to the settlement of the tribes may be found in Mayes, who provided a powerful corrective to some of the abuses of Noth's amphictyonic concept, and Weippert, who surveyed modern critical scholarship since 1925.

6. Old Testament scholars disputed the location of Bezek. Most commentators favored a city north of Judah in the territory of Ephraim (cf. Baly, p. 170). It seems preferable to conclude that this stronghold lay within the territory of Judah and Simeon. It was not uncommon for more than one place to bear the same name (e.g., Bethlehem, Carmel) and in time to bear a qualifying name indicating its locality (e.g., Caesarea Philippi).

7. C. E. Macartney, *Chariots of Fire* (New York: Abingdon, 1951), pp. 76–77.

8. *Māsā'* in the Niphal stem often means: "to find, to catch, to capture," and even "to overpower" (cf. *TWOT*, 1:521).

9. Bush, p. 13; cf. also J. Kitto, *Daily Bible Illustrations* (Grand Rapids: Kregel, 1981), 1:508–9.

10. N. Avigad, *Discovering Jerusalem* (Nashville: Nelson, 1980), 270pp.; K. M. Kenyon, *Digging Up Jerusalem* (New York: Praeger, 1974), pp. 67–97; and G. F. Owen, *Abraham to the Middle East Crises* (Grand Rapids: Eerdmans, 1957), 429pp.

11. Bush, p. 15.

12. Baly, pp. 181–82; G. F. Owen, *The Holy Land* (Grand Rapids: Baker, 1977), pp. 184–94.

13. Baly, pp. 140–43; Owen, pp. 14–89.

14. Baly, pp. 12, 36, 57, 73, 91–94, 98, 100–03, 139, 181–85; *NIDBA*, pp. 232–33.

15. G. A. Larue, *JBL* 33 (1965), pp. 337–39; P. C. Hammond, *BA* 28 (1965), pp. 30–32.

16. Y. Aharoni, *EAEHL*, 1:171–78.

17. Fausset, p. 21.

18. Soggin (p. 22) concluded that the text is in error. Wood (p. 168), however, offered plausible evidence for Othniel's humility.

19. In this connection, W. B. Hunter's book *The God Who Hears* (Downers Grove, Ill.: InterVarsity, 1986), 224pp., is profitable reading.

20. Cf. W. F. Albright, *Archaeology and the Religion of Israel* (Baltimore, Md.: Johns Hopkins University, 1955), pp. 57–58, 75, 140, 166; idem, *CBQ* 15 (1963), pp. 1–11.

21. *NIDBA*, pp. 258–60.

22. For recent studies of the Philistines, see E. H. Hindson, *The Philistines and the Old Testament* (Grand Rapids: Baker, 1971), pp. 105–39; K. A. Kitchen, "The Philistines" in *POTT*, pp. 53–78; and Y. Yadin, *The Art*

of Warfare in Bible Lands (New York: McGraw–Hill, 1963), 2:248–53, 336–45, 354f.

23. Wood, pp. 140–41.

24. Josephus, *Antiquities of the Jews,* 5.2.7.

25. Kenyon, pp. 34, 41–48, 50, 76, 92, 98.

26. R. K. Harrison, ed., *Major Cities of the Biblical World* (Nashville: Nelson, 1985), pp. 49–57.

27. *NBD*, p. 348.

28. Cf. C. F. Pfeiffer and H. F. Vos, *Historical Geography of the Holy Land* (Chicago: Moody, 1967), pp. 101, 119, 122–23.

29. J. A. Thompson, *The Bible and Archaeology.* 3d ed. (Grand Rapids: Eerdmans, 1982), pp. 63f., 114f., 262–66.

30. For a discussion of these gods, see M. H. Pope, *El in the Ugaritic Texts* (Leiden, The Netherlands: Brill, 1955), 116pp.; Pritchard, *Palestinian Figurines in Relation to Certain Goddesses Known Through Literature* (Philadelphia: University of Pennsylvania, 1943), 99pp.; A. S. Kapelrud, *The Violent Goddess* (Oslo, Norway: Universeits–forlaget, 1969), 149pp.; U. Cassuto, *The Goddess Anath* (Jerusalem: Magnes, 1971), 194pp.; J. Gray, *The Legacy of Canaan* (Leiden, The Netherlands: Brill, 1965), 348pp.; E. O. James, *The Cult of the Mother Goddess* (London: Thames and Hudson, 1959), 300pp.; S. N. Kramer, *The Sacred Marriage Rite* (Bloomington, Ind.: Indiana University, 1969), 289pp.; R. Patai, *The Hebrew Goddess* (New York: Ktav, 1965), 349pp.; U. Oldenburg, *The Conflict Between El and Baal in Canaanite Religion* (Leiden, The Netherlands: Brill, 1969), 217pp.

31. Wood, pp. 139–40, 147–50.

32. A. Edersheim, *Bible History* (Grand Rapids: Eerdmans, 1954), 1:2:112.

33. J. A. Boreland, *Christ in the Old Testament* (Chicago: Moody, 1978), pp. 34–144.

34. Cf. *TWOT*, 1:107–8.

35. Examples of such treaties may be found in Pritchard, *ANET* (1959), pp. 203ff.; D. J. Wiseman, *The Vassal–Treaties of Esarhaddon* (London: British School of Archaeology in Iraq, 1958), 99pp.; M. G. Kline, Treaty of the Great King (Grand Rapids: Eerdmans, 1963), 149pp.

36. A. R. Millard, "The Canaanites," in POTT, pp. 29–52.

Chapter 2

1. C. R. Swindoll Growing Strong in the Seasons of Life, (Portland: Multnomah, 1983), p. 93.

2. Wood (pp. 10–11, 123–31) dealt with the chronological problems as well as Joshua's prowess as a leader. For an analysis of this passage, see N. Stemmer, Jewish Quarterly Review 57 (1967), pp. 237–41.

3. Culver, pp. 53, 76–77, 119, 125, 130, 132–34, 139–41, 144–45, 202.

4. False forms of worship were intimately connected with the basic necessities of life: fruitful harvests, increasing the size of one's flocks and herds, bearing children (especially sons), success in trade, and victory in time of war.

5. W. F. Albright, *History, Archaeology and Christian Humanism* (New York: McGraw–Hill, 1964), pp. 99, 150–53, 175n, 240; idem, *Yahweh and the Gods of Canaan* (New York: Doubleday, 1968), 294pp.; J. Gray, *The Canaanites* (New York: Praeger, 1965), 244pp; H. C. Habel, *Yahweh Versus Baal* (New York: Bookman Associates, 1964), 128pp.

6. *NIDBA*, pp. 460–61. Cf. Gray, *The Legacy of Canaan,* 348pp.; A. S. Kapelrud, *The Ras Shamra Discoveries and the Old Testament* (Norman, Okla.: University of Oklahoma Press, 1962), pp. 32–81.

7. Cf. Albright, *Archaeology and the Religion of Israel,* pp. 74ff.; H. Ringgren, *Religion of the Ancient Near East* (Philadelphia: Westminster, 1973), pp. 141–42.

8. W. L. Reed, *The Asherah in the Old Testament* (Fort Worth, Tex.: Christian University Press, 1949), 116pp.; *TDOT*, 1:438–44; Albright, *Archaeology and the Religion of Israel,* pp. 77–79.

9. McClain, pp. 91–95.

10. Cundall, p. 69.

11. The importance of our identification with Christ in his death, burial, and resurrection appears to have dropped out of the teaching of the church. J. R. W. Stott in *Men Made New* (London: InterVarsity, 1966), 108pp., dealt effectively with these issues. His insights are refreshing and stimulating.

12. The word used is *zānā*, not *qādēš*. For an explanation of its distinctive usage, see *TWOT*, 1:246; 2:786–89.

13. Cf. P. C. Craigie, *The Book of Deuteronomy.* New International Commentary on the Old Testament (Grand Rapids: Eerdmans, 1976), pp. 18f., 22–36, 62f., 79–89, 147f., 164ff., 249ff., 318–35, 254ff.; and J. A. Thompson, *Deuteronomy.* Tyndale Old Testament Commentaries (Downers Grove, Ill.: InterVarsity, 1974), pp. 102–59, 279–85.

14. Bush, p. 28.

15. In the Near East, war was generally a sacred undertaking. Wars were fought in the name of the local god(s). What set Israel apart from the nations around her was that Yahweh, her God, was transcendent. His esteem did not rise or fall with the fortunes of his people. Certain OT scriptures bear on the theme of *ḥērem* : Exod. 15:3; 1 Sam. 17:45;

1 Kings 22:19; 2 Chron. 20:22; Isa. 42:13. Cf. *TWOT*, 1:324; and P. C. Craigie, *The Problem of War in the Old Testament* (Grand Rapids: Eerdmans, 1978), pp. 45–63.

16. Fausset, pp. 46–47.

17. R. A. S. Macalister, *The Philistines, Their History and Civilization* (London: British Academy, 1914), 136pp.; G. E. Wright, *BA* 22 (1959), pp. 54–66; T. C. Mitchell, *AOTS*, pp. 404–27; K. A. Kitchen, *POTT*, pp. 53–78.

18. A. Poidebard and J. Lauffray, *Sidon* (Beyrouth, France: Ministere des trevaux publics, 1951), 102pp. For an explanation of Phoenician inscriptions from Sidon, see W. Beyerlin, ed., *Near Eastern Religious Texts Relating to the Old Testament,* Old Testament Library (Philadelphia: Westminster, 1978), pp. 227–68.

19. H. A. Hoffner, *Tyndale Bulletin* 20 (1969), pp. 27–37.

20. Henry, 2:132. A recent work of outstanding merit by W. C. Kaiser, Jr., entitled *Quest for Renewal* (Chicago: Moody, 1986), 163pp., expands on this theme.

21. J. B. Jordan's commentary *Judges: God's War Against Humanism* (Tyler, TX: Geneva Ministries, 1985), 334 pp., is an able polemic. Jordan and his associates in the Institute for Christian Economics adhered to a postmillennial eschatology. They apparently overlooked the fact that postmillennialism is simply a veiled form of humanism.

Chapter 3

1. The concept of corporate personality in ancient Israel is important. Several writers have attempted to extrapolate the biblical data; cf. H. W. Robinson, *Corporate Personality in Ancient Israel* (Philadelphia: Fortress, 1980), 64 pp., which formerly appeared under the title *The Group and the Individual in Israel* (1937), and A. R. Johnson, *The One and the Many . . .* (Cardiff, Wales: University of Wales Press, 1961), 44 pp.

2. L. H. Wiseman, *Practical Truths from Judges* (Grand Rapids: Kregel, 1985), p. 64.

3. *Hārâ*, "to burn, to be kindled" (cf. Num. 22:27; Jonah 4:1). The term originally signified "nostril," which was thought of as the locale of anger and an indication of a person's indignation.

4. Cf. G. Rawlinson, *Five Great Monarchies of the Ancient Eastern World* (London: Murray, 1871), 2:61; E. Taubler, *HUCA* 20 (1947), pp. 136–42; R. T. O'Callahan, *Aram Naharim* (1948), pp. 122ff.; A. Malamat, *JNES* 13 (1954), pp. 321–42; and Cundall, p. 73. Various conjectures have been made as to Cushan–rishathaim's identity. Several scholars

have been in favor of emending the MT to make Cushan the "chief of Teman," a town in north Edom. Wood (pp. 92–96, 162–71) provided convincing evidence for retaining the text as it has come down to us.

5. Watson, p. 73.

6. L. J. Wood, *The Holy Spirit in the Old Testament* (Grand Rapids: Zondervan, 1976), pp. 41f.; cf. J. F. Walvoord, *The Holy Spirit* (Grand Rapids: Zondervan, 1958), pp. 47, 71–77.

7. Cf. KD, pp. 237, 241–46; *TWOT*, 2:947–49.

8. The question naturally arises: Was Othniel the brother or was he the nephew of Caleb? Joshua 14:6–15 and Judges 1:13; 3:9 imply that he was Caleb's brother. A difficulty arises, however, when we notice that Othniel's father is spoken of as Kenaz. Caleb's father was Jephunneh (Num. 32:12; Josh. 14:6; cf. 15:17). This has led some scholars to assume that both Caleb and Othniel were the sons of Jephunneh and descendants of Kenaz. Such an explanation fits Judges 1:13 and 3:9, but not 1 Chronicles 4:13. Seraiah is not mentioned as being a brother of Caleb; so the Kenaz in this context must be someone who bore the name of his illustrious ancestor. The difference can be resolved by noting the age difference between Caleb and Othniel. Caleb's father, Jephunneh, must have died. His mother remarried. Her second husband was Kenaz, the father of Othniel.

9. C. J. Barber, *Nehemiah and the Dynamics of Effective Leadership* (Neptune, N.J.: Loizeaux, 1976), pp. 179–85, concludes with a chapter profiling the ideal leader. Cf. Barber and Strauss, *Leadership: The Dynamics of Success,* pp. 25–118.

10. Wood, p. 169.

11. Ibid., pp. 146–55.

12. Glueck, *The Other Side of Jordan* (Cambridge, Mass.: American Schools of Oriental Research, 1970), pp. 138–91; idem, *The River Jordan* (New York: McGraw–Hill, 1968), pp. 102–04, 145; cf. A. H. van Zyl, *The Moabites* (Leiden, The Netherlands: Brill, 1960), 240pp.

13. N. Glueck, *The Other Side of Jordan,* pp. 138–91.

14. F. M. Abel, *Géographie de la Palestine* (Paris: Gabalda, 1933–38), 2:270–73.

15. E. G. Kraeling, *JBL* 54 (1935), pp. 205–10; Wood, pp. 173–75.

16. Bush, p. 34.

17. Yadin, 2:216–17, 424–26.

18. Bush (p. 35) provides an illustration of this process. Cf. *MBA,* 74.

19. Boling, p. 86.

20. Kitto, 1:515–18.

21. Cf. E. G. Kraeling, *JBL* 54 (1935), pp. 205–10; F. C. Fensham, JNES 20 (1961), pp. 197f.; E. Danelius, *JNES* 22 (1963), pp. 191–93; A. van Selms, *VT* 14 (1964), pp. 294–309; P. C. Craigie, *JBL* 91 (1972), pp. 239–40; Wood, pp. 175–79.

22. G. Bush, p. 41.

23. Kitto, 1:518–19.

Chapter 4

1. Jabin was probably not a personal name but a dynastic title (Josh. 11:1; Ps. 83:9) like Pharaoh in Egypt or Abimelech in Philistia. Cf. A. Malamat, *JBL* 79 (1960), pp. 12–19. He oppressed the Israelites for twenty years, 1257–1237 B.C.

2. Watson, pp. 93–94. Cf. Lang and Kirk, 1:37.

3. Cundall, p. 81.

4. Bush (p. 44) described her as holy, prudent, and knowledgeable, acting as God's mouthpiece to his wayward people. Her name in Hebrew means "a bee." The manner in which she was introduced, *'ēšet lappîdōt*, has been thought by some scholars to be unusual. Those who are quick to emend the text dismiss the thought of her being married and look instead for some significance in the word *lappîdōt* (see #6 below). The same kind of terminology was used, however, when introducing other prophetesses, as was illustrated in 2 Kings 22:14; 2 Chronicles 22:11; 34:22.

5. Watson, p. 93.

6. "Lappidoth" was a Hebrew name meaning "the torch." Those who are fond of finding significance in names will appreciate the combination of "industry" (Deborah) and "illumination" (Lappidoth) provided by this pair.

7. Cf. deVaux, *The Early History of Israel*, pp. 766–73; H. C. Thompson, *Transactions of the Glasgow University Oriental Society* 19 (1961–62), pp. 74–85; deVaux, *Ancient Israel*, pp. 143–63.

8. E. Hubbard, *A Message to Garcia* (New York: Crowell, 1924), pp. 9–24.

9. Cf. Cundall, p. 83.

10. The term "to draw [out or near to]" (4:6–7) has been hotly debated. Bush (pp. 46–47) has an extended discussion of its meaning. Cf. C. F. Burney, p. 87.

11. Cf. A. S. Peake, *Heroes and Martyrs of Faith* (London: Hodder and Stoughton, n.d.), pp. 152–60.

12. Cundall, p. 84.

13. Lang and Kirk, 1:41. Lang errs in one particular, viz., in ascribing to Barak the title "mighty man of valour."

14. Cf. C. J. Barber, *Ruth: A Story of God's Grace* (Neptune, N.J.: Loizeaux Brothers, 1989), pp. 88–91, 97–101. This work demonstrates that no sexual impropriety took place when Ruth visited Boaz's threshing floor.

15. L. Kohlberg in his *Essays on Moral Development* (San Francisco: Harper and Row, 1981–), 1:16–19 outlined three levels or stages in the development of values: (1) the *preconventional* level, in which emphasis is laid on "proper behavior" and adherence to culturally imparted norms mediated through parental authority; (2) the *conventional* level, in which stress is placed on conformity and the maintaining of expectations of one's family and/or peers; and (3) the *postconventional* level, in which decisions are made according to autonomous moral principles that have validity and application apart from external authorities (whether individuals or groups).

Although some have challenged certain of Kohlberg's assumptions, his basic stages of moral development—from dependency to maturity—are valid. When applied to the attitudes and teaching of some of our churches, we can readily see why some believers remain caught in the trap of legalism and do not grow into the image of Christ (cf. Eph. 4:13–14*a*; Col. 3:10). True maturity involves growth in five specific areas:

• A well-developed sense of *autonomy* by which we become self-determining and are able to make wise choices. Such autonomy should not be equated with irresponsibility, for irresponsibility only demonstrates the immaturity of the person who does not know how to use his/her freedom (cf. C. R. Erdmans's exposition of 1 Cor. 8:1–11:1 in *The First Epistle to the Corinthians* [Philadelphia: Westminster, 1938], pp. 73–96). For the believer a mature autonomy enables him/her to voluntarily submit his/her will to Christ (cf. 2 Cor. 10:5; see also 5:15). Such submission results in perfect freedom (Matt. 11:28–30).

• A well-developed sense of our own *sexuality,* which causes a man to feel comfortable in his role as a male and enables a woman to feel comfortable in her role as a female. Such maturity makes possible the appropriate interaction illustrated in scripture (e.g., when Paul accepted the hospitality of a single woman named Lydia [Acts 16:14–15] or as we find in the case of Ruth and Boaz when they spent time together at night on a threshing floor [Ruth 3:6–15]).

• A well-developed *internalized sense of morality* by which we make wise moral choices and discern between good and evil. We can cultivate such knowledge only by a daily, continuous meditation on scripture (cf. Pss. 1 and 119; Col. 2:6–7; Heb. 5:13–6:2; Jude 20). By

building our moral principles on internal rather than external fac-
tors, our actions will result from conviction, not ever–changing
social mores.

   • Our *career choice,* which should be in keeping with the gifts
that the Holy Spirit has sovereignly bestowed on us (Rom. 12; 1 Cor.
12–14; Eph. 4).

   • A clear *hope* for the future. This will include both temporal and
eternal realities and embrace short–range and long–range goals.

16. This reference to Dan proves that they had already migrated to the
    northern limits of the territory allotted to Israel (cf. Josh. 19:47 and
    Judg. 1:34 with Judg. 18:1–31, noting vv. 1, 7, 27–29).

17. The Hebrew word *pārad* means "to divide, to separate" (cf. Prov.
    16:28). In the Niphal it implies continuous action (Gen. 13:9; Prov.
    18:1). For a brief discussion, see *TWOT,* 2:733. For the location of
    Zaanannim as well as the scene of the battle, see *MBA,* 75.

18. An abundance of literature is available on the subject: cf. Bush, pp.
    52–56; J. Kitto, 1:524–26; W. M. Thomson, *The Land and the Book*
    (New York: Harper and Brothers, 1886), 1:436, 3:312; F. C. Fensham,
    BASOR 175 (Sept. 1964), pp. 51–54; and an extensive discussion in
    H. C. Trumbull, *The Threshold Covenant* (Edinburgh: Clark, 1896),
    335pp.

19. Cundall (pp. 88f.) believed the *semîkā* to be a "fly net." *TWOT,* 2:879
    (#2269a), adheres to the belief that this was a rug or thick coverlet.

20. Josephus, *Antiquities of the Jews,* 5.5.4; cf. Bush, p. 55.

21. A. Cohen, *Joshua and Judges.* Soncino Books of the Bible (London:
    Soncino, 1961), pp. 191–92, 201.

22. Bush, pp. 55–56; J. Kitto, 1:525–26. Cf. Soggin (p. 77) and Cundall (p.
    89) for mediating points of view.

23. J. C. Geikie, *Old Testament Characters* (New York: Pott, 1903), p. 138.

24. The ethical dilemma posed by Jael's action has been discussed by
    K. Barth in *Ethics,* ed. D. Braun, trans. G. W. Bromiley (New York:
    Seabury, 1981), pp. 147–48; L. B. Smedes in *Mere Morality* (Grand
    Rapids: Eerdmans, 1983), pp. 101–2; and W. C. Kaiser, Jr., *Toward Old
    Testament Ethics (Grand Rapids: Zondervan, 1983), pp. 176–80.*
    Kaiser drew attention to Deuteronomy 7:12–16 and 23:6 and claimed
    that "principles [applying to us today] do exist for the defense of an
    attacked home or city (either by a lawless criminal or an invading
    enemy)." He continued, "War [or an act of aggression in defense of
    one's country] is God's ultimate, but reluctant, method of treating
    gross evil that resists every other patient and loving rebuke of God."
    When we note the angel of the Lord's indictment of Meroz (Manas-
    seh) for not cutting off the retreat of Sisera's army (5:23), with the

praise given Jael in the very next verse, then plainly our view of the ethics involved needs to be modified.

25. A vast body of literature has been written on Judges 5. Soggin (pp. 60–61), in keeping with the European system, prefaced his comments on the text with an extensive bibliography. The following works augment his research: A. Baker, CBQ 27 (1965), pp. 124–36; P. C. Craigie, JBL 87 (1969), pp. 253–65; idem, VT 22 (1972), pp. 349–53; A. Globe, *JBL* 93 (1974), pp. 493–512; idem, *Biblica* 55 (1974), pp. 168–78; J. Ackerman, *BASOR* 220 (Dec. 1975), pp. 5–13; A. Globe, *ZAW* 87 (1975), pp. 169–84; idem, *VT* 25 (1975), pp. 362–67; Z. Weisman, *VT* 26 (1976), pp. 116–20; P. C. Craigie, *Journal of the Evangelical Theological Society* 20 (1977), pp. 15–22; M. D. Coogan, *CBQ* 40 (1978), pp. 143–66; P. C. Craigie, *ZAW* 90 (1978), pp. 374–81; S. G. Dempster, *Westminster Theological Journal* 41 (1978), pp. 33–53; G. Garbini, *Journal of Semitic Studies* 23 (1978), pp. 23–35; E. Tov, *VT* 28 (1978), pp. 224–32; A. J. Hausch, *JBL* 99 (1980), pp. 23–41; J. F. A. Sawyer, *VT* 21 (1981), pp. 87–89.

26. D. R. Hilliers, *Treaty–Curses and the Old Testament Prophets* (Rome: Pontifical Biblical Institute, 1964), 101pp.

27. Boling, p. 114.

Chapter 5

1. Lang and Kirk, 1:86–89.

2. A. Malamat, PEQ 84 (1953), pp. 61–65.

3. Lang and Kirk, 1:89–90.

4. Cf. Isaiah 11:14; Jeremiah 49:28; Ezekiel 25:1–10.

5. Josephus, *Antiquities of the Jews,* 5.6.1.

6. Three important articles are worth consulting: J. D. Whiting, *National Geographic Magazine* 28 (Dec. 1915), pp. 512–50; T. Chapelle and D. Chapelle, *National Geographic Magazine* 103 (April 1953), pp. 545–62; and R. A. M. Conley, *National Geographic Magazine* 136 (Aug. 1969), pp. 202–27.

7. Kitto, 1:531ff.

8. *Minhārôt* is a hapax legomenon from the root *nhr* and suggests a valley or ravine. The "dens" may well have been clefts or defiles in the mountains caused by water erosion.

9. Fausset, pp. 104–5; Bush, p. 82.

10. H. P. Liddon, *The Divinity of Our Lord and Saviour Jesus Christ* (Minneapolis: Klock and Klock, 1978), pp. 45–99; J. F. Walvoord, *Jesus Christ Our Lord* (Chicago: Moody, 1969), pp. 52–55.

11. J. Bruce, *The Life of Gideon* (Edinburgh: Edmonston and Douglas, 1870), pp. 18ff.; Gray, p. 297; Lang and Kirk, 1:83 (cf. Judg. 6:24 and 8:32 with Josh. 18:23 and 1 Sam. 13:17).

12. The obstacles in Gideon's way were, from a human standpoint, very real. His family was poor when compared with their "thousand" (Exod. 18:25). Cf. Bush, p. 86.

13. Lang and Kirk, 1:83ff. Lang also has an interesting summary of Gideon's greatness (which differs from the criteria used at the beginning of this chapter).

14. deVaux, *The Early History of Israel,* pp. 813–19; Robinson, 3:137, 605; Thomson, 3:180.

15. Lang and Kirk (1:98ff.) has an excellent summary of the Lord's progressive revelation of himself to Gideon.

16. B. L. Montgomery, *The Path to Leadership* (London: Collins, 1961), pp. 15, 17–19.

17. Cf. Bush, p. 86.

18. The word *minḥāh* and is usually translated "offering," cf. G. B. Gray, *Sacrifice in the Old Testament* (New York: Ktav, 1970), pp. 13–17, 47, 398–402; *TWOT,* 1:514–15.

19. Cf. Burney, p. 192; Lang and Kirk, 1:102–3; Moore, p. 189.

20. Gideon worshiped the Lord as *Yahweh Shalom,* exemplifying the peace that has filled his heart. Lang's comparison of Gideon's altar with the altars of other great men of the OT is worth noting (Lang and Kirk, 1:106).

21. Ibid., 1:109–10.

22. If the Midianites had *not* invaded the land by the time of the events of 6:11, then we must seek for an explanation of Gideon's fear of being detected. Verse 33, however, implies that the annual invasion took place after Gideon's sacrifice and before the Spirit of the Lord came on him. Most commentators have ignored the problem. A plausible explanation in given with the comments on verse 11. For the location of Mount Moreh, as well as the flight taken by the Midianites after being routed by Gideon, see the *MBA,* 76.

23. Gideon stood in awe of the proud and haughty Ephraimites. He feared their rejection. He realized that if they declined to accompany him, the other tribes would lose heart. Jephthah likewise had problems with these sons of Joseph (cf. 8:1–3 and 12:1–6).

24. Bush, pp. 94–96; Lang and Kirk, 1:119–25.

25. Fausset (pp. 113–18) provided a valuable summary of the lessons to be derived from this passage. His views differ from the application of the text that we have adopted. His comments are often judicious. Cf. Bush, pp. 94–96.

Chapter 6

1. H. Haag, *ZAW* 79 (1967), pp. 305–14; J. A. Emerton, *JTS* 27 (1976), pp. 289–312.
2. Thompson, 2:178–86.
3. Baly, pp. 21, 38–39, 149, 151, 173–74, 189.
4. A problem arises with the mention of Mount Gilead in 7:3, for this mountain is in Transjordan. Most of the older commentators ignored the problem. Some modern, generally conservative, scholars are in favor of emending the MT to read "Mount Gilboa." This is always a dubious expedient. Burney (pp. 207–8) proposed changing the Hebrew to *Galud* (thus introducing into Gideon's statement a similarity of sound with the name of the spring, *'Ain Jalud*, "let those who are fearful decamp from 'Mt. Fearful.'"). He was followed by Boling (pp. 144–45). Others such as Moore (p. 201) and Soggin (p. 136) admitted the problem but offered no real solution. KD (pp. 341–42) suggested the possibility that a large number of people from Gilead had settled in the area west of the Jordan allotted to the tribe of Manasseh and had given names to certain places that were reminiscent of the land they had left behind them. This view was followed by F. D. Lindsay in *The Bible Knowledge Commentary* (Wheaton, Ill.: Victor, 1985), 1:393–94. P. Cassel in J. P. Lange's *Commentary on the Holy Scriptures* (Grand Rapids: Zondervan, 1960), 4:122, postulated that the name had become synonymous with the character of the tribe of Manasseh, having been given to Manasseh's son (Num. 26:29; cf. 32:40; Josh. 17:1). Although it is impossible to decide this issue with certainty, the views of KD and Cassel offer two plausible explanations.
5. Bush (pp. 97–100) and Lang (1:129–32) give excellent descriptions of these events.
6. The expression *hᵃmušîm* has been translated "armed men" as well as "ranks of five" or even "fifty." Boling (p. 146) referred to Joshua 1:14 and 4:12 where the term is used for an army advancing in battle array. Cf. Bush, p. 101.
7. Boling (p. 146) translated *sᵉliwl lehem' sᵉ'ōrîm*, as a "stale" or "moldy [loaf of] barley bread." It was eaten only by the poorest of the poor. As such it was a graphic description of the poverty of the people of Israel (as well as the smallness of Gideon's army). Cf. Josephus, *Antiquities of the Jews,* 5.6.4.
8. The use of the article with the word "tent" implied that Gideon's attack was directed on the supreme authority of the coalition. Later we read of *two* princes of Midian and still later find Gideon pursuing the *two* kings of Midian. The article used with the singular noun

"tent" implied a solitary individual. The problem may be resolved when we reflect on the use of the name "Jerubbaal" in 7:1 (with which this account begins). This would indicate that the attack was directed at Baal. "The [one] tent" was symbolic of the whole army. To demolish it was to destroy the entire host.

9. *ZPEB*, 1:162–64.

10. The commentaries by Bush, Lang and Kirk, Wiseman, and Wood can be consulted with profit.

11. Josephus, *Antiquities of the Jews*, 5.6.5, believed these were rams' horns similar to those used by Joshua at the overthrow of Jericho.

12. Cf. A. Malamat, *PEQ* 84 (1953), pp. 61–65; C. Herzog and M. Gichon, *Battles of the Bible* (New York: Random, 1978), pp. 54–62. Cf. *MBA*, 77.

13. Lang and Kirk, 1:158–59.

14. Baly, p. 13.

15. Wood, pp. 223ff.

16. A monarchy would be instituted later. When the people called for a "king," Saul was anointed a "prince" over God's people. He was to exercise authority *under* God's rule. Culver (pp. 171, 173, 176, 282) and McClain (pp. 4–6, 17, 19–21, 97, 113, 268–86, 307–18, 369–84) have good discussions of God's intent for a monarchy. Cf. G. H. Davies, *VT* 13 (1963), pp. 151–57; and B. Lindars, *JTS* 16 (1965), pp. 315–26.

17. Robinson, 2:275, 287–302; Baly, pp. 113–19, 137, 154, 178–80.

18. Montgomery, p. 13.

19. Preachers will find Lang's comments (in Lang and Kirk, 1:144–52) worth noting. His application of the text differs from the approach followed in this chapter.

Chapter 7

1. D. Seward, *Napoleon's Family* (New York: Viking, 1986), 216pp.

2.

3. Ibid., p. 9.

4. Aharoni, pp. 57–62, 146–50; B. W. Anderson, *BA* 20 (1957), pp. 10–19; W. Harrelson, *BA* 20 (1957), pp. 2–10; S. H. Horn, *JEOL* 6 (1964), pp. 284–301; G. E. Wright, *Shechem: The Biography of a Biblical City* (New York: McGraw–Hill, 1965), p. 270; M. Reviv, *IEJ* 16 (1966), pp. 252–57; G. R. H. Wright, *ZAW* 80 (1968), pp. 1–35; idem, *VT* 20 (1970), pp. 75–82; idem, *ZAW* 87 (1975), pp. 56–65.

5. Although Gideon was probably much older than his Shechemite concubine, she was probably glad to marry such a prominent Is-

raelite. For a discussion of the legal rights and responsibilities of concubines, see E. Neufeld, *Ancient Hebrew Marriage Laws* (London: Longmans, Green, 1944), pp. 118–34, and deVaux, pp. 24–25, 53–54, 115–17. As deVaux showed, this included an inheritance when her husband died.

6. The capture of Shechem is not recorded in the book of Joshua. At the covenant–renewal ceremony held there (Josh. 8:30–35), it appears in Israelite hands. This would have been impossible unless Shechem had been captured (or, less likely, had been on friendly terms with the invading Hebrews). Probably Shechem was one of the cities captured by the Israelites and only sparsely populated. This would have made possible its gradual repopulation by Canaanites (cf. 9:28, which seems to provide a definite link with the past). In time it became predominantly pagan. If true, it explains why it was the site for the central sanctuary for only a short time (cf. A. E. Cundall, *Vox Evangelica* 4 [1965], pp. 12–17), giving way first to Bethel and then to Shiloh.

7. Cf. W. L. Moran, *JNES* 22 (1963), pp. 173–76; D. R. Hilliers, *BASOR* 176 (December 1964), pp. 46–47; W. Bruggemann, *CBQ* 32 (1970), pp. 532–42.

8. In this connection, O. Kernberg's book *Internal World and External Reality* (New York: Aronson, 1985), 359pp., is of particular importance. He described the dynamics involved in society as well as in individuals and explained why some of the most unworthy people rise to positions of prominence.

9. Cf. Bush, p. 120; R. J. Bull and J. F. Ross, *BASOR* 169 (1963), pp. 27–32; R. E. Clements, *Journal of Semitic Studies* 13 (1968), pp. 21–32.

10. The phrase *'al-'eben 'ehāt*, "upon one stone," (9:5) gives evidence of Abimelech's superstitious nature. By concentrating the blood in one place, he sought to limit the cry for blood–vengeance to a single spot. This was in marked contrast to the execution of the princes of Midian (cf. 7:25), where the men of Ephraim did not fear retaliation for their act from family, friends, or subjects of Oreb and Zeeb.

11. Cf. Bush, p. 122. Jotham's words "Listen to me . . . and may God listen to you" obviously indicate that he now stood before the people of Shechem as God's representative. Cf. A. D. Crown, *'Abr Nahrain* 3 (1961–62), pp. 90–98; J. Harvey, *Biblica* 43 (1962), pp. 172–96. For an explanation of the parabolic form of communication, see E. H. Maly, *CBQ* 22 (1960), pp. 299–305; B. Lindars, *JTS* 24 (1973), pp. 355–66. Other biblical illustrations of OT parables used to convey an important message may be found in 2 Samuel 12:1–4 and 2 Kings 14:9–10. For some excellent illustrations of nonbiblical parables, see Bush, p. 123.

12. Cundall (pp. 129–30) has a fine summary of these events.

13. The issue of integrity (cf. 9:15–16) was prominent in Jotham's parable. The Hebrew *be'emet* , "in truth," was commonly found in covenants (such as the one the Shechemites must have entered into with Abimelech when they plotted with him and later proclaimed him their king). The term *be'emet* implied fidelity and was the basis of the covenant(s) between God and man.

14. The word *šiphâ* , "concubine," receives a full explanation in E. Neufeld, pp. 121–25, and in N. Avigad's article in *IEJ* 3 (1953), pp. 137–52.

15. For an explanation of "God sent an evil spirit," see Bush, p. 128; KD, pp. 365–66; and Fausset, pp. 174–77.

16. Cf. R. G. Boling, *VT* 13 (1963), pp. 479–82; idem, *Judges,* pp. 176–79.

17. R. J. Tourney, *Revue Biblique* 66 (1959), pp. 358–68, identified Mount Zalmon with Mount Ebal; cf. W. F. Albright, *HUCA* 23 (1950–51), p. 23.

18. The term *wayyizrā'eha melah* , "to sow with salt," has no immediate parallel in the OT. Explanations vary. Burney (pp. 285–86) and Moore (pp. 263–64) considered it a ritual act, symbolically implying perpetual desolation. W. R. Smith, *Lectures on the Religion of the Semites* (New York: Ktav, 1969), pp. 594–95, and S. Gevirtz, *VT* 13 (1963), pp. 52–62, thought the act implied placing a *hērem* or "ban" on the city. F. C. Fensham, *BA 25 (1962), pp.* 48–50, believes Abimelech placed Shechem under a covenantal curse; A. M. Honeyman, *VT* 3 (1953), pp. 192–95, saw in the act further evidence of Abimelech's superstitious nature, for salt was regarded as having purgative and protective powers (especially in decomposing blood) and so would reduce blood–guiltiness. Cf. J. Pitt–Rivers, *The Fate of Shechem* (Cambridge: Cambridge University Press, 1977), pp. 157–58.

19. *Pelah rekeb* , "stone of riding." Cf. *ZPEB,* 4:227.

20. Montgomery, p. 9.

21. Ibid., p. 11.

Chapter 8

1. T. Hardy, *The Dynasts,* Act 2, Scene 5.

2. Montgomery, pp. 14–15, 17.

3. Wood, pp. 265–68. Cf. A. J. Hauser, *JBL* 94 (1975), pp. 190–200.

4. J. S. Wright, *Revell's Dictionary of Bible People* (Old Tappan, NJ: Revell, 1978), p. 229.

5. Cf. Barber, *Nehemiah and the Dynamics of Effective Leadership,* p. 167.

6. "Tola" was a name given to a crimson worm as well as the dye from the cochineal beetle. The word was translated crimson in Isaiah 1:18

and purple in Lamentations 4:5. These colors were frequently mentioned in the tabernacle furnishings (cf. Exod. 25:4; 26:1, 31, 36 et al.), where the same root word was used. The name may have described the appearance of Jacob's grandson at birth (Gen. 46:13). Whatever the origin, Tola became the chief of one of the four clans of Issachar (Num. 26:23–25). The Tola of the book of Judges was descended from Puah (also spelled Puvah [Gen. 46:13; Num. 26:23; 1 Chron. 7:1–2]). He lived (*yōšēb*) in the hill country of Ephraim at Shamir (the location of which is now unknown, even though some have sought to identify it with Samaria. Cf. Burney, pp. 99–102; Moore, pp. 270–73; and Noth, pp. 99–102).

7. BDB, p. 446.

8. Boling, p. 187.

9. Fausset, p. 197.

10. Wood, pp. 268–70. Cf. M. Noth, *Die Israelitischen Personennamen im Rahmen der gemeinsemitischen Namengebung,* pp. 7, 28, 204, 216.

11. Fausset, p. 200; cf. Bush, p. 137.

12. During the intervening time, their number had increased to thirty. The writer provided an interesting play on words by using *'ārîm* , "towns," and the unusual word for donkey,*'yārîm*. Cf. Boling, *VT* 16 (1966), pp. 295–96.

13. The importance of maintaining an adequate defense was stressed by Winston Churchill in his famous speech, "The Sinews of Peace," delivered at Westminster College, Fulton, Mississippi, on March 5, 1946, and underscored in more recent times by Charleton Heston, following a visit to the Atomic Testing Laboratory, University of California, and preserved in an address to the National Center for Legislative Research, Washington, D.C. The full text is to be found in *Vital Speeches of the Day* (1984), 50:20–21. Here is an excerpt:

> Peace is the cry on every hand. From politicians sniffing a breeze bearing votes, from scholars, bishops, and earnest and frightened school children taught to draw crayon mushroom clouds instead of Easter bunnies, we hear it. "Peace, God, give us peace." Amen to that surely.
>
> The curious thing is, we *have* peace. Since Hiroshima, there has been no global war. Peace has been preserved for almost 38 years by the nuclear deterrent maintained by the United States and her NATO allies. This force has restrained the only conceivable enemy in such conflict: the Soviet Union.
>
> Nevertheless, throughout the Western democracies in the last two years, thousands of decent

people, chilled by the fear of nuclear war, have concluded that the way to avoid it is to toss away the shield
that has protected us from it. War is a terrible thing; to
fear it is reasonable, and common to us all. But fear is
not a reasonable guide for human actions.

To this must be added Christ's own words to his disciples when He
told them that division rather than peace would characterize house-
holds as well as nations (Luke 12:51; cf. Matt. 24:6; Luke 18:8). Since
no one can predict when the Lord will come, it is unwise for Western
countries to neglect the very reason for the present peace. The
Israelites at the time of Jabin failed to be watchful, and the results
are recorded in Judges 4.

14. Montgomery, pp. 13, 16.
15. For an interesting account of the worship and mythology of Baal, see
    J. C. L. Gibson, *Canaanite Myths and Legends* (Edinburgh: Clark,
    1978), pp. 2–19, 38–81.
16. M. Tadmor, "Female Cult Figurines in Late Canaan and Early Israel,"
    in *Studies in the Period of David and Solomon,* ed. T. Ishida (Winona
    Lake, Ind.: Eisenbrauns, 1982), pp. 139–73.
17. Wiseman, pp. 223–24.
18. See Notes, chapter 1, footnote 30.
19. Henry, 2:187.
20. Cundall, pp. 138–39.
21. *ZPEB,* 4:885–87. Cf. R. R. Wilson, *Prophecy and Society in Ancient Israel*
    (Philadelphia: Fortress, 1980), pp. 189–91, 210–12, 230, 238–39, 247–
    51, 276.
22. Cf. the famous "Moabite Stone," in which Mesha, king of Moab,
    attributed the defeat of his people to the anger of Chemosh. The text
    may be found in *ANET*, pp. 320–21.
23. Pagan priests derive their control over people from the power to
    curse. Only in Judaism and Christianity is there inherent in the
    God–man relationship the power to bless.
24. *Za'aq* implies a "cry of pain" (cf. Hos. 7:14).
25. Cundall, p. 139.
26. Ibid.
27. Bush, p. 140.
28. Defined as "the attribution of human characteristics, activities, or
    emotions to God" (see V. A. Harvey, *A Handbook of Theological Terms*
    [London: Allen and Unwin, 1964] p. 21).
29. Bush, p. 141.
30. *Quote* (June 15, 1975), p. 569.

31. I am indebted to Larry Richards for directing my attention to 2 Kings 4:26 where the word *shalom* is used three times to describe what is "right" or "good."

32. L. O. Richards, *Expository Dictionary of Bible Words* (Grand Rapids: Zondervan, 1985), p. 479.

Chapter 9

1. A. Whyte, *Bible Characters: Old Testament* (London: Oliphants, 1952), pp. 188–89.

2. Bush (p. 142) drew attention to the verb *was*, which he preferred to translate "had become." "The original *hāyāh*, was not merely a verb of existence, but denoted the transition of its subject, from one state to another. When its meaning was simply 'is,' or 'was,' it was almost invariably omitted in the original. Here, however, it is inserted, and probably hints at the process by which Jephthah had gradually become distinguished." For an excellent summation of Jephthah's character, see Wood, pp. 281–301.

3. For a discussion of the word *zānāh*, "prostitute," see B. A. Brooks, *JBL* 60 (1941), pp. 227–53; R. Gordis, *HUCA* 25 (1954), pp. 9–35; H. H. Rowley, *Bulletin of the John Rylands Library* 39 (1956–57), pp. 200–33; D. J. Wiseman, *Tyndale House Bulletin* 14 (1963), pp. 8–11; and O. E. Collins, "The stem *znh* and prostitution in the Hebrew Bible" (Ph.D. diss. Brandeis University, 1977), 298pp. Neufeld, p. 127, has some important comments on the rights of inheritance of firstborn sons.

4. Robinson, 3:290, 319.

5. The word is rêq, "vain, empty, worthless" (cf. Prov. 12:11; 28:19). Boling (p. 197) stated, "his partners were drawn from the dregs of society."

6. Bush, p. 143.

7. Cundall, p. 141.

8. *NIDBA*, p. 24.

9. Thompson, 3:576–77.

10. *MBA*, 78.

11. Montgomery, p. 12; cf. J. C. Geikie, *Old Testament Characters,* pp. 160, 162–63; Wood, pp. 282–83.

12. There is a mistaken view (encountered frequently in the literature) that claims Gilead was not Jephthah's father but that "the *district* is personified as his father." Cf. Burney, p. 308; Boling, p. 197, et al. The context militates against such a view.

13. *Rō'š,* "head, chief." Cf. Barlett, VT 19 (1969), pp. 1–10.

14. KD, p. 380.

15. This is the first mention of the name *Yahweh,* and it is significant that it came from Jephthah's lips. Bush (p. 145) stated, "The spirit of pious dependence on the divine blessing, argues strongly in favor of his general [godly] spirit." Cf. Geikie, pp. 161–62.

16. I.e., he entered into a solemn covenant with the people, *and called on God to be his witness.*

17. Cooperation and compromise are two words with widely divergent ideas. We may, in a given situation, cooperate with a person or organization, even if we disagree with certain plans that may have been formulated. Compromise, however, implies a willingness to sacrifice principles for the sake of some supposed gain. In Jephthah's case cooperation was out of the question, and, unlike politicians today, he was not prepared to compromise.

18. Bush, p. 146; cf. J. van Seters, *JBL* 91 (1972), pp. 182–97; and A. Malmat, *JBL* 79 (1960), pp. 12–19.

19. A. Haldar, *Who Were the Amorites?* (Leiden, The Netherlands: Brill, 1971), 93pp.

20. Bush, pp. 150–58. The majority of Bible scholars believe that Jephthah sacrificed his daughter as a "burnt offering." Cf. I. Mendelsshon, *IEJ* 4 (1954), pp. 116–69; R. deVaux, *Studies in Old Testament Sacrifice* (Cardiff, Wales: University of Wales Press, 1964), pp. 65ff.; J. A. Emerton, *ZAW* 85 (1973), pp. 220–23; A. R. W. Green, *The Role of Human Sacrifice in the Ancient Near East* (Missoula, Mont.: Scholars Press, 1975), pp. 161f., and nearly all commentaries. In contrast to the preponderance of those favoring a bloody sacrifice, there are some who find the evidence in the Bible to support a different and more consistent view. Cf. the exceptionally good article on "Jephthah" in the J. McClintock and J. Strong, eds. *Cyclopedia of Biblical, Theological, and Ecclesiastical Literature* (Grand Rapids: Baker, 1969), 4:818–20; S. Shibayama's discussion of *yāraḏ* and *ʿālāh* in the *Journal of Bible and Religion* 34, 4 (1966), pp. 358–62; R. D. Culver's clear and logical explanation in *The Evangelical Christian* (February 1959), pp. 69–70; and Wood's extensive treatment (pp. 287–95).

21. ZPEB, 5:890–91.

22. Apparently even after his victory over the Amorites, some people (perhaps from among the prominent families, or even his half-brothers) openly opposed his leadership.

23. The Hebrew text reads that the daughters of Israel would "go up" (presumably to the sanctuary at Shiloh) and "tell to the daughter of Jephthah the Gileadite, four days in the year" (11:40). The word *tell to* in the MT is *tānāh*, and has been translated "to recount, rehearse, commemorate, tell" (cf. BDB, p. 1072). While we would like to know

more of the details, the use of the word in this context does not support the idea of "to lament."

24. Hebrews 11:32, where Jephthah is mentioned alongside Samuel, David, and other great men of God.

25. C. J. Barber, *Give Me This Mountain* (Winona Lake, Ind.: Brethren Missionary Herald Press, n.d.), p. 145.

26. Lang and Kirk, 1:60–61. Cf. F. Willesen, *VT* 8 (1958), pp. 97–98; and D. M. Gunn, *JBL* 93 (1974), pp. 513–18.

27. A. P. Stanley, *History of the Jewish Church* (London: Murray, 1875), pp. 303, 306; Geikie, pp. 165–66; cf. Wood, pp. 295–96.

28. Cf. Barber and Strauss, *Leadership: The Dynamics of Success,* pp. 12–73.

29. Montgomery, p. 12.

Chapter 10

1. Moore, p. 325; A. Jeremias, *The Old Testament in Light of the Ancient Near East* (New York: Putnam's, 1911), 2:169ff.; J. G. Frazer, *The Golden Bough* (London: Macmillan, 1936), 3:390ff.; S. A. Cook, *Encyclopaedia Britannica,* 11th ed., 24:119; and for a clear refutation, G. G. Cohen, *EQ* 42 (1970), pp. 131–34.

2. "Samson Agonistes," *The Works of John Milton,* ed. D. Bush (Boston: Houghton–Mifflin, 1965), lines 374–75.

3. Cf. *The Minister's Library* (Chicago: Moody, 1985), 1:439–40, for books with explanations of the lure of cults and false religions.

4. Wood, pp. 270–74.

5. deVaux (pp. 26–40) has an excellent discussion of marriages in OT times. He noted in particular the need for negotiations regarding the *mōhar*. Cf. J. A. Thompson, *Handbook of Life in Bible Times* (Downers Grove, Ill.: InterVarsity, 1986), pp. 85–88; and C. J. Barber and A. A. Barber's discussion of biblical marriage in *Your Marriage Has Real Possibilities* (Grand Rapids: Kregel, 1981), 165pp., where issues pertaining to *mōhar* are discussed in connection with the union of Jacob and Rachel.

   Manoah did not select a bride for Samson. The possibility exists that in such a small community none was suitable. And even though the tribe of Judah was close, the general apostasy may have rendered the available women unfit to be wives of judges.

6. Josephus, *Antiquities of the Jews,* 5.7.15.

7. Boling, p. 216.

8. Kitchen, *POTT,* pp. 53–78; *ZPEB,* 4:767–73. Cf. A. R. Burn, *Minoans, Philistines, and Greeks* (New York: Knopf, 1930), 273pp.; Albright, pp.

110–22; C. H. Gordon, *Antiquity* 30 (1956), pp. 22–26; G. E. Wright, *BA* 22 (1959), pp. 54–66; idem, *BA* 29 (1966), pp. 70–86; G. A. Wainwright, *VT* 9 (1959), pp. 73–84; Yadin, pp. 248–53, 336–45.

9. *MBA,* 80, 82. Cf. B. J. Beitzel, *Moody Atlas of Bible Lands* (Chicago: Moody, 1985), p. 107 (map 35).

10. J. Blenkinsopp, *JBL* 82 (1963), pp. 65–76; J. A. Wharton, *Interpretation* 27 (1973), pp. 48–66; and J. C. Exum, *JBL* 99 (1980), pp. 43–59, provide far more elaborate, structural outlines.

11. *MBA,* 80, 82.

12. F. M. Abel, *Géographie de la Palestine,* 2:468–69.

13. Pfeiffer and Vos, pp. 110–16.

14. *EAEHL,* 1:248–53; Robinson, 2:224; F. M. Cross and G. E. Wright, *JBL* 75 (1956), pp. 202–06; Y. Aharoni, *BASOR* 154 (1959), pp. 35–39; W. F. Albright, *BASOR* 173 (1964), pp. 51–53.

15. J. Hall, *Contemplations on the Historic Passages of the Old and New Testaments* (London: S.P.C.K., n.d.), p. 124.

16. Ibid., p. 125. There is an interesting change in the tense of the Hebrew verbs from "you shall conceive" to "you [are] pregnant," which has been ignored by most commentators.

17. Cundall, p. 157.

18. Ibid.

19. Ibid.

20. Lang and Kirk, 2:16. For an extended treatment, see also J. Bruce, *The Life of Samson* (Edinburgh: Edmonston and Douglas, 1872), 389pp.; and J. L. Crenshaw's *Samson: A Secret Betrayed, A Vow Ignored* (London: S.P.C.K., 1979), 168pp.

21. Cundall, p. 157.

22. Bush, p. 176.

23. Each child deserves to receive from its parents a sense of belonging, worth, and competence. As we study the benefits of being in God's family, we find that this is exactly what He provides us (1 John 3:2–3; 4:9, 16, 18). Cf. C. J. Barber, *Searching for Identity* (Chicago: Moody, 1975), pp. 21–22. The same author, in collaboration with G. H. Strauss, identified three basic styles of parenting: authoritarian, authoritative, and permissive (see *The Effective Parent* [San Bernardino, Calif.: Here's Life, 1980], 147pp.).

24. McClintock and Strong, 12:332–33.

25. Bush, p. 177.

26. For a study of fear, see Barber, *Dynamic Personal Bible Study,* (Neptune, NJ: Loizeaux, 1981), pp. 75–85; and R. E. Morosco, *Journal of Psychology and Theology,* 1:2:43–50.

27. Lang and Kirk, 2:27–28.

28. G. G. Cohen, *EQ* 42 (1970), pp. 131–41; *ZPEB*, 1:658–60. For the contrary position, see T. H. Gaster, *Myth, Legend and Custom in the Old Testament* (New York: Harper, 1969), pp. 434ff.; idem, *Thespis* (New York: Gordian, 1975), pp. 127, 220–21, 227, 272ff.

29. R. van der Hart, *VT* 25 (1975), pp. 720–28.

30. Lang and Kirk, 2:31–33. Kirk concluded with four practical observations that differ from the two with which this chapter closes. Preachers will find his thoughts most stimulating.

31. J. Hall, p. 126.

32. *The Poetical Works of William Cowper,* ed. H. S. Milford, 4th ed. (London: Oxford University Press, 1963), p. 450.

Chapter 11

1. P. Tournier, *The Person Reborn* (New York: Harper and Row, 1966), pp. 74–75.

2. Cf. Bush, pp. 183ff.; J. Claypool, *Glad Reunion* (Waco: Word, 1985), pp. 55ff.; Crenshaw, pp. 43ff.; Geikie, pp. 167ff.; J. G. Frazier, *Folklore in the Old Testament* (London: Macmillan, 1919), 2:480–84; Kitto, 1:549–65; Lang and Kirk, 1:5–79; 2:53–147; C. E. Macartney, *The Way of a Man with a Maid* (Nashville: Abingdon, 1931), pp. 100ff.; idem, *Chariots of Fire,* pp. 137ff.; J. O. Sanders, *Robust in Faith* (Chicago: Moody, 1965), pp. 102ff.; A. P. Stanley, *Scripture Portraits* (London: Allen, n.d.), pp. 38ff.; I. Williams, *Characters of the Old Testament* (London: Rivington's, 1869), pp. 147ff.; Wiseman, pp. 290–347; and Wood, pp. 310–31.

    Watson (p. 280) summarized the general (though erroneous) view: "So [Samson] went his own way an admired hero, a lonely giant among smaller beings. Worst of all he was an easy prey to some kinds of temptation. Restrained on the one side, he gave himself license on others; his strength was always undisciplined, and early in his career we can almost predict how [he] will end. He ventures into one snare after another. The time is sure to come when he will fall into a pit out of which there is no escape."

    Fausset (pp. 226–63) offered a refreshing alternative. E. L. Shostrom in *Actualizing Therapy* (San Diego: EDITS, 1976), 345pp., enlarged on the polarities of strength (cf. 13:25; 14:6, 19; 15:14) and weakness (cf. 14:19b; 15:9–13). He also dealt with two other related issues: anger and love. His insights into the process of maturity are weighty. Preachers will find entirely new vistas of truth open up to them as they interact critically with the issues Shostrom presented. (Cf. E. L. Shostrom and D. Montgomery, *God in Your Personality*

[Nashville: Abingdon, 1986], 191pp., for a popular version of the material presented in *Actualizing Therapy*.)

3. Bush, p. 184.

4. See Chapter 4, note 15.

5. Bush, p. 184.

6. deVaux, *Ancient Israel*, p. 29 (cf. pp. 20, 28–34).

7. For a discussion of circumcision, see *ZPEB*, 1:866–68; cf. Judges 15:18; 1 Samuel 14:6; 17:26, 36; 31:4; 1 Chronicles 10:4. Boling (p. 229) stated, "In the matter of circumcision Israel participated in the wider culture, the Philistines being, so far as we know, the sole uncircumcized people in Israel's vicinity."

8. The Bible allows for greater flexibility in the marital relationship than we may at first be prepared to concede. The basic criteria are outlined in Genesis 2:24–25. These involve "leaving father and mother" (necessitating personal maturity on the part of the new husband who is to take responsibility for establishing a new family), "cleaving to his wife" (which highlights the importance of the development of unity in the husband–wife relationship), and the "two becoming one flesh" (a phrase expressing the mystical oneness into which a couple enter, and intimating the necessity of working toward sexual harmony). Finally, the biblical writer emphasized that Adam and Eve were "naked and unashamed." This may be identified as true mutual transparency. It expresses that neither had anything to hide from the other. Although these verses applied to the first man and woman before sin entered into the world, the same principles remain intact to this day. These tenets have been expanded in C. J. Barber and A. A. Barber, *You Can Have a Happy Marriage* (Grand Rapids: Kregel, 1984), 191pp.

9. Cf. M. Noth and D. W. Thomas, eds. *Wisdom in Israel and the Ancient Near East* (Leiden: Brill, 1955), 301 pp.; G. von Rad, *Wisdom in Israel* (Nashville: Abingdon, 1972), 330pp.; R. Gordis, *The Word and the Book* (New York: Ktav, 1976), 388pp.; C. H. Bullock, *Introduction to the Poetical Books of the Old Testament* (Chicago: Moody, 1979), pp. 49–112, 155–222.

10. E. O. James, *Marriage and Society* (London: Hutchinson's University Library, 1952), pp. 59–65. Cf. Bush, p. 185; J. L. Crenshaw, *ZAW* 86 (1974), pp. 470–504; J. A. Wharton, *Interpretation* 27 (1973), pp. 48–67.

11. Cf. C. J. Barber, *Journal of Psychology and Theology* 2, 1 (1974), pp. 48–59.

12. Cundall, p. 162. Cf. Mishnah, *Kethuboth* 16b, 17a; *Sota* 49a; *Gittin* 57a; and *Yebamoth* 60b.

13. Most commentators have jumped to the conclusion that Samson disappeared among the growing vines to pick grapes. They then have castigated him for what they believe to be a breach of his Nazirite vow. There is no evidence in the text that the grapes were even ripe at this time of year; and if they were, the townspeople would surely have been harvesting them. A more plausible explanation of Samson's action is that "he turned aside" to relieve himself. If Samson had gone among the vines to pick ripe grapes, then killed the lion and left the body behind him, why didn't harvesters find the carcass of the lion a short time later? Since no one found the lion's body, evidently the harvest was over. This would allow adequate time for the body to decay (or to be eaten by scavengers) and for bees to make their hive in it *before* Samson returned approximately nine months later to claim his bride. So maybe Samson "turned aside" for a different purpose than the one generally assumed.

14. Lang and Kirk, 2:60.

15. Neufeld, pp. 142–47; cf. L. M. Epstein, *Marriage Laws in the Bible and the Talmud* (Cambridge: Harvard University Press, 1942), pp. 49ff., 145ff.

16. Neufeld, pp. 148–51; James, pp. 28–76.

17. J. R. Porter, *JTS* 13 (1962), pp. 106–09.

18. Bees are fastidious creatures. They would never build a hive in anything decaying or unclean. Two possibilities suggest themselves: (1) the carcass of the lion had decayed or been eaten by scavengers (e.g., ants, hyenas, jackals, or vultures); (2) it had completely dried out in the hot sun and turned to dust and bones. Whatever happened, a certain amount of time had passed, demonstrating conclusively that Samson's marriage did *not* take place within a few days or weeks (as has been assumed by those who believe that his bride was a widow or a divorcee). Cf. G. Cransdale, *Animals in Bible Lands* (London: Paternoster, 1970), pp. 244–46; V. Moller–Christensen and K. E. Jordt Jorgensen, *Encyclopedia of Bible Creatures,* ed. M. T. Heinecken (Philadelphia: Fortress, 1965), pp. 197–202.

19. J. R. Porter, *JTS* 13 (1962), pp. 106–09.

20. A. Van Selms, *JNES* 9 (1950), pp. 65–75.

21. One of the leading Philistine cities, situated about thirty miles southwest of Zorah (*MBA,* 82). Cf. *EAEHL,* 1:129–30; *NIDBA,* pp. 75–76.

22. Tournier, *The Strong and the Weak* (Philadelphia: Westminster, 1966), pp. 18f.

23. Cf. idem, *To Resist or Surrender* (Richmond, Va.: John Knox, 1964), p. 20.

24. Idem, *The Strong and the Weak,* pp. 169f.

Chapter 12

1. P. Tournier, *The Strong and the Weak,* pp. 169ff.

2. Ibid., p. 185f.

3. The term *śānē'* is used in Deuteronomy 22:13, 16 and 24:3 as part of the so–called formula of repudiation. It is variously translated "hate" (Gen. 26:27), "to be unable or unwilling to put up with someone" (Deut. 22:13), "enemy" (Gen. 24:60). Cf. BDB, p. 971; *TWOT,* 2:879–80.

4. Bush, p. 196; Neufeld, pp. 176–90; deVaux, pp. 34–36.

5. Hall, p. 131.

6. Bush, p. 197.

7. Ibid.

8. The Hebrew word can also mean jackals; cf. Cransdale, *Animals of Bible Lands,* pp. 124–26.

9. D. N. Freedman, *Biblica* 52 (1971), p. 535.

10. Cf. S. Mendelsohn, *Criminal Jurisprudence of the Ancient Hebrews* (New York: Hermon, 1968), pp. 38–44, 67–77; *ZPEB,* 1:1032–33. Samson, as a judge appointed by God, included his wife's family within the law of his people. He knew that no Philistine tribunal would execute justice on those who had planned the death of his wife and her father. He, therefore, carried out the teaching of the law of Moses on those who were guilty of premeditated murder.

11. F. Willesen, *Journal of Semitic Studies* 3 (1959), pp. 495–508.

12. Lang and Kirk, 2:116.

13. Bush, p. 200.

14. Lang and Kirk, 2:118.

15. Ibid., 2:123.

16. Ibid., 2:124–25.

17. The text specifically states that the jawbone was "fresh," not old, dried out, and brittle. We have no way of knowing when the donkey died (or was killed). To those who are quick to indict Samson for his supposedly frequent breach of his Nazirite vow, I would say that this animal had either been devoured quickly by scavengers or had become dehydrated in the hot sun, which turned the carcass to dust. All that remained was the jawbone. Samson, therefore, did not come into contact with a *decaying* carcass. This incidental reference also casts light on the decomposition of the lion's body (14:5–9).

18. Kitto, 1:557; Wood, pp. 316–22. Modern psychological research into humor has revealed some interesting facts; cf. D. E. Berlyne, *Conflict, Arousal, and Curiosity* (New York: McGraw–Hill, 1960), 350pp. For example, Berlyne's empirical research led him to identify a form of

humor as a "jag." It occurs when one experiences threat, discomfort, or uncertainty and then the cause is suddenly removed, leaving the individual in a position of safety and with the pressure gone. The emotional release produces a neurophysiological state of arousal that gives rise to the kind of humorous expression found in Samson's paronomasiac expression.

19. Bush, p. 201.
20. Lang and Kirk, 2:135.
21. Ibid., 2:137.

Chapter 13

1. David's outlaw years, when he was hunted by King Saul, followed closely the period of Samson's judgeship (c. 1025–1011 B.C.). David became king over Judah in 1011 B.C. Attempts on his life probably continued for a considerable period of time. He recorded the dangers he faced in the psalms he wrote. They have a bearing on the kinds of strategies the Philistines may have used to bring about Samson's demise. These could have included entrapment involving nets (Pss. 9:15; 25:15; 31:4; 35:7; 57:6 et al.) or pits covered with dried grass or sand (Ps. 119:85) and the ever–present possibility of ambush (Pss. 10:8; 59:3; cf. 91:5). Wood (pp. 322–24) held to a contrary point of view. His thesis, however, is not entirely incompatible with the position adopted in this chapter; and while it was not necessary for biblical writers to follow a similar line of thought or form of expression, it should be noted that a statement like the one in 1 Samuel 7:13*a* is not made in connection with Samson's victory over the Philistines. One is left to conclude, therefore, that his judgeship involved continual skirmishes with Israel's enemies.

2. This is validly inferred from 16:31. The record is very brief, passing over all but the most important details, and concentrating on how Samson finally was given into the hands of his enemies by a woman. If his father died first, then with the passing of his mother there would be even more reason for the kind of conduct evidenced in this chapter.

3. Cf. C. J. Barber and S. Aspenleiter, *Through the Valley of Tears* (Old Tappan, N.J.: Revell, 1987), pp. 27–40.

4. Baly, pp. 112–27, 138–42; W. M. F. Petrie, *Ancient Gaza*, 4 vols. (London: British School of Archaeology in Egypt, 1931–34). V. Rappaport, *IEJ* 20 (1970), pp. 75–80; *EAEHL*, 3:408–17.

5. Thompson, 2:68 (cf. 1:170–87).

6. Bush, p. 203.

7. *ZPEB*, 2:655–56.

8. Of importance is whether or not those who have accused Samson of "lust" are using the term in its biblical sense. *Nepeš,* "soul, breath, desire" (cf. Exod. 15:9; Ps. 78:18 AV), *šerîrût,* "imagination" (Ps. 81:12 AV) in the OT, and *epithymia* in the LXX and the NT denote any strong desire, good or evil. In this connection the translators of the NASB and NIV often differ. As is always the case, the context in which a word appears has a direct bearing on its meaning. *Ta'avāh*, denoting the object of one's desire (cf. Ps. 78:30 AV) is not used in this passage. And in the LXX and the NT rarely does *epithymia* imply sexual passion (except in 1 John 2:16). A general reference with strong negative overtones, but not necessarily implying sexual indiscretion, is found in James 1:14. What appears to have been ignored by the majority of commentators is that the usual words for sexual desire (*pathos* [cf. Rom. 1:26; Col. 3:5; 1 Thess. 4:5], *orexis* [Rom. 1:27], and [only one of the ten occurrences of] *pleonexia* [Eph. 4:19]) are not used to describe Samson's conduct. To imply that Samson was consumed with lust places the burden of proof on the accuser. Accuracy in interpreting the biblical text requires that we seek to understand a passage in light of the historical–textual–cultural principles of hermeneutics.

9. H. L. Mencken, *The Vintage Mencken,* ed. A. Cooke (New York: Knopf, 1955), p. 240.

10. There is some ambiguity over whether Samson carried the gates of the city to the top of a hill outside of Gaza and facing Hebron or to a hill adjacent to Hebron thirty-eight miles away. Cf. Bush, pp. 204–5; Cundall, pp. 174–75; Lang and Kirk, 2:160–61; Moore, pp. 349–50; A. Schreiber, *Jewish Quarterly Review* 50 (1959–60), pp. 176–80; idem, *JQR* 51 (1961–62), pp. 35–40; Soggin, pp. 253, 256.

    Samson's act further underscores the polarities of power versus powerlessness. Soggin (p. 256) said, "The action of Samson [in carrying away the gates of the city] is a joke pure and simple, meant to make the inhabitants of Gaza seem utterly ridiculous and robbing them of the last shreds of their reputation [as the most powerful of the Philistine cities]."

11. Young women usually married soon after puberty. It was not unusual for a girl to become the wife of an older man. The prospect of widowhood, therefore, was highly likely. Soggin (p. 237) hinted at the probability of the Timnahite being Samson's *first wife,* leaving open the possibility of a second, similar kind of marriage to Delilah. The biblical writer, with the benefit of hindsight, used the term *'iššāh*, "woman," to subtly show his disapproval of Delilah as a person.

Although it may be validly argued that the passage before us does not mention a wedding ceremony per se, neither does Genesis 24:67; yet no one doubts the commitment of Isaac and Rebekah to one another as husband and wife. Furthermore, in a *sidîqâ* marriage the formalities in the case of a widow were negligible and may have involved nothing more than mutual consent (cf. the expression "took to himself a wife" in Gen. 11:29; 21:21; 25:1, 20 et al.). This, however, did not make the union any less binding on the couple. The basis of marriage (regardless of its outworking in the cultural-economic milieu of the couple) has always been for them to live together in a unique and lasting relationship.

12. Josephus, *Antiquities of the Jews* (5.8.11), claimed that Delilah was a Philistine prostitute. In matters of this nature, he often distorted the truth to put his people in a favorable light. A close reading of the text fails to support his view.

13. Considering the fact that few people of the tribe of Dan lived in houses, and that houses of the poor generally had only one room, Delilah (had she been married previously) must have been accustomed to wealth, for her house had at least two rooms.

14. Soggin, pp. 257.

15. Lang and Kirk, 2:167–68.

16. BDB, p. 847.

17. Lang and Kirk, 2:176–77.

18. F. C. Fensham, *EQ* 31 (1959), 97ff.

19. The Hebrew text presents difficulties in translation. Soggin (p. 252) rendered Samson's prayer as follows: "O Lord, Yahweh, remember me and give me strength just once again, O God! With one blow let me be avenged of the Philistines for my two eyes." Cf. J. A. Emerton, *ZAW* 85 (1973), pp. 200–203.

20. *TWOT*, 1:12–13, 44–45, 210–12; *TDNT*, 3:1058–86; *TDOT*, 1:59–72; 5:500–21. Cf. R. Abba, *JBL* 80 (1961), pp. 320–28; W. F. Albright, *JBL* 54 (1973), pp. 175–92; idem, *Yahweh and the Gods of Canaan*, pp. 168–72; L. R. Bailey, *JBL* 87 (1968), pp. 434–38; F. M. Cross, *Harvard Theological Journal* 55 (1962), pp. 226–59; idem, *JSS* 1 (1956), pp. 25–37; C. H. Gordon, *JBL* 54 (1973), pp. 140–44; J. A. Kelso, *JBL* 20 (1921), pp. 50–55; H. G. May, *JBL* 60 (1941), pp. 114–45; M. H. Segal, *JQR* 46 (1952), pp. 89–115; R. D. Wilson, *Princeton Reformed Review*, 18:460–92; F. Zimmerman, *VT* 12 (1962), pp. 190–95.

21. Josephus, *Antiquities of the Jews*, 5.8.12; cf. Wood, pp. 332–34.

22. C. Forbes, *The Religion of Power* (Grand Rapids: Zondervan, 1986), pp. 17–20.

23. Ibid., p. 20.

24. Ibid., pp. 44f., 79–82.
25. Nehemiah's case illustrates the manner in which this kind of pressure may be brought to bear on an individual (cf. Barber, *Nehemiah and the Dynamics of Effective Leadership,* pp. 58–111).
26. Forbes, p. 35.

Chapter 14

1. G. Gallup and D. Poling, *The Search for America's Faith* (Nashville: Abingdon, 1980), 153pp.
2. Such trends within our society have been explored by M. E. Marty, *A Nation of Behavers* (Chicago: University of Chicago Press, 1976), 239pp.
3. A. E. Wilder–Smith, *He Who Thinks Has To Believe* (San Diego, Calif.: Master, 1981), 94pp. Cf. N. L. Geisler, *Is Man the Measure?* (Grand Rapids: Baker, 1983), 201pp.; idem, *The Roots of Evil* (Grand Rapids: Zondervan, 1978), 96pp.; and the classic works of J. G. Machen, of which his *Christian Faith in the Modern World* (Grand Rapids: Eerdmans, 1967), 258pp. is representative. Other works on the defense of Christianity may be traced through *The Minister's Library.*
4. Three publications have a bearing on this subject: D. R. Groothuis, *Unmasking the New Age* (Downers Grove, Ill.: InterVarsity, 1986), 192pp.; I. Hexham and K. Poewe, *Understanding Cults and New Religions* (Grand Rapids: Eerdmans, 1986), 170pp.; and J. Sire, *Scripture Twisting: Twenty Ways the Cults Misread the Bible* (Downers Grove, Ill.: InterVarsity, 1980), 180pp.
5. Cf. M. E. Marty, *Varieties of Unbelief* (New York: Holt, Rinehart, and Winston, 1964), 231pp.
6. Cf. C. Brown, *Philosophy and Christian Faith* (Downers Grove, Ill.: InterVarsity, 1969), 319pp.; N. L. Geisler and W. D. Watkins, *Perspectives* (San Bernardino, Calif.: Here's Life, 1984), 269pp.; O. Guinness, *The Dust of Death* (Downers Grove, Ill.: InterVarsity, 1973), 419pp.; J. Sire, *The Universe Next Door* (Downers Grove, Ill.: InterVarsity, 1976), 236pp.; R. C. Sproul, *Lifelines* (Old Tappan, NJ: Revell, 1986), 220pp. Other standard works by N. L. Geisler, G. R. Lewis, J. G. Machen, F. A. Schaeffer, and R. C. Sproul can also be consulted with profit.
7. From Joshua 6:25 we know that Rahab was still alive at the time the book of Joshua was written. The migration of the Danites must have occurred early in the settlement of the land. Cf. Burney, pp. 408–36; Garstang, pp. 29, 229f., 245–47; A. H. Jones, *Bronze Age Civilization* (Washington, D.C.: Public Affairs, 1975), 182pp.; A. Malamat, *Biblica* 61 (1970), pp. 1–16; J. M. Miller and J. H. Hayes, *A History of Ancient Israel and Judah* (Philadelphia: Westminster, 1986), pp. 100–103, 106,

108; Moore, pp. 365–408; M. Noth, *Israel's Prophetic Heritage,* ed. B. W. Anderson (London: SCM, 1962), pp. 68–85; H. H. Rowley, *Expository Times* 51 (1940), pp. 466–71; idem, *From Joseph to Joshua* (London: Oxford University Press, 1952), pp. 79–86; Weippert, pp. 16–18, 142; and Wood, pp. 191, 210, 212–13.

8. The ideological parallel between the religious beliefs of Micah's day and our own may be deduced from the following books (as well as some works already cited in this chapter): J. N. D. Anderson, *Christianity and World Religions* (Downers Grove, Ill.: InterVarsity, 1984), 216pp.; H. O. J. Brown, *Heresies* (Garden City, N.Y.: Doubleday, 1984), 477pp.; and J. W. C. Wand, *The Four Great Heresies* (London: Mowbray, 1955).

9. Cf. C. J. Barber and J. D. Carter, *Always a Winner* (Ventura, CA: Regal, 1977), pp. 63–69.

10. Cf. Albright, *Archaeology and the Religion of Israel,* pp. 129ff., 150–52; J. Bright, *The History of Israel,* 3d ed. (Philadelphia: Westminster, 1981), pp. 170–72; A. Cody, *History of the Old Testament Priesthood.* Analecta Biblica (Rome: Pontifical Biblical Institute Press, 1969), 216pp.; deVaux, pp. 307f., 359; *ISBE,* 3:965–68; E. O. James, *Nature and Function of the Priesthood* (London: Thames and Hudson, 1961), pp. 73–90; 100–04; T. F. Torrance, *Scottish Journal of Theology* 11 (1958), pp. 225–52; *ZPEB,* 4:852–57.

11. KD, p. 431. Cf. E. O. James, *Myth and Ritual in the Ancient Near East* (London: Thames and Hudson, 1958), pp. 58–67.

12. *ZPEB,* 3:682, #2; J. Bright, pp. 172f., 237–38.

13. Cf. rise of liturgy and drama in E. O. James, *Myth and Ritual in the Ancient Near East,* pp. 291–309; and T. H. Gaster, *Thespis,* p. 515.

14. Pagan priests were skilled in the art of duplicity. Their oracles were invariably interpreted in terms of the inquirer's vested interests and personal desires. If and when events turned out contrary to the expectations of the devotee, the priests could easily change the sense of their words (cf. Dan. 2:1–11). Examples may be traced through the works of P. J. Alexander, *The Oracle of Baalbek* (Washington: Dunbarton Oaks Center for Byzantine Studies, 1957), 151pp.; R. H. Charles, ed., *The Apocrypha and Pseudepigrapha of the Old Testament* (Oxford: Clarendon, 1913), pp. 2:368–406; J. H. Charlesworth, ed., *The Old Testament Pseudepigrapha* (Garden City, N.Y.: Doubleday, 1983), pp. 1:317–472; T. Dempsey, *The Delphic Oracle* (New York: Blom, 1972), 192pp.; H. W. Parke and D. E. W. Wormell, *The Delphic Oracle* (Oxford: Blackwell, 1956), pp. 2:1–228.

15. L. O. Richards and C. Hoeldtke explained this tendency, together with the biblical alternative in *A Theology of Church Leadership* (Grand Rapids: Zondervan, 1980), 425pp.

16. Cf. Kaiser, Jr. *Toward Old Testament Ethics,* p. 282.

17. Cf. N. L. Geisler, *Bibliotheca Sacra* 144 (1987), pp. 79–104; and F. Bulle, *God Wants You Rich* (Minneapolis: Bethany House, 1983), 223pp.

18. Albright, *Yahweh and the Gods of Canaan,* 276pp.; L. R. Bailey, *HUCA* 42 (1971), pp. 97–115; *Encyclopedia of Religion and Ethics,* ed. J. Hastings (Edinburgh: Clark, 1915), pp. 7:138–42; and James, *The Ancient Gods* (New York: Putnam's, 1960), 359pp.

19. *ZPEB,* 5:677–78; cf. E. O. James, *The Cult of the Mother Goddess*; idem, *Myth and Ritual in the Ancient Near East,* pp. 58–60, 63–64, 105, 110, 113, 122, 132f., 141f., 243, 301.

20. Mishnah, *Aboth* 5.9. (The index, pp. 812–44, provides easy access to the teachings of the rabbis on these themes.)

21. Cf. *The Minister's Library,* 1:439–59; 2:477–93.

22. M. E. Wagner, *Put It All Together* (Grand Rapids: Zondervan, 1974), 162pp.; idem, *The Sensation of Being Somebody* (Grand Rapids: Zondervan, 1975), 251pp.

Chapter 15

1. W. Dyer, *Your Erroneous Zones* (New York: Funk and Wagnalls, 1976), pp. 1–2.

2. Wood, pp. 150–55, 295.

3. McClintock and Strong, 8:144–45; *ZPEB,* 4:777.

4. The laws governing the taking of concubines were complex. The state into which she entered was intended to be permanent. In certain contexts the words "concubine" and "wife" are used interchangeably (cf. Gen. 30:3–4 with 37:2). A distinction, however, was generally maintained (cf. 2 Sam. 5:13; 19:5; 2 Chron. 11:21; Song of Sol. 6:8–9; Dan. 5:2–3), with a wife occupying status on a socially higher plane, but not necessarily enjoying the same affection from her husband. Although not representing God's ideal for his people, He had nonetheless sanctioned such an arrangement at Mount Sinai (Exod. 21:10). Neufeld, pp. 121–32, discussed the rights of Hebrew concubines as distinguished from women taken captive from the nations conquered by Israel (cf. Lev. 25:44; Num. 31:9, 18; Deut. 20:14; 2 Sam. 5:13). Woolley, in *Family, State, and Church—God's Institutions,* p. 18, clarified some of the mental blocks Occidentals experience when considering Oriental institutions. Cf. deVaux, pp. 24–25, 29, 115–17; Epstein, pp. 34–76; idem, *The Jewish Marriage Contract* (New York: Arno, 1973), pp. 9–10, 123n; and James, *Marriage and Society,* pp. 63–64, 76–78, 154–55.

5. J. Simons, *Jerusalem in the Old Testament* (Leiden, The Netherlands: Brill, 1952), pp. 60–61, 246–47; M. F. Unger, *Archaeology and the Old Testament* (Grand Rapids: Zondervan, 1954), pp. 92–93, 206–09; G. E. Wright, *Biblical Archaeology* (Philadelphia: Westminster, 1962), pp. 127–29.

6. W. F. Albright, *BASOR* 52 (1933), pp. 6–12; L. A. Sinclair, *Annual of the American Society for Oriental Research* 34–35 (1954–56), pp. 5–52; P. Lapp, *BA* 28 (1965), pp. 2–10.

7. D. W. Riddle, *JBL* 57 (1939), pp. 141–54; *ISBE*, 2:105–6.

8. J. P. Free, *Archaeology and Bible History* (Wheaton, Scripture Press, 1962), pp. 62–63.

9. *Bᵉlīya'al,* "worthless, without profit"; cf. *TWOT*, 1:111.

10. Ibid., 2:724; Neufeld, pp. 121–24.

11. The origin of the rite is wrapped in the shrouds of antiquity. As H. C. Trumbull, *The Threshold Covenant,* pp. 64, 203–22, 238, showed, however, elaborate ideas had become associated with the crossing of the threshold. It implied a "pass-over" or "cross-over" and guaranteed protection, security, and freedom from harm. Without question the Levite's host felt caught between a sacred obligation on the one hand and the total disregard of the men of the city for the laws governing hospitality on the other.

12. Cundall, pp. 197–98.

13. *ZPEB*, 2:255–57.

14. Yadin, *Art of Warfare in Bible Lands,* 2:364; *ZPEB*, 1:81.

15. *MBA,* 81; Cundall, pp. 201–6.

16. J. Pedersen, *Israel, Its Life and Culture* (London: Cumberlege, 1940), 3–4:11–12, 456ff. Real fasting implies being so given over to prayer and so intent on waiting on the Lord that one becomes oblivious to the passing of time and the needs of the body. It is totally different from the pharisaical type of "fasting" that is becoming popular in certain segments of the church today. True fasting was never intended to be a way to obligate God to bestow his favors on us. Cf. C. Brown, *New International Dictionary of New Testament Theology* (Grand Rapids: Zondervan, 1975), pp. 1:611–13.

17. Bush, pp. 246–47; *ZPEB*, 5:203–9.

18. *MBA,* 86; Robinson, 1:440, 443.

19. Ibid.

20. Twelve is symbolic of completeness. That is why when Judas took his own life, Christ's disciples felt it necessary to select another for the sake of unity and testimony (Acts 1:16–22). At no time, however, did the leaders of the tribes inquire of the Lord as to his will

concerning the perpetuation of the tribe of Benjamin. They relied solely on human ingenuity.

21. *ZPEB*, 5:850–52.

22. *ISBE*, 2:946.

23. Woolley, pp. 8–25.

24. S. B. Clark, *Man and Woman in Christ* (Ann Arbor, Mich.: Servant, 1980), pp. 3–63. Although lip service is often paid the family as the "basic unit of society," politicians and employees frequently make decisions or impose principles or policies on individuals that, as these chapters show, destroy the autonomy of the husband/father and fragment the family. Only by adhering to the three distinct, God-appointed spheres of authority (viz., family, church, and state) can familial unity and social solidarity be maintained.

25. Mishnah, *Nedarim,* pp. 264–80.

SCRIPTURE INDEX

PERSON AND TITLE INDEX